PENGUIN  CLASSICS

AKENFIELD

RONALD BLYTHE, critic and writer, is the author of *The Age of Illusion*, a social history of England between the wars, *Akenfield: Portrait of an English Village*, *The View in Winter*, *From the Headlands* and *Divine Landscapes*. He is editor of *Writing in a War* (originally published as *Components of the Scene*), *The Penguin Book of Diaries* and *Private Words: Letters and Diaries from the Second World War*. Many of these are published by Penguin or Viking. He has edited Thomas Hardy's *Far From the Madding Crowd*, Henry James's *The Awkward Age* and William Hazlitt's *Selected Writings* for Penguin.

RONALD BLYTHE

Akenfield

Portrait of an English Village

PENGUIN BOOKS

To John Nash

PENGUIN BOOKS

Published by the Penguin Group
Penguin Books Ltd, 80 Strand, London WC2R 0RL, England
Penguin Group (USA) Inc., 375 Hudson Street, New York, New York 10014, USA
Penguin Group (Canada), 90 Eglinton Avenue East, Suite 700, Toronto,
Ontario, Canada M4P 2Y3 (a division of Pearson Penguin Canada Inc.)
Penguin Ireland, 25 St Stephen's Green, Dublin 2, Ireland (a division of Penguin Books Ltd)
Penguin Group (Australia), 250 Camberwell Road, Camberwell, Victoria 3124, Australia
(a division of Pearson Australia Group Pty Ltd)
Penguin Books India Pvt Ltd, 11 Community Centre,
Panchsheel Park, New Delhi – 110 017, India
Penguin Group (NZ), cnr Airborne and Rosedale Roads, Albany,
Auckland 1310, New Zealand (a division of Pearson New Zealand Ltd)
Penguin Books (South Africa) (Pty) Ltd, 24 Sturdee Avenue,
Rosebank 2196, Johannesburg, South Africa

Penguin Books Ltd, Registered Offices: 80 Strand, London WC2R 0RL, England

www.penguin.com

First published by Allen Lane 1969
Published in Penguin Books 1972
Reprinted with a new Preface 1999
Published in Penguin Classics 2005
009

Copyright © Ronald Blythe, 1969, 1999
All rights reserved

The moral right of the author has been asserted

Printed in England by Clays Ltd, St Ives plc

ISBN-13: 978–0–141–18792–1

www.greenpenguin.co.uk

ALWAYS LEARNING   **PEARSON**

Contents

Contents

Preface

This book was written in 1966-7 and first published in May 1969. I was then living at Debach, a tiny parish of some eighty souls which adjoined the larger village of Charsfield. I remember walking the ancient boundaries of flat-land Debach and hollow-land Charsfield on a grey winter's day and thinking of the ritual toil which had engaged them, and thousands of villages like them, since those who settled them made the first field. All around were similar settlements with 'field' names, so I called my book *Akenfield* after the oaks which stood in the field opposite my old house. 'Acen' = Old English for 'oak'. Also because I was born in the Suffolk village Acton. 'Actun' = 'the homestead by the oaks'. *Akenfield* is chiefly based on Charsfield, but with the surrounding countryside and myself drawn into it. My excuse for the former extension is that, like man, no village is an island, entire of itself, but has always relied on the blacksmith, wheelwright, schools, transport, butcher, and now priest of the area. The book is more the work of a poet than a trained oral historian, a profession I had never heard of when I wrote it. My only realy credentials for having written it was that I was native to its situation in nearly every way and had only to listen to hear my own world talking. Thus a thread of autobiography runs strongly through it. Having been born between the wars during the last years of the great agricultural depression, I was in a kind of natural conversation with all three generations who spoke to me in the mid-sixties, and I was able to structure their talk over farming, education, welfare, class, religion and indeed life and death in terms such as I myself was experiencing these things, although now with a writer's vision of them. I saw the two World Wars as extraordinary intrusions, walling-off two successive generations from each other, and giving each of them a distinctive voice. And I was delighted as always with those who bent the rules, dodged the system and who managed to be 'different' within the rigidities which rural communities like to impose. There is no place like the countryside for the most imaginative – and blatant – non-conformity.

The most unlooked-for change of fortune during the rural sixties would have been that for agriculture thirty years on. Then it was grow all the grain you can, never mind what eccentrics calling themselves 'ecologists' said. An often brutal and ignorant rationalization of the old field system which so upset John Clare when his village was enclosed was government-inspired and payed for. One Suffolk village, Tannington, was in the van of such change, with scarcely a tree or hedge to its name.

Although cornfields had to expand to take combine harvesters, it was shocking to see centuries' old hedgerows bulldozed, the pouring on to the land of chemicals about which the average farmer understood very little, and stubble-burning as an economy. Now there is official and social condemnation of such practices, and because of the eventual withdrawal of subsidies, plus European laws, there is a feeling of insecurity among today's farmers such as most of them have only read about and would never have imagined could return. The labour force was small enough then but is now minute. A couple of men on eight hundred acres. The 'old people', that is, those who truly belong to a village, are the least surprised. Ups and downs are in their blood, and although vague about agronomics they don't expect anything to last. But some farmers today are nerve-racked and fearful. Gone is that first fine careless confidence when the grain grew as it never had grown before. Thus a recovered respect for nature, often brought about, I sometimes think, by their children, who have been thrillingly 'ecologized' at school and university, not to mention by television. One of my hardest tasks in the nineties has been to make the villagers *look* at their fields, not drive through them as though nothing existed between their houses and the supermarket. An almost total lack of contact with its growing acres by the majority of people now living in the countryside has, more than anything else, brought about its increasing urbanization. The old work ground is seen only when it becomes a playground. But the locals as well as the visitors are walking more, which is something they would have found difficult to do during the sixties when the ancient village paths petered out in seas of grain.

My father had fought at Gallipoli in the Suffolk Regiment and it was while listening to Len Thompson about what to me, as a boy, was a half-glamorous, half-terrible experience, that I recognized the 'iceberg' quality in those I thought I knew pretty well. Only the tip of them showed, all the rest ran deep. A similar revelation occurred when I listened to our retired district nurse. She was the secretary of the P.C.C. and I was a churchwarden, and we had every reason to believe that there was not much we could tell each other which was not already known. Many years after *Akenfield* I sat by her death-bed and watched the old 'authority' come and go in her dark eyes.

The earlier poet of this region was Edward FitzGerald who lies buried under rose-trees seeded from those which grow round Omar's tomb at Naishapur in Boulge churchyard, just a mile or two from my house. How often he would have seen it, and how often I sat in what was once his lodge-cottage distributing our Flower Show prizes – mainly to two grimly competitive farm-workers who yearly cleared the board. Tramping and cycling about, I frequently found myself haunted by FitzGerald. Many of his lanes had been obliterated by the American bomber base across which the Welsh rector and myself would take our blowy walks. The poet in *Akenfield* is James Turner, my first writer friend, who lived three miles away, and with whom over many years I explored Suffolk – a vivid, sometimes testy man whose wife moved him on and on until he reached Cornwall.

There was the question of dialect. 'Suffolk' being my first language, so to speak, I did not find it wholly impossible to write even if it is thought to be notoriously hard to get right. I sat with the wheelwright's nephew as we asked each other the meaning of words in Forby's *The Vocabulary of East Anglia*, 1830, and found that we were rarely stumped. Eventually I decided to keep to what was being said, and to a certain personal rhythm in each speaker, using a story, 'Tom-tit-Tot', from the Suffolk Folk-lore Society's collection to give a wonderfully accurate example of our dialext. It has always intrigued East Anglians how their speech gradually broadens out between the Stour and the Wash. This is one thing which hasn't altered much since the sixties. In fact, certain 'country' groups may be re-establishing the local speech of their grandparents.

One can compare the economics of then and now but it would need an expert to explain the real difference. The Rural Dean's annual stipend in 1969 was £1,175; in 1998 it is £15,000. The farm-worker's weekly wage then was £11.11; now it is £200 with overtime. But the long struggle against the poverty wages and grim conditions of the inter-war years continues to lie like a barely credible memory at the heart of today's prosperity and leisure. The middle-aged, let alone the aged, have to shake themselves to admit that things were so. There are various ways to describe a time, a place, a condition. One can come to them from outside and say what one saw. Or one can emerge from within a community, as so many rural writers do, and be at a particular moment its indigenous voice.

Ronald Blythe
May 1998

Acknowledgements

I would like to thank all those many friends and neighbours in Suffolk whose great kindness made it possible for me to plan and complete this statement about living in an East Anglian village at the beginning of the second half of the twentieth century. All the facts about the economy, population, and social life of Akenfield are drawn from a village in East Suffolk; only the names of the village and the villagers have been changed. My countless enquiries were everywhere answered with patience and courtesy, and the warmth lurking just behind that famous Suffolk taciturnity made my many visits to the farms and cottages a remarkable collective experience.

As always, I owe a special debt to Miss White, the Borough Librarian of Ipswich, and her staff, and among the various public bodies which gave me invaluable assistance, particular thanks must go to the National Union of Agricultural Workers (Lord Collison of Cheshunt and Alderman J. M. Stewart), the Ministry of Agriculture, Fisheries and Food for allowing me to see the Parish Summaries of Agricultural Census Returns; and to the Agricultural Training Centre, Witnesham.

I would also like to acknowledge the help I received from the following books:

T. Eastwood. *Industry in the Country Towns of Suffolk and Norfolk.* O.U.P., 1951.

G. Fussell. *The English Rural Labourer.* Batchworth, 1949.

P. Wilson Fox. *Report on the County of Suffolk.* Royal Commission on Agriculture, 1958.

W. P. Baker. *The English Village.* O.U.P., 1953.

E. Morris. *History and Art of Change-Ringing.* Chapman and Hall, 1931. *Fream's Elements of Agriculture.* Murray, 1962.

A. Klaiber. *Story of the Suffolk Baptists.* Highgate, 1931.

C. D. Harris. *Geography of the Ipswich-Orford Area.* Unpublished thesis, Ipswich Reference Library.

Reg Groves. *Sharpen the Sickle! The History of the Farm Workers' Union.* Porcupine Press, 1959.

H. Rider Haggard. *Rural England.* Longmans, 1902.

C. Gurdon. *County Folk-lore: Suffolk.* Folk-lore Society, 1893.

A. K. Giles and W. J. G. Cowie. *The Farm Worker: His Training, Pay and Status.* Bradley, 1964.

Pay of Workers in Agriculture in England and Wales. H.M.S.O., 1967.

W. E. Tate. *The English Village Community.* Gollancz, 1967.

Lord Ernle. *English Farming, Past and Present.* Heinemann, 1961.

L. Dudley Stamp. *Man and the Land.* Collins, 1967.

George Ewart Evans. *The Horse in the Furrow.* Faber, 1967.

W. M. Williams. *The Sociology of an English Village.* Routledge and Kegan Paul, 1956.

Introduction

The village lies folded away in one of the shallow valleys which dip into the East Anglian coastal plain. It is not a particularly striking place and says little at first meeting. It occupies a little isthmus of London (Eocene) clay jutting from Suffolk's famous shelly sands, the Coralline and Red crags, and is approached by a spidery lane running off from the 'bit of straight', as they call it, meaning a handsome stretch of Roman road, apparently going nowhere. This road suggests one of those expensive planning errors which, although cancelled in the books, will mark the earth for ever. It is the kind of road which hurries one past a situation. Centuries of traffic must have passed within yards of Akenfield without noticing it.

It is a 'round' village, with the houses lining the edges of the perimeter lanes, but with shops, church, pub, school, chapel, etc. spread along a central road following the bank of a creek officially known as the Potsford River but called locally the 'Black Ditch'. This stream is a tributary of the Deben, one of a dozen or more which wind towards its right bank and which drew the Danish and Saxon settlers to their secluded pastures. By the time the Normans arrived, the village was part of the most densely populated belt in Britain. Details in the Little Domesday Book (1086) describe its take-over by the French and provide some of the few recorded facts in all its long history.

Lands of Earl Alan: ... 16 free-men ... 12 of these under commendation to Edric the Grim, and 1 under St Ethelreda, and over 3 others [the saint?] had half commendation – [held] a caracute of land. Then 5 plough teams, now 4. An acre of meadow.

In Akenfield Thurston son of Wido holds a free-man Brihtmar [who was] under St Ethelreda's commendation in King Edward's time with 30 acres. Always 1 plough team, 1 acre of meadow .... This Thurston holds of Roger Bigot.

Lands of the Bishop of Bayeux ... 14 free-men [held a caracute] of land. Roger Bigot holds this and Ralph de Savigni [holds it] of him – and 13 acres. Then 5 plough-teams, now 3. An acre of meadow ... then valued at 60 shillings.

Lands of Hugh de Montford ... in Akenfield [were] 2 free-men under commendation to St Ethelberga.

Lands of Robert Malet [the Conqueror's great friend] ... Lands of Geoffrey de Magnaville.

and so on, this same sloping heavy soil, so tough to plough, which dominates every view still, this same bright hard climate of wind-chilled sunshine. An oceanic climate maintained by the North Sea, which is a dozen or so miles away on the other side of a great tract of heath full of rare steppe flora, fossils and the bones of ancient men, and in which lies the royal burial ground of Sutton Hoo. The rainfall here is the lowest in Britain, averaging 24.6 inches annually. Before the mains water arrived in 1944, there were droughts most summers. So the ponds and wells are likely to belong to the old habitation pattern. Most houses and groups of cottages possess one or the other, usually a pond, and 'pond pox' was a normal hazard of life up until the last war.

Like the majority of Suffolk villages, Akenfield was enclosed centuries before the notorious Georgian enclosure acts destroyed peasant England. But its hedges – now being slaughtered – were planted in the eighteenth century and, where they remain, shelter all the wild life of the particular fields they surround. Earlier field boundaries can be easily traced by ridges and ditches, and here and there a great tree spreads itself out in Time, making no sense at all. The clay acres themselves are the only tablets on which generations of village men have written, as John Clare did, *I am*, but nothing remains of these sharp straight signatures.

The centre of the village remains self-contained and quiet in spite of farm machines, motor-bikes and the dull murmur of summer holiday traffic on the bit of straight. Jets from the American base at Bentwaters occasionally ordain an immense sound and the place seems riven, splintered – yet it resumes its wholeness the second the plane vanishes. Nobody looks up. In Breughel's painting of Icarus Auden noticed:

> *How everything turns away*
> *Quite leisurely from the disaster; the ploughman may*
> *Have heard the splash, the forsaken cry,*
> *But for him it was not an important failure; the sun shone,*
> *As it had to …*

Could this be village indifference or village strength? Insensitivity or a discipline? These East Anglian field workers are the descendants of men who were given battlefield leave to return home and get in the harvest. There is, in the bony quiet of their faces, not insularity or an absence of response, but a rational notion of 'first things first', as they say. The peculiarly English social revolution which began immediately after the war has dramatically changed the countryman's life, though not nearly so dramatically as that of his cousin's life in the town. He has his 1960s comforts and luxuries, as well as a fair inkling of popular sixties culture, but these things, though grabbed for by one who has a long memory of bleakness, are apt to be regarded as trimmings. The earth itself has its latest drugs and fertilizers poured into it to make it rich and yielding, but it is still the 'old clay'. In both its and his reality, the elemental quality remains uppermost. Science is a footnote to what he really believes. And what he *knows* is often incommunicable.

The villager may be anyone from an old horseman who, aeons away in social-change time, belonged to a family used serf-fashion as a field-gang, to a rich agricultural technician for whom the word 'farmer' is beginning to sound a quaint description, yet both will be one in the great division which separates the growers from the mere consumers of food the world over. Deep in the nature of such men and elemental to their entire being there is the internationalism of the planted earth which makes them, in common with the rice-harvesters of Vietnam or the wine-makers of Burgundy, people who are committed to certain basic ideas and actions which progress and politics can elaborate or confuse, but can never alter. Where the strict village existence is concerned it is *Plus ça change, plus c'est la même chose*. The villager is often imprisoned by the sheer implacability of the 'everlasting circle', as the poet James Reeve described the fertility cycle. His own life and the life of the corn and fruit and creatures clocks along with the same fatalistic movement. Spring-birth, winter-death and in between the harvest. This year, next year and for ever – for that was the promise. Such inevitability cuts down ambition and puts a brake on restlessness. The villager saw the 'promise', distorted and monstrous though it was, all through the great agricultural depression which began in the late 1870s and lasted long enough to leave its mark on every farmer and farm-worker over forty. The East Anglian corn plateau then sank into heaths, sporting estates and, in many places, simply 'went back', yet still the voice could be heard saying, 'Spring, summer, harvest, winter ...'. The words echoed in the most ruined field and at the most despairing of seasons.

The townsman envies the villager his certainties and, in Britain, has always regarded urban life as just a temporary necessity. One day he will find a cottage on the green and 'real values'. To accommodate the almost religious intensity of the regard for rural life in this country, and to placate the sense of guilt which so many people feel about not living on a village pattern, the post-war new towns have attempted to incorporate both city and village – with, on the whole, disheartening results. A number of such towns are spreading into East Anglia, arriving suddenly on the loamy flats where there never was habitation before, and claiming that they can offer the best of both worlds. Trees are landscaped into the concrete. There are precincts, ways, conurbations, complexes ... enlightened civic nouns. There are open spaces, air and every amenity. Yet the inhabitants, many of whom are the descendants of the great village exodus of the nineteenth century, often look bewildered. They have, in three or four generations, over-filled London and are now spilling back home. Except that the estate-towns aren't home, so more than ever the old, settled, recognizable village represents the ideal community. More and more are making it. With general car-ownership, perhaps the greatest single factor in village change since the war, a vital new class of countryman has come into existence. Only a generation or so ago, a villager who had to 'go away to work' was obliged to give up the close-knit and meaningful village background of which he was an important part for lodgings in an Ipswich or Norwich backstreet. Or, conversely, village life became so suffocating and inhibiting because he had no way of occasionally getting away from it, that a young man would join the army or simply the age-old drift away from his home village which was also his prison. The new villagers commute to the county and market towns. In Akenfield they include school-teachers, technicians from the Ipswich factories, office workers and an architect. These 'young marrieds' go less and less for the converted cottage and more for picture-windowed bungalows set in gardens so spectacularly neat that they look as though they had been bought by the yard from a nurseryman – which many of them have. They travel to work daily in Anglias and on mopeds. The towns are numerous and near. There are as many as twelve to choose from and none much more than twenty miles off. Three, Framlingham, Woodbridge and Wickham Market are almost within walking distance, or would have been thought so when walking was a normal human activity.

But the villager who works in the near-by town does not think of himself as belonging to an urban district any more than his ancestor was very conscious of belonging to a Hundred. The first thing a newcomer does when arriving in a village is to begin to claim it. He doesn't state or stake his claim, he simply starts to feel his way towards the village's identity, recognize it for what it is and shape himself to fit it. He will often envy the old indigenous stock – there are eighteen families in Akenfield descended from people living in the village in *c.* 1750 – but in effect his life will be far freer than theirs. The sometimes crushing, limiting power which the village exerts on families which have never escaped will be unknown to him.

The new villager's attitudes are deeply coloured by the national village cult. In Akenfield, evidence of the good life, a tall old church on the hillside, a pub selling the local brew, a pretty stream, a football pitch, a handsome square vicarage with a cedar of Lebanon shading it, a school with jars of tadpoles in the window, three shops with doorbells, a Tudor mansion, half a dozen farms and a lot of quaint cottages, is there for all to recognize. Akenfield, on the face of it, is the kind of place in which an Englishman has always felt it his right and duty to live. It is patently the real country, untouched and genuine. A holy place, when you have spent half your life abroad in the services. Its very sounds are formal, hieratic; larks, clocks, bees, tractor hummings. Rarely the sound of the human voice. So powerful is this traditional view that many people are able to live in the centre of it for years and see nothing more. As G.E. Coulton observed, 'Village happiness is often exaggerated beyond all reason ...'. Perhaps it would be fairer to say that two contrasting conceptions of this happiness, the new – i.e. the literate and informed – and the old – i.e. the mysterious and intuitive – are now existing side by side in Akenfield, and with scarcely any awareness of each other.

The villager who has never moved away from his birthplace for anything more than military service retains the unique mark of his particular village. If a man says that he comes from Akenfield he knows that he is telling someone from another part of the neighbourhood a good deal more than this. Anything from his appearance to his politics could be involved. But on the whole the villagers don't volunteer much about themselves. They are not loquacious people. The old ones have emerged from indignities and sufferings which taught a man how to hold his tongue, and a guarded note marks much of their conversation. On the whole, they will admit certain information about their lives during the 'bad days' and will courteously rake up a few old customs as makeweight, but they remain intrinsically private folk and their characters cannot be termed open. The young men are beginning to realize that the farming scene has no future for them unless they happen to be farmers' sons and can inherit. The middle-aged workers bore them with their tales of thirty-bob-a-week-and-all-hours but the more intelligent teenager has already discovered that his farming life must in essence be his father's farming life repeated – plus sufficient training to allow him to cope with the new agricultural machinery. What most modern farms need is a good tractor-driver or two, as once they needed good ploughmen – or horsemen, as they were called in Suffolk – and for the majority of farm-workers this job has to be the ceiling of their expectations. Agriculture is one of Britain's crucial industries but its skilled workers are the lowest paid and, socially, lowly rated. In East Anglia it remains embedded in a conservatism as heavy as the clay lands themselves.

The nearer native and new villager come together, the more obvious their difference. If the latter is no longer young, he relaxes in what seems to him the security of an undisturbed and benevolent class pattern. He finds life clearly sign-posted once more and knows where he is. He will obey village rules and take immense care not to offend against the least of its little foibles. But he never becomes joined to the place. Whilst the atavistic thread, whether he likes it or not, remains unbroken for the village man. It is both his advantage and his fetter, allowing him certain instincts, knowledge and emotions which can only be inherited through unbroken contact with the life of the earth itself. It is this thread – and it is classless – which creates such lasting barriers as must exist between the agriculturalist and the non-agriculturalist in the modern village setting.

This book is the quest for the voice of Akenfield, Suffolk, as it sounded during the summer and autumn of 1967. The talk covers half a century of farming slump and the beginning of what is being called the second agricultural revolution. It begins with the memories of men who were children when much of the land changed hands towards the end of the nineteenth century. Described as an estate of five farms, 'all in the occupation of respectable and punctual yearly tenants', and combining 'accommodation lands, small-holdings, the advowson of the church and the manor itself, in all 712 acres of tithe-free property', it passed from Earl Howe to a Kentish yeoman, whose grandsons farm it today. The new owners were Unitarians and fitted comfortably into Suffolk's dissenting background, although their property was bounded in on all sides by the pheasant acres of sporting feudalists, chiefly the Duke of Hamilton and Lord Rendlesham. The new owners switched much of their land from cereals and roots to orchards and produced the greatest farming change which Akenfield can have seen for hundreds of years. It is not a total change: there are still many acres of wheat, sugar-beet, barley and peas, but the presence on the valley slopes of many thousands of apple, plum and pear trees has created a feeling of enclosure from the customary bleakness which is luxurious and slightly foreign. The fruit plantations have also done something else for the communal life of Akenfield – they have perpetuated the old crowded harvest scene. A single youth is now the undoubted lord of the harvest as he steers his vast scarlet pterodactylic combine across the lonely acres, but it takes a full turn-out of many families to gather in the apples.

Down by the river lie the currant and gooseberry fields – literally the fruit of the potter's field, for the loam there is littered with Roman earthenware. Just above, the bit of straight – or the 'Army Path', as the Saxon farmers called it – shoots past towards the coast. The heights are crowned with mill sites and within the village proper there exists an empty secondary horse village, a deserted complex of packways, stables, smithies, chaff and collar houses, loose boxes, abandoned wagons, carts, harness rooms and tackle. Nothing has contributed more to the swift destruction of the old pattern of life in Suffolk than the death of the horse. It carried away with it a quite different conception of time.

The old farmsteads, snowcemmed and trim, ride high on the hills. They must remain remote unless some huge housing project thrusts up to meet them. And this is not likely. Akenfield itself has no development plans and even if Ipswich's overspill ever threatened it, it is doubtful if any preservationist society would launch an appeal to save it. It is not that kind of village. One or two new houses have gone up recently, usually in the depths of the valley and at the side of the stream and its meadows, with its carrs and its mosses, where a millennium of villagers have preferred not to live. This, on the quiet face of it, is as ordinary a group of country folk as one would meet anywhere in 1967. Or is it? How much is preserved? How much lost?

Politically, the over-fifties are still locked in the distresses and indignations stemming from the 'Revolt of the Field' of almost a century ago. A champion hedge-cutter named Joseph Arch led the revolt, which was to result in the first National Union of Agricultural Labourers – and a subsequent lock-out by the farmers. In Clopton, a parish four miles from Akenfield, the church-wardens gave this notice:

The Society calling itself the National Agricultural Union having ordered strikes in a portion of the county of Suffolk, all members of the same in this parish have notice to give up their allotments, and will be struck off the list of parochial and bread charities.

From this trade-unionism, which was more active in Norfolk and Suffolk than anywhere else in Britain, came years of farmers versus farmworkers skirmishing which embittered the countryside. The social and economic divisions widened to an extent unknown before and the position was worsened by the ruthlessness with which the farmers, deprived of cheap labour during hard times, ignored the Education Act of 1870 by taking boys away from school at eleven and twelve. The older farmers, too, are still emotionally caught up in what they called at the time the 'coming down process' and have vivid memories of being young in a twitch-ridden landscape, with water spread in thin lakes on top of the undrained clay and buildings sliding down into nettles. Both groups belong to 'those who stayed at home' during the great abandonment of the villages which began in 1881, when 700,000 British agricultural workers and their families, helped by Union funds, emigrated to the colonies. 'It was not the idlest and wastrels who sailed,' wrote Herbert Paul, 'but the strongest, the healthiest, and the most industrious men in the prime of life....' Two and a half million acres of arable became grass between 1872–1900 and the cornlands which remained needed far fewer workers because of the invention of the binder and other machines. Ironically for the Suffolk farm-worker, the best of these machines were pouring out of factories 'just over the way' – from Richard Garrett's great ironworks at Leiston and from Ransome's of Ipswich. These events and their consequences have touched all but the post-war generation. It is clear that much of the self-confidence of many of the middle-aged men has been either shaken or destroyed, resulting in protective good manners. They are grave, almost remote. Most remote of all is Davie, born in 1887 and who looks like Meredith at eighty, who cannot read or write a word and who insists that he has nothing to say.

Davie's life is not really of Akenfield – or of anything. It has been a coda to the old existence. He has never had to protest or state his case because it seems never to have occurred to him that he has a case. He is considered dirty by the village, though quite unnervingly white of skin and hair. Tall and straight, with vast blue child's eyes, he has lived in one half of the same double-dweller for eighty-one years. The house is turned away from the village and overlooks a sweep of barley and the valley made by the next tributary stream. This view is perfect and Davie hates it. During the 1920s there were rumours that a new road would be cut through it, carrying the traffic to Yarmouth, and then Davie exulted. But nothing happened. Next, it was said that the pylons carrying nuclear power from the Sizewell generator would pass his door, and then that 'they would be having his garden up' for the North Sea gas pipes, but again nothing happened. Davie is convinced of a curse.

He has been to the war, one of the strange host of 30,000 farm labourers called up in 1917, when the victims were running out. He was thirty and had already been hard at work in the Akenfield farms for twenty-one years. Then this sudden and amazing journey to the battlefield, equipped with a gun which he understood, because of rabbiting, and a New Testament, which he alternately smoked or used for lavatory paper.

'Did you kill men, Davie?'

'I got several' – the same answer to a question on how he did on a rook-drive.

'What was the worst thing, Davie?'

'Why, the wet, of course!'

He has lived alone since his parents died during a diphtheria epidemic which broke out when he was ten, never marrying, never inviting anyone to his cottage, which is crammed with polished furniture, wine-bottles and rag rugs which he makes himself. He knows of no blood relations. He was baptized in the font in the parish church, the bowl of which is supported by carved stone 'woodmen' – the forest gods of Suffolk – but it is the register and not Davie which gives this information. He likes to believe that he has 'never set foot in the ol' place – nor in that chapel neether!' Absence of commitment is a tremendous relief to him. He likes to think that there is nothing to tell. Yet the first thing one notices about him is not negation and recluse-like rejection, but an almost greedy, urgent positivity. It is such a vital existence which informs him. He is, he breathes – though what air? one sometimes wonders. The village fool? So obviously and completely not. Some slight imbalance, some occasional fall due to 'nerves', as all illnesses beyond the immediately identifiable and accidents are called in Akenfield, might have placed him – might have enrolled him in the tolerated company of the 'touched'. Yet the one certain thing about Davie is his crushing sanity. His isolation is due, maybe, to some snapping of the communication links between his world and ours. Scraps of old farming practice can be dragged out of him – nothing special. Twenty men and boys scythed the corn and sang as they went.

'What was the song, Davie?'

'Never you mind the song – it was the singing that counted.'

High up on the wall of the biggest barn in the village, almost at the apex of the east wall's pediment, on the inside and armorial beneath its mantling of cobwebs, there is a deep and perfect impression of a small hand with the fingers fanned out. It is Davie's hand, pressed into the wet plaster when he was fourteen, after he had helped to mend the barn. A chink in the roof spotlights the clean lines of this dusty answer. 'There – that's something,' says Davie. 'Or you could say, "that's all".'

The wind catches at his house. The East Anglian wind does far more than move the barley; it is doctrinal. Probably no other agent except, per-haps, the great forests which once covered this plain, has done more to shape the character of the people who have dwelt on it. It is a quite unmysterious wind, dispelling the fuzziness of things. On a clear day – and they are mostly clear days in this part of the world – you can see as far as you can bear to see, and sometimes farther. It is a suitable climate for a little arable kingdom where flints are the jewels and where exist-ence is sharp-edged.

Population and Houses

Population, 1961=298. (146 males, 152 females.) The figures show a dramatic drop from the 1931 census, when 416 people lived in the village.

Houses:

Ten farmhouses dating from the late fifteenth to the mid seventeenth centuries, all built of stud and plaster, and with tiled roofs. The largest of these farmhouses is The Hall but each has been constructed on the same principle of timber uprights spaced out along a great wall-plate beam, with the sections infilled with either split oak lathes over which clay bound with flax stems, straw and tow has been smoothed. A lime plaster completed the process. The wall-plate usually rests on a dwarf masonry wall which is pitched on the outside to prevent rising damp. The roofs are steep and the ground floors paved with bricks. A great and often ornate brick chimney complex rises through the centre of these substantial farms. Most have been modernized, and five are not now connected with farming.

Two sixteenth-century cottages made of wattle and daub. The wattles were the hazel-branch infillings between the oak posts. One of these cottages is the only thatched dwelling left in the village.

Six seventeenth-century cottages. Stud and plaster. On some of these the plaster has been combed or lined with a stick into patterns called 'bird's foot', 'the dot' and 'the rope' – the basic motifs of Suffolk 'stick-work'.

Twenty-four eighteenth-century cottages. Stud and plaster, clapboard and brick. Nearly all of these, and indeed some forty-two buildings in the village all told, are pantiled. Sometimes called 'Roman' tiles in the district, these large orange tiles glow in the hard Suffolk light. They originated in Holland and first entered East Anglian ports as ballast during the seventeenth century. They were manufactured here a century later and are a dominating feature of the local architecture.

Twenty-three nineteenth-century cottages and houses, nearly all of local brick. These include 'double-dwellers' put up at an average cost of £70 each during the worst days of Victorian farm labour exploitation. Some remain much as they were, plus television, others have been successfully extended to form good agricultural cottages.

1900–20. Only three houses were built in the village during this period.

1920–40 – nineteen houses built, including sixteen council houses and bungalows. The latter stand in an attractive position in the main street but reveal their authority's brutal indifference to taste, feeling and imagination. Although built in the late 1930s, bathrooms and water closets are only now being installed (1968).

Post-war. Twelve houses have been built, mainly since 1950. They include four excellent estate cottages for the orchard workers and a few bungalows for professional people. One of these, put up by a young architect a year ago, is one of the most beautiful buildings in the village. All the houses are surrounded by, usually well-kept, gardens.

Work in the Village

Farmers:

Roger Cable	(fruit and arable)
Eric Milburne	(fruit and arable)
Duncan Campbell	(sheep, dairy and arable)
Bernard Nunn	(livestock and arable)
Roger Adlard	(weaner pigs and chickens)
Colonel West	(weaner pigs and arable)
Jamie McIver	(mainly arable)

Small-holders:

Adrian Ranson	(fruit, catch crops)
L. and J. Oldfield	(market gardeners)
Barney Tucker	(fruit and catch crops)
Winston Plummer	(dairyman)
Geoffrey Whitehead	(market gardener)
Oliver Quantrill	(battery hens and pigs)
Sammy Whitelaw	(fruit)
Terry Lloyd	(pigs)

Farm manager:
 Robert Palgrave

Farm foremen:
 Ken Baker
 Dana Appleby
 Charles Holden
 Alan Mitton

Farm mechanic:
 Laurence Honeywood

Pigman:
 Abel Paternoster

Road-workers:
 Donald Cooper
 Andrew Fletcher (foreman)

Gravedigger:
 William Russ

Odd-jobbers:

Persis Ede	(fruit-farm work, dealer)
Kitchener Mead	(clock-winder, sweep and barber)

Publican:
Barnaby Palmer

Van-drivers:
Stella Fletcher   (travelling shop)
Hector Watson   (travelling shop)
Dawn Parsons   (travelling shop)
'Hickey' Briggs   (travelling shop)
David Parsons   (travelling shop)

Shop-keepers:
Alec Rix   (general store and post office)
Chris Kilderbee   (general store)
Janet Smith   (general store and petrol pump)

Veterinary surgeon:
Tim Swift

Insurance agents:
'Ted Hughes
John Stennett

Gardener:
Christopher Falconer

Shepherd:
Anthony Summer

Tractor-drivers:
Tom Dix
Derek Warren

General farm-workers:
Alan Ling
Kurt Fischer (ex-prisoner of war)
'Angle' Double
Mervyn Watson
Stanley Ling
Hugh Paternoster
Douglas Cooper
George Keeble
Eddie Toogood

Women who do occasional work on the farms:
May Ling   (fruit-picking)
Olive Watson   (fruit-picking)

Greta Paternoster	(fruit-picking)
Mary Paternoster	(fruit-picking)
Sheila Keeble	(fruit-picking)
Winifred Reeve	(fruit-picking)
Phyllis Briggs	(fruit-picking)
Jeanette Appleby	(fruit-picking)
Ivy Kempe	(fruit-picking)
Molly Gaunt	(fruit-picking)
Mary Mitton	(fruit-picking)
Sue Crawford	(fruit-picking)
Flora Appleby	(fruit-picking)
Margaret Ransom	(fruit-picking)
Millie Double	(general farm work)
Peggy Nunn	(general farm work)
Deirdre Cant	(general farm work)

Creative artists:
| J— W— | (poet) |
| Stephen Welham | (painter) |

Vicar:
The Rev. Gethyn Owen, M.A.

Baptist pastor:
Mr Dermott Thompson

School-teachers:
| Mrs Sullivan | (headmistress) |
| Daphne Ellington | (assistant mistress) |

School caretaker:
Theresa Judd

Craftsmen:
Gregory Gladwell	(blacksmith)
Bruce Buckley	(forge apprentice)
Francis Lambert	(forge worker)
Ernie Bowers	(thatcher)
Horry Rose	(saddler)
Jubal Merton	(wheelwright and carpenter)

Civil defence worker:
Major John Paul, M.C.

Housekeepers: four

Housewives (i.e. married women):
    thirty-three

Widows: ten

People who live in the village but work outside it:

James Gaunt	(building trade)
Errol Creed	(building trade)
Dennis Creed	(building trade)
Barry May	(building trade)
Rayner Creighton	(schoolmaster)
Hugh Hamblin	(schoolmaster)
Sheila Brooke	(schoolmistress)
Robert Munro	(primary school-teacher)
Alice Steed	(nurse at mental hospital)
Jack Barton	(farm manager)
Derek Riley	(nurseryman)
Dick Goodman	(seedsman's lorry-driver)
Lesly Judd	(clerk on U.S.A.A.F. base)
James Law	(flour-mill worker)
Adam Scott	(coal merchant's driver)
William Ridge-Powell	(city businessman)
Moreton Gage	(county council architect)
Bob Kenyon	(grocer's driver)
Ray Kenyon	(office worker, Ipswich)
Keith Robinson	(fruit-canner)
Geoffrey Riddleston	(bank cashier)

Retired people:

John Grout	(farmer)
Emily Leggett	(domestic servant)
Leonard Thompson	(farm-worker)
Luke Last	(farm-worker)
Fred Mitchell	(farm-worker)
Bill Scott	(tailor)
Sidney Summers	(schoolmaster)
Frederick Whittaker	(hotelier, Great Yarmouth)
Samuel Gissing	(farm-worker)
Ted Mallett	(fishmonger, Ipswich)
Marjory Jope	(district nurse)
Peter Morley	(builder and decorator)
Albert Wolfson	(civil servant)

The above analysis doesn't include every name but attempts to show the main work pattern of the village people. Altogether, some eighty-five men and women are full-time earners, whether self-employed or wage or salaried employees.

Some eighty-two men and women are directly or indirectly connected with agriculture and horticulture. This number includes retired farming people, farmers' wives and part-time workers. Also people who work in flour mills, drive corn lorries or who work in farm-machinery works.

Only one man commutes to London each day (ninety-two miles), but there has been a steady increase in Ipswich (ten miles) commuting over the last seven years.

Domesday for 1936 and 1966: The Second Agricultural Revolution

The following figures, taken from the official agricultural returns for Akenfield, reveal the immensely increased yield from the village's 1,355 acres during the last thirty years.

Acres	1936	1966
wheat	185	238
barley	147	572½
oats	19	23
potatoes	¾	36½
beans and peas for stock-feeding	107	27
turnips, swedes and fodder beet for stock	3	—
kale for stock-feeding	—	5¼
sugar-beet	76	116¾
vetches, taws and lucerne	14	—
clover, sainfoin for mowing, grazing	136	26
permanent grassland for mowing, grazing	486	131
rough grazing	31	1½
vegetables for human consumption (not potatoes)	7	127½

Orchards and other Fruit

Acres	1936	1966
commercial orchards	76	120¾
other orchards	9	7¼
small fruit	14	53¾

Bare Fallow

Acres	1936	1966
fallow	61	17½

Akenfield

Stock

	1936	*1966*
cattle	266	111
sheep	115	750
pigs	674	1278
poultry	3293	24105

1 · The Survivors

Leonard Thompson ·
aged seventy-one · farm-worker

Len and his wife live in a solitary house which stands not more than a
yard off the Roman road. The foundations of the house must rest in the
ditch made by the road-builders when they dug out earth for the
camber. The mixture of fragility and tenacity which marks the cottage
is somehow indicative of Len himself. Although there is nothing
particularly frail about him in the physical sense – he is a little brown
bull of a man with hard blue eyes and limbs so stretched by toil that
they seem incapable of relaxing into retirement – he has stood firmly in
the apocalyptic path of events which have wrenched the village from its
serfdom. He is astute, unsentimental and realistic. He is neither proud
nor regretful to have endured the bad times. He is political and holds
large, simple convictions which make a lot of today's social hopefulness
sound oddly irrelevant. In fact, his evident political nature makes him
untypically East Anglian, for politics on the corn plain are notoriously
vague, furtive and unreal.

Len is also an extraordinarily interesting survivor of Britain's village
lost generation, that mysterious army of horsemen, ploughmen and field
workers who fled the wretchedness of the farms in 1914. The army had
provided – along with the railways – an escape route for many years
before this, but it was the First World War which swept Len and his
contemporaries off the hated land to conditions which forced the thinking countryman to decide to halt a system of degradation when they
returned. The climate of the 1920s and 1930s suited Len perfectly for
what he had to do. The war had given those who survived it confidence.
Len showed his by stolidly denying the village farmers their virtual
ownership of the labourers and their families. He organized the union
branch. The successes and defeats of the struggle, which was basically
a nineteenth-century one and little different from that of Joseph Arch

and his colleagues, suited him excellently. He wanted 'improvement', not metamorphosis. But for a man of Len's age, the change which has swept through the village *is* metamorphosis, neither more nor less, and so one sees him, a fine old man, doing his utmost to comprehend the foreign place in which he happened to have been born. Grandchildren arrive during the university holidays. Nephews and nieces fly in from Canada, while the ash at the end of the road, which marked the last point at which soldier and emigrant sons could turn and wave before walking to Ipswich to catch the train to Gallipoli or Quebec, still blocks the view.

*

There were ten of us in the family and as my father was a farm labourer earning 13s. a week you can just imagine how we lived. I will tell you the first thing which I can remember. It was when I was three – about 1899. We were all sitting round the fire waiting for my soldier brother to come home – he was the eldest boy in the family. He arrived about six in the evening and had managed to ride all the way from Ipswich station in a milk-cart. This young man came in, and it was the first time I had seen him. He wore a red coat and looked very lively. Mother got up and kissed him but Father just sat and said, 'How are you?' Then we had tea, all of us staring at my brother. It was dark, it was the winter-time. A few days later he walked away and my mother stood right out in the middle of the road, watching. He was going to fight in South Africa. He walked smartly down the lane until his red coat was no bigger than a poppy. Then the tree hid him. We never saw him again. He went all through the war but caught enteric fever afterwards and died. He was twenty-one.

Very soon after this it was very hard living indeed for the family. There were seven children at home and father's wages had been reduced to 10s. a week. Our cottage was nearly empty – except for people. There was a scrubbed brick floor and just one rug made of scraps of old clothes pegged into a sack. The cottage had a living-room, a larder and two bedrooms. Six of us boys and girls slept in one bedroom and our parents and the baby slept in the other. There was no newspaper and nothing to read except the Bible. All the village houses were like this.

Our food was apples, potatoes, swedes and bread, and we drank our tea without milk or sugar. Skim milk could be bought from the farm but it was thought a luxury. Nobody could get enough to eat no matter how they tried. Two of my brothers were out to work. One was eight years old and he got 3s. a week, the other got about 7s. Our biggest trouble was water. There was no water near, it all had to be fetched from the foot of a hill nearly a mile away. 'Drink all you can at school', we were told – there was a tap at school. You would see the boys and girls filling themselves up like camels before they left school so that they would have enough water to last the day. I always remember the bitter metal taste of the tap in my mouth; it was cold – beautiful! I remember once coming home from school and feeling almost mad for water. My mother was washing the linen on the doorstep and when her back was turned I swigged two cupfuls from the tub. Up it came at once – it was all soapsuds! Mother did no more than box my ears. That is how they thought about you at that time.

Our parents and all the cottage people were very religious and very patriotic. The patriotic songs and the church hymns seemed equally holy. They took our breath away. The boys marched through the village singing,

Lords Roberts and Kitchener, Generals Buller and White,
All dressed in khaki, going out to fight ...

and their faces would look sincere and important. It was all 'my country' – country, country, country. You heard nothing else. There was no music in the village then except at the chapel or the church and our family liked it so much that we hurried from one to the other to hear all we could. People like us, who went where we fancied on a Sunday, were called 'Devil-dodgers'. We all went to one service after another and ate packets of bread-and-jam in between. People believed in religion then, which I think was a good thing because if they hadn't got religion there would have been a revolution. Nobody would have stuck it. Religion disciplined us and gave us the strength to put up with things. The parson was very respected. He could do what he liked with us when he felt like it. One day he came to our house and told my eldest sister, who was eleven, to leave school. 'I think you needn't finish,' he said. 'You can go and be maid to old Mrs Barney Wickes, now she has lost her husband.' Mrs Barney Wickes was blind and my sister was paid a penny a day out of Parish Relief to look after her.

People were strict. Parents were strict. All the village children thought of was how to get away, how to 'get on'. But we had our games and treats. We had a game called 'Hudney'. A stone was placed on a brick and had to be knocked off by another stone when it was aimed at it. When you ran to retrieve the stone a boy would try and hit you with a ball and if he did you were out of the game. We played this for hours on end. We had no toys, no books and we didn't play cricket or football.

But all the boys and young men swam naked in the river in the summer-time. It was our biggest happiness. Boys were washed until they were about two, then their bodies didn't see water again until they learned to swim. We didn't look dirty. We were healthy, strong children, but small. One of our great desires was to have cake. Nearly all our food was boiled on account of there being no oven in most of the cottages. A 'treat' was any party where you could eat cake.

I walked two miles to school. There were so many children you could hardly squeeze in the room. All the same, it was very cold in the winter. Most of the boys had suits and boots on with nothing underneath. Every now and then we used to have to stand on the outside of our desks and mark-time to get our circulation back. We did left-right, left-right for about five minutes – good God, what a row we made! Later on, I heard this sound again in Gallipoli. It seemed homely and familiar. We must have been bashing some landing-stage. The school was useless. The farmers came and took boys away from it when they felt like it, the parson raided it for servants. The teacher was a respectable woman who did her best. Sometimes she would bring the *Daily Graphic* down and show us the news. I looked forward to leaving school so that I could get educated. I knew that education was in books, not in school: there were no books there. I was a child when I left but I already knew that our 'learning' was rubbish, that our food was rubbish and that I should end as rubbish if I didn't look out.

When I was six we moved to another house. It was a tied-cottage with a thatched roof and handsome beams. My father said, 'We shall be better off, boys, we shall have a nice spring of water just across the road, and that will be a great relief. Also we shall have a nice big garden with two apple trees, a Doctor Harvey and a Blenheim Orange.' We moved to this house in 1904. As soon as we got there, mother went stone-picking in the fields. She didn't have to do this because we were living in a tied-cottage but because we had to buy some new clothes. We helped her when we got back from school at five o'clock. She had to pick up twenty-four bushels of stones a day to get 2s. Each parish had to mend its own lanes then and the stones were used for this. A tumbril was put in the field and a line was chalked round it. When you had filled it up to the line you got the 2s. It would take the whole day. We did it every minute we weren't at school and all through the holidays. It was all I can remember.

But during the harvest holiday we had a change – gleaning. The women would meet and say, 'Is Scarlets ready for gleaning yet? Is Great Mosses?' – these were the names of the fields. They meant, not has

the field been cut but have they cleared the 'policeman'. The policeman was the name given to the last trave or stook which the farmers
would leave standing in the middle of the field so they could have time
to rake-up all the loose corn they could before the gleaners arrived. There
was one farmer who made a habit of keeping the gleaners waiting and
one night a young man stole the 'policeman'. The next morning the
gleaners hurried in and gleaned masses – the field hadn't been raked,
you see. The whole village was laughing – except the farmer. He raked-
up quick the next year, I can tell you!

I gleaned all my boyhood. I ran away from it once but came to grief,
and since the results have been with me all my life, I will tell you about
it. When I was six I got fed up with being in the gleaning-field with all
the women, so I ran off to help the boy who worked the cattle-cake
machine. In no time my hand was caught and my fingers were squashed.
The farmer was just coming up by the granary on his horse when he
heard me screaming. 'What have you been up to, you young scamp?' he
shouted. 'My fingers – they're in the cake-breaker!' And he said – I
shall never forget it – 'Get you off home then!' But when he saw my
hand he changed his tune and said, 'Get up to the house'. The farmer's
wife tied some rag round my hand and took me home and my mother
wheeled me miles to the doctor's in a pram. My sister was home from
service, so she came with us and held me while the doctor scraped the
grease out of my wounds with a knife, stitched up one finger, cut another,
pared it like a stick and tied what was left to the bone, and then moved
on to the next finger. I lifted the roof, I can tell you. There was no anaesthetic, nothing. My sister began to faint and the doctor got on to her
something terrific. 'Damn silly girl – clear off outside if you can't stand
it! Fetch my groom in.' So the groom came and held me until it was
finished. All the time the doctor worked he shouted. 'What did you do
it for? Why? Damn little nuisance! Stupid little fool!'

Nobody used pity then, and especially not to children, and particularly not to boys. The farmer told my father and he said, 'I'll give him
something to think about when I get home!' It was harvest so it was
late when he returned. 'Where's that boy Leonard?' he said 'I'm
going to give him a good hiding.' 'He's gone to bed, he's had enough,'
said mother. My father didn't realize how bad it was, you see. The tops
of three of my fingers had been cut off. So he didn't touch me.

There were a lot of hidings then. My father was a good man and didn't
like giving them to us, but some people did. Father never smoked or
drank, and he looked after his children. He had a wonderful character
in the parish. He would go to work with three-quarters of a loaf of

bread and a little bit of cheese, and maybe a couple of onions, but when we ran to meet him after his day's work, he would give us the cheese. He had saved it for us. 'I can do without that,' he would say. We were thrashed a lot at school. Fathers would be ordered to the school to hold their sons while the mistress thrashed them. Most of the teachers were big thrashers. But we were tough, very tough. Everybody said, don't-don't to boys then and after awhile we didn't listen. We were wondering how we could get away.

I left school when I was thirteen, on April 20th when the corn was low. I helped my mother pulling up docks in the Big Field for a shilling an acre, which my mother took. She could see that I was too big to have money taken from me like this, so when the farmer came round she said, 'Can't you give my boy a proper job?' She meant a regular job with a wage. But the farmer just laughed and rode away. So the next week I tried my luck at another farm. Mr Wakeling, this farmer, was very tall and he had three sons of about eighteen to twenty-one who were all over six feet. They all stood looking down at me and smiling. 'So you are thirteen and you have left school, but what can you do?' 'I can do anything.' 'Well, there's a mangold field over there – you do that.'

'What are you going to get?' asked my mother when I told her. 'I never asked and he never said,' I replied. It was the beginning of being grown-up.

I had a week in this field, singling mangolds, and I did well because I had often done the job before after school. The farmer came and looked and said, 'You've done very well, my little man. How much have I got to give you?' 'My mother said half-a-crown but perhaps you would sooner give me a rise.' But the farmer thought half-a-crown was good, which was what I got for sixty hours' work. When the harvest came along, the boy who was doing the milking, and who was seventeen and strong, was told to load corn and I had to take over the cows. The farmer's riding ponies and then his sons' ponies were added. Then the farmer said, 'You'll have to work Sundays now, but I shall be giving you another sixpence.' So I got 3s. a week. Mother said, 'How lucky you are!'

Shortly after this my father came to grief with his farmer and we had to leave the tied-cottage. We moved down by the river and when we were settled father took my brother and myself to his new employer and, twizzling me round so that I could be seen, said, 'Here's a good strong boy. I want 4s. 6d. a week for him.' 'We'll see about that at the end of the week,' said the farmer. Then my father made my brother stand forward – he was fifteen – and said, 'Look what a fine lad. I want 8s.

a week for him.' The farmer thought for a minute, looked us up and down and said, 'All right.'

The second week that I was at this new farm I had to drive a herd of cattle to Ipswich. I was thirteen and had lived only ten miles away all my life, but I had never been to this big town before. The farmer went ahead in his trap and waited for me at Ipswich market. He sold the cows and bought some more, and told me to drive them back to the farm. Most of my work was like this, walking cattle along the roads backwards and forwards to the market – about twenty-five miles a day. The farmer was a dealer. I stayed with him a year and four months and was paid 4s. 6d. a week. And then I got into a hell of a row. I'd driven a flock of sheep from Ipswich and the next morning they found that one had died. The farmer was in a terrible stew. He ran down the field and met my mother on her way to chapel and told her all about it. I had driven the sheep too hard, he said. 'And you drive boys too hard!' said my mother – she had no fear at all. Well, the truth of the matter is that she said a lot of things she'd only thought until then, and so I left the farm. It must seem that there was war between farmers and their men in those days. I think there was, particularly in Suffolk. These employers were famous for their meanness. They took all they could from the men and boys who worked their land. They bought their life's strength for as little as they could. They wore us out without a thought because, with the big families, there was a continuous supply of labour. Fourteen young men left the village in 1909–11 to join the army. There wasn't a recruiting drive, they just escaped. And some people just changed their sky, as they say, and I was one of them.

Every week in the *Suffolk Chronicle and Mercury* there was an advertisement which said, 'Lads for Yorkshire. Milk or Ploughing. Good Homes. Fares Paid. Apply: Woods of Stowmarket.' All the Yorkshire farm-workers, you see, had left the land to work in the factories and mills. So they hit on this idea of getting workers up from Suffolk, where things were desperate, to cultivate the Yorkshire farms. So I thought, right, I'll go! I was getting 9s. a week for a seventy-five-hour week in a cow-shed. I had four hours off a week, from 10–2 on a Sunday. So I went to Yorkshire. I met Mr Woods on Bury St Edmunds station and he gave me my ticket. I went to a farm in the West Riding. It was the first time I had been away from home. I lived in a little old room on the farm with two other boys and was told that I would get £12 at the end of the year, which was 5s. a week, but also my food and keep. The food was good; we ate it with the servant in the kitchen. We worked like little donkeys until we were a bit unsteady on our feet, then it was bed. Then work. I had to pay a pound a year to an old woman to do my washing, pay a pound to get home again and a pound for boots and corduroys, but I came to Suffolk with eight golden sovereigns in my hand and felt a millionaire.

I returned to my old farm at Akenfield for 11s. a week, but I was unsettled. When the farmer stopped my pay because it was raining and we couldn't thrash, I said to my seventeen-year-old mate, 'Bugger him. We'll go off and join the army.' It was March 4th 1914. We joined the army a few hours after we had made our decision. We walked to Ipswich and got the train to Colchester. We were soaked to the skin but very happy. At the barracks we kissed the Bible and were given a shilling. The recruiting sergeant said, 'You can't go home in all this rain, you can sleep in a bed in the recruiting room'. In the morning he said, 'Go home and say good-bye, and here's ten shillings each for your food and fares. Report back on Monday.'

In my four months' training with the regiment I put on nearly a stone in weight and got a bit taller. They said it was the food but it was really because for the first time in my life there had been no strenuous work. I want to say this simply as a fact, that village people in Suffolk in my day were worked to death. It literally happened. It is not a figure of speech. I was worked mercilessly. I am not complaining about it. It is what happened to me.

We were all delighted when war broke out on August 4th. I was now a machine-gunner in the Third Essex Regiment. A lot of boys from the village were with me and although we were all sleeping in ditches at Harwich, wrapped in our greatcoats, we were bursting with happiness. We were all damned glad to have got off the farms. I had 7s. a week and sent my mother half of it. If you did this, the government would add another 3s. 6d. – so my mother got 7s. My father died early this year and my mother lived on this 7s. a week for the whole of the war, adding a scrap to it by doing washing, and weeding in the fields. Neither of my parents lived long enough to draw the Old Age Pension. I can remember, when work was short, a group of unemployed young men coming to where some old men were sugar-beeting, which is the worst job there is, and shouting, 'Now that you grandfathers have got the pension' – it was 5s. a week – 'why don't you get out of the field and give us a chance?' These 'old' men were only in their fifties but the hardness of their lives had made them ancient.

All this trouble with the village fell behind us now. I was nineteen and off to the Dardanelles, which is the Hellespont, I discovered. I had two boys from the village with me. We'd heard a lot about France so

we thought we'd try Turkey. The band played on the banks of the
river as we pulled out of Plymouth and I wondered if we would ever
come home again. We were all so patriotic then and had been taught to
love England in a fierce kind of way. The village wasn't England;
England was something better than the village. We got to Gib and it
was lovely and warm. Naked Spanish boys dived round us for coins.
There were about fifty nurses on the top deck and they threw tanners.
You could see they were having an eye-opener. We stopped to coal-up.
The dust blew all over the decks and all over us. We were packed like
sardines and eating rubbish again. Water and salt porridge for breakfast. Beans and high salt pork for dinner. The pork was too bad for
land-men to eat so we threw it into the coaldust and the coolies snatched
it up and thrust it into their mouths, or put it into sacks to take home
for their families.

We arrived at the Dardanelles and saw the guns flashing and heard
the rifle-fire. They heaved our ship, the *River Clyde,* right up to the
shore. They had cut a hole in it and made a little pier, so we were able to
walk straight off and on to the beach. We all sat there – on the Hellespont! – waiting for it to get light. The first things we saw were big
wrecked Turkish guns, the second a big marquee. It didn't make me
think of the military but of the village fêtes. Other people must have
thought like this because I remember how we all rushed up to it, like
boys getting into a circus, and then found it all laced up. We unlaced it
and rushed in. It was full of corpses Dead Englishmen, lines and lines
of them, and with their eyes wide open. We all stopped talking. I'd
never seen a dead man before and here I was looking at two or three
hundred of them. It was our first fear. Nobody had mentioned this. I
was very shocked. I thought of Suffolk and it seemed a happy place for
the first time.

Later that day we marched through open country and came to within
a mile and half of the front line. It was incredible. We were there – at
the war! The place we had reached was called 'dead ground' because it
was where the enemy couldn't see you. We lay in little square holes,
myself next to James Sears from the village. He was about thirty and
married. That evening we wandered about on the dead ground and
asked about friends of ours who had arrived a month or so ago. 'How
is Ernie Taylor?' – 'Ernie? – he's gone.' 'Have you seen Albert Paternoster?' – 'Albert? – he's gone.' We learned that if 300 had 'gone' but
700 were left, then this wasn't too bad. We then knew how unimportant
our names were.

I was on sentry that night. A chap named Scott told me that I must only put my head up for a second but that in this time I must see as much as I could. Every third man along the trench was a sentry. The next night we had to move on to the third line of trenches and we heard that the Gurkhas were going over and that we had to support their rear. But when we got to the communication trench we found it so full of dead men that we could hardly move. Their faces were quite black and you couldn't tell Turk from English. There was the most terrible stink and for a while there was nothing but the living being sick on to the dead. I did sentry again that night. It was one-two-sentry, one-two-sentry all along the trench, as before. I knew the next sentry up quite well. I remembered him in Suffolk singing to his horses as he ploughed. Now he fell back with a great scream and a look of surprise – dead. It is quick, anyway, I thought. On June 4th we went over the top. We took the Turks' trench and held it. It was called Hill 13. The next day we were relieved and told to rest for three hours, but it wasn't more than half an hour before the relieving regiment came running back. The Turks had returned and recaptured their trench. On June 6th my favourite officer was killed and no end of us butchered, but we managed to get hold of Hill 13 again. We found a great muddle, carnage and men without rifles shouting '*Allah! Allah!*', which is God's name in the Turkish language. Of the sixty men I had started out to war from Harwich with, there were only three left.

We set to work to bury people. We pushed them into the sides of the trench but bits of them kept getting uncovered and sticking out, like people in a badly made bed. Hands were the worst; they would escape from the sand, pointing, begging – even waving! There was one which we all shook when we passed, saying, 'Good morning', in a posh voice. Everybody did it. The bottom of the trench was springy like a mattress because of all the bodies underneath. At night, when the stench was worse, we tied crêpe round our mouths and noses. This crêpe had been given to us because it was supposed to prevent us being gassed. The flies entered the trenches at night and lined them completely with a density which was like moving cloth. We killed millions by slapping our spades along the trench walls but the next night it would be just as bad. We were all lousy and we couldn't stop shitting because we had caught dysentery. We wept, not because we were frightened but because we were so dirty.

We didn't feel indignant against the Government. We believed all they said, all the propaganda. We believed the fighting had got to be done. We were fighting for England. You only had to say 'England' to stop any argument. We shot and shot. On August 6th they made a landing at Suvla Bay and we took Hill 13 again, and with very few casualties this time. We'd done a good job. The trench had been lost yet again, you see. When we got back for the third time we found a little length of trench which had somehow missed the bombardment. There were about six Turkish boys in it and we butchered them right quick. We couldn't stay in the trench, we had to go on. Then we ran into machine-gun fire and had to fall flat in the heather, or whatever it was. Suddenly my mate caught fire as he lay there. A bullet had hit his ammunition belt. Several people near jumped up and ran back, away from the burning man and the machine-gun fire. I could hear the strike of the gun about a foot above my head. I lay between the burning man and a friend of mine called Darky Fowler. Darky used to be a shepherd Helmingham way. I put my hand out and shook him, and said, 'Darky, we've got to go back. We *must* go back!' He never answered. He had gone. I lay there thinking how funny it was that I should end my life that night. Then my mate began to go off like a firework – the fire was exploding his cartridges. That did it! I up and ran.

There is nobody can say that you have killed a man. I shot through so many because I was a machine-gunner. Did they all die? – I don't know. You got very frightened of the murdering and you did sometimes think, 'What is all this about? What is it for?' But mostly you were thinking of how to stay alive. The more the killing, the more you thought about living. You felt brave and honoured that you should be fighting for England. You knew that all the people at home were for it. We believed we were fighting for a good cause and so, I expect, did the Turks. You didn't think personally. You can't get on with wars if you think personally. You can't say you *shot* a man, although you know you hit him, because there were so many guns going at the same time. But I should think that I killed several. [Several means quite a few or many in Suffolk.]

After Gallipoli I went to France. I went through the Somme and through the battle of Arras, after which I was captured. It was 14th April 1917. We ran and gave ourselves up, there was nothing more we could do. The Germans lined us up and marched us off. I thought, 'We're safe now. We're out of it ...' I didn't know what was going to happen. If I had I would sooner have gone through all the fighting again. It was the worst thing which ever happened to me in my life. We were taken to Lille, where the Germans had to make us ill and wretched in a week in order to march us through the town, so that they could say to the people, 'Look at the great British army, look what it has been reduced to!' We were driven into dark dungeons, straight off the battle-field, starved, made filthy and in only *six days* we were ill and we looked

Akenfield

like scarecrows. The Germans knew how to do this to men. After the parade about 300 of us were packed into a half-built mansion and there we lived on pearl barley boiled in coppers and bread or cake made of weed-seed. Then we were put into a forest to make charcoal and some- times the Germans shot into our legs as we marched. We never knew what they would do next. They chose boys to thrash. I don't know why I was chosen but I was a favourite for this thrashing and was always being taken off for a beating. George Holmes, a farmer's son from the village, was one of the people who died from the ill-treatment.

At Christmas 1917 they took us to Germany, right down to Kiel. It was snowing and we were in rags. No shoes. They gave us wooden clogs. We dug on the Kiel railway, making a track to the Baltic for the big guns. Many people died. On November 5th 1918 some German sailors arrived and set us free. They cut all the barbed wire and left just one guard in charge. 'You can leave if you like,' they said. 'The war will soon be over. There is going to be a revolution, so keep off the roads. You could go and help the farmers pick up potatoes. That would be sensible.'

So this is what we did. And when the war ended, there we were, Ger- mans, Poles, Russians and Englishmen, working in the fields and realiz- ing that there was damn little growing in them.

The soldiers who got back to the village recovered very quickly. People who had lost their sons felt strange. Generally speaking, we were thankful that it was all over and we could get back to our work. Yet things *had* changed and people were different. The farm-workers who had been soldiers were looked at in a new way. There were a few more privileges around than there used to be. They'd let you take a rabbit or two, for instance. Before 1914, if you'd caught a rabbit, my God, the world would have come to an end! The sack was the least you'd get. We felt that there must be no slipping back to the bad old ways and about 1920 we formed a branch of the Agricultural Labourers' Union.

1920 looked like being a good year. The awards made by the Central Wages Board were enforced in the spring and we were getting 38s. 6d. a week on the farms. We worked fifty-four hours a week and had a half- holiday, and if we worked overtime it was 1s. 1d. an hour. What a change from 1914, when it was 13s. a week and just enough grub and sleep to keep you on the move! The farmers were able to pay the new wages because of the prices guaranteed by the Corn Act of 1917, so we didn't feel that we were diddling them. Only two or three hundred men belonged to the Union before the war, now thousands and thousands joined. This was the summer one of our members, Mr Edwards, won

South Norfolk for Labour. He was the second farm-worker to get into Parliament. We were so pleased with the way things were going that we felt we must consolidate. We had never had anything before, you see. We felt glad but unsafe. So we demanded 50s. a week and said that we would strike if we didn't get it. Then things began to go wrong. It had nothing to do with the strike plans.

The slump set in during the great hot summer of 1921. I remember it well. We had no rain from March right through to October. The corn didn't grow no more than a foot high and most of it didn't even come to the ear. We harvested what we could and the last loads were leaving the field when we heard, 'the wages are coming down this week'. It was true. The farmers told the men that they would be given 42s. 6d. Then it was 38s. 6d. A fortnight later on the farm where I worked it was 'You'll have to be on short-time – the boss can only afford to give you 27s. 6d. a week'. And that is what we lived on all that bad winter.

It was the Government's fault. They ended the Corn Act less than a year after it had been made law. They said it was best if the farmers made their own bargains, which meant that they wouldn't pay the subsidies. The price of wheat was quartered in a year. Cattle were sold for next to nothing because the farmers couldn't afford to keep them. The farmers became broke and frightened, so they took it out on us men. We reminded them that we had fought in the war, and they reminded us that they had too! So it was hate all round. Then we had to close down our Union Branch because nobody could afford to pay the 4d. a week membership fee. I remember the week this happened. I drew 27s. 6d. from the farmer and after I had given my wife 24s. and paid my Union 4d. and my rent 3s. 1d., I had a penny left! So I threw it across the field. I'd worked hard, I'd been through the war and I'd married. A penny was what a child had. I wasn't having that. I would sooner have nothing.

The farmers were utterly against the Union and utterly against the Wages Board. Now, in our village, we had no Union, no Board – nobody to look after us. Sixteen men fell out of work but there was no dole for farm labourers. An unemployed married farm-worker got parish relief but a single man got nothing. So the young men began to walk to the other villages, searching for odd jobs. Soon East Anglia was full of these men and, by 1930 or so, you'd get up to fifty of them passing the cottage every night as they tramped from workhouse to workhouse. The farmers knew about our Union activities from their grooms and gardeners, who had always reckoned themselves above the men who worked in the fields. They would return from the pub and tell their masters all they had heard. There would be fights sometimes between the field workers and the farmers' creepers. It took a brave man to show his politics in Suffolk all through the 1930s. If you weren't a Tory you were a trouble-maker. All the same, we got the Union going again in 1934. Things changed after this, first very slowly, then faster and faster.

I am old now. I read library books about the Great War – my war. The one I am reading now is called *The Sword-Bearers*. I have these deep lines on my face because I have worked under fierce suns.

Emily Leggett · aged seventy-nine · horseman's widow

I have been wed and widowed twice. My first husband was head horse-man at Round Wood Farm and when we married his wages were 13s. a week. He used to give me 12s. and keep a bob for his pocket. We were children together, then lovers, then I married him. He lived in the next door double-dweller. We were both nineteen when we wed. A beautiful boy he was. It seems a long time now since I saw him. He had six horses to look after and he used to get up at five o'clock every morning to bait* them.

When the war came he was sent at once to join the cavalry at Curragh Camp in Ireland because he was such a fine horseman. He was trained there for about three months and then he was given three days' leave before going to the Western front. But the water was so rough that he only had one day and one night with me. That was the only time I saw him between his joining-up and his going. One day. He was blown off his horse and blown to pieces. There was nothing of him left to find. So he hasn't got a grave. The chaplain wrote and told me all about it. When the telegram came and I read of his death I couldn't possibly believe it. I couldn't think that it was true. My poor young husband! I had only just got his last letter – I still have it. It said not to worry. He was just twenty-five.

I was born in this house, so was my father and his father. It is a charity house – or was – we have to pay rent and rates now. Nearly all the people I used to know are gone. I went to school here – what little I went. I was blinded by eye ulcers a lot of my childhood and so I didn't do much schooling. We took our poorness naturally. We knew within a little what we were going to get and that there would never be any more. So that was that. My father was one of eight and I've often

* Feed.

heard him say that he didn't know what it was like to have a new pair of shoes on his feet. He only had shoes which other folk passed on to him. We ought to be thankful to be as we are today. Whatever would our poor old mothers and fathers have thought if they could see all the money we get now! We know that it doesn't go far but we touch it.

I can remember the men mowing by hand, twenty-four of them in the one field, and each behind the other. The children helped in their own way. We started field work when we were five or six. I used to carry my father's food to the harvest field. It would be crowded with men and when they saw the food they would laugh and cheer. The farmers gave each man two bushels of malt and a pound of hops for doing the harvest. They would have cost 6s. if you had to buy them. Then they got £5 or £5 10s. largess or bonus when it was all over. The quicker they got the harvest in the more money they got. Of course they worked all hours God ever made to get this money. My father would go to the beanfield at two in the morning to get the beans when they were dew-damp, so that they didn't shell-out. Just when there was enough light to see. People now get as many pounds in the week as they got shillings!

We women and children went gleaning when the last wagons had left the field. We picked up the corn for mother and she cut the ears off with her pig-knife and put them in a sack. We were allowed to keep all this. We fed it to the fowls or ground it into flour.

A lot of people shared bedrooms in those days – I mean four and five to a room because of the big families. We never saw anything wrong. People think we did but we didn't. My sister and me and my brother shared a room until we married but we knew nothing. I'm sure of this. Today they hear too much about sex too early. My father was church-warden and a good man. He never went to bed without kneeling against his chair and saying his prayers.

After I had been a widow for five years I married Bob – another horseman! We had no children of our own but we brought up a foster-daughter. We managed all right although it was hard. I walked ten miles, there and back, to Woodbridge every Friday for the shopping, and if it was a dry summer, so that the pond disappeared, I walked two miles there and back for a couple of pails of water. This water came from a spring and it was a treat after the pond, I can tell you! Worth going after. The dust from the roads in the summertime was enough to blind you and if it rained the mud squirted up into your long skirts and made them filthy. People got very dirty then.

When the second war came it changed the village more than it had ever been changed before, or so I believe. It was because they sent the

Irishmen to build the aerodrome. Blackies as well. Hundreds of Irish and Blackies concreted the fields. They got the stones for the concrete from Shingle Street. Two of the Irish boys were billeted on me because I had two bedrooms. The Germans came to bomb the aerodrome and when this happened the Irishmen used to run outside and stand in the pond! Me and my husband we sat in our chairs and waited. Things would fall off the mantelpiece and the village would shake. It was awful.

My husband began to be ill then. On the days when I had to take him into Ipswich for treatment I always came back to find the tea ready. The Irishmen had done it. I have been blessed with beautiful boys.

My second husband had an awful death – worse than the first I sometimes think. I never had my clothes off except for washing for twenty weeks. I never left him for an hour. The doctor wanted me to have him put away – they always do – but I said no. Men should die where they have lived. The nurse came in and washed him every day. It didn't cost me nothing. So I saw the end of him. He died on the Friday and was buried on the Sunday because he was a bad corpse. It was cancer of the throat. The war was over then and they were smashing up the aerodrome and putting back the corn. 'I shan't live to see it,' he said. And he didn't. Nobody could have wished for two better husbands. My horsemen – both gone!

Fred Mitchell · aged eighty-five · horseman

I worked with horses. I came from the West. Have you been to Ched-burgh – Wickhambrook way? I came from that direction. I lived there two years. Then I lived at Whepstead – have you been to Whepstead? I had a few years along of a farmer there – horseman, machinery man and most everything else. The farmer was a big chapel man from Clare. Do you know Clare? Then on I moved. To Poslingford. Do you know Poslingford? That's a rum old village. It was there that I met the farmer who brought me to the East and brought me bad luck, as it happened. The farmer had a hold of me. You see, the Great War broke out and he got exempts for me, one after another, until it was all over, so he had me.

I was living at Depden when I first started ploughing. The farmer said to me, 'You're going to plough today'. I was something pleased. The horses were in the stable. I soon got hold of them and off I went! I was fifteen years old and I had been at work for seven years. I kept about on this Depden farm – do you know Depden? – for one year and then, after the harvest, I thought I'd have a go at Newmarket. Newmarket was crowded with village boys who had a handy way with horses. They hoped the toffs would fancy them and put them in the racing stables. I soon found a job there; it was to do with the heavy horses. The man who employed me would cart anything anywhere. He'd got over fifty horses, including a pair of blacks for funerals, a pair of greys for weddings, and everything up to date. Yes, I've been about – but it hasn't done me much good. The trouble is, I shouldn't have met this Poslingford farmer, then I could have gone on getting about.

I saw the big change. My father worked on a farm – and his father. They both got very near to ninety, I believe. They were hardy old sorts. They never had a thing amiss with them. They worked and lived, and then kind of toppled over at the end. I should have been like them but my accident made the difference to me. The horses ran away with me on the farm. It was only two fields away from this house. It was a terrible accident; it jagged me all to pieces. The horses bolted in the field and ruined me. We were using the self-binder at the time. It was the second year I was in this village and thirty-eight year ago or more. I was at the top of the field whole and then at the bottom of the field broken, and all in minutes. I should not have come here. I wasn't in the hospital much more than a month. They sent me out on stilts. Hang on, they said, you'll soon manage. Today, if you've only got a finger-ache they'll let you stay comfortable until it's better. I wasn't half looked after. They had to lift me out of the hospital to get me home. 'Have you got a nurse?' they said. 'I don't know of one,' I said. 'Oh, dear,' they said. 'Then however will you get on?' I had to be massaged but nobody I knew could do that kind of thing for me. So my leg healed but became short and walking on it has wrung me over. It hurts me a bit all the time. But still, I'm lucky to be alive!

I got no compensation at all. My governor, being a tidy well-off farmer, made my club money up to my wages, but of course there was the family and they were all young. I had a rough old time from then on, I can tell you! But I pulled through. I've got to eighty-five in spite of it all. They tell me I don't look it.

I had a struggle to bring the family up. You had to nearly perish to bring a family up then. It was too much. There wasn't a penny for nothing. They have money now, don't they? We didn't have money. I never had no good times. Nothing began to happen until my boys were all grown up and I was getting old. But there, I wasn't the only one! The farmers were sharp with us. If you couldn't do a job you were reminded that plenty more could. So you had to be careful. I had to accept everything my governor said to me. I learnt never to answer a word. I dursn't say nothing. Today you can be a man with men, but not then. That is how it was. It will never be like that again. I lived when other men could do what they liked with me. We feared so much. We even feared the weather! Today a farmer must pay for the week, whatever the weather. But we were always being sent home. We dreaded the rain; it washed our few shillings away.

I have this invalid-chair now. I had a three-wheel bike up to a few years ago but it got harder and harder to push it along. Then this chair came. The village had bought it for me – they all clubbed together like. The young men made them do it, I'm told. So perhaps it isn't such a bad village after all. It must have cost pounds and these boys just gave it to me. These boys play a lot. Look up any time and ten-to-one you'll find them playing. Football, riding around. I never did any playing in all my life. There was nothing in my childhood, only work. I never had pleasure. One day a year I went to Felixstowe along with the chapel women and children, and that was my pleasure. But I have forgotten one thing – the singing. There was such a lot of singing in the villages then, and this was my pleasure, too. Boys sang in the fields, and at night we all met at the Forge and sang. The chapels were full of singing. When the first war came, it was singing, singing all the time. So I lie; I have had pleasure. I have had singing.

I had all these sons and no money. I had to make a decision – food or clothes? Never mind the clothes, I thought. I sent my sons to the chapel raggedy. 'We can see your boys a-filling out!' the mawthers used to laugh. 'If you're looking that close, you can also see that they are spotless,' I said. They were fed, they were clean; I couldn't dress them too. Sometimes, when I look back on it all, it makes me feel bad. But I shall have to forget, shan't I? Wise people are men who have learnt how to forget. There were times when I didn't know what to do. Before I had my accident I just got away. I up-sticks and went. But now I was stuck in one place like a tree, and perhaps the shopkeeper was after me. 'Had I forgotten this little account ... ?' Oh, dear, oh dear! 'I'll give you a little on account,' I'd say, and hap as not the little would be my all. Not Tommy Ramsey at Framlingham, though. He'd let me have any mortal thing, money or no money. He knew he'd get it in time. Tommy never worried a man. There were shop-keepers round here who were like little worrying terriers.

We all had heaps of children in the village when I was young. Boys and girls were piled up in one bedroom. It wouldn't be allowed nowadays, would it? I don't know what they got up to – nothing very dreadful, I fancy. My family was decent enough. We had a nice little house with three bedrooms, so we all laid proper, two by two.

My wife died three years ago. She was a good sort. I could read to her from the paper of an evening. But as for writing, I can just about sign my name for my money. She did all the writing. But when the money went over the mark, it was me they'd come after! It would sometimes make me feel very queer. But we ate well. My wife made her own bread and there was something cooked every day, no matter how broke we were. She was a great hand at long puddings with plenty of suet and lemon peel in them, which she made in a boiler. Today, they make a dinner out of nothing. You can hear the paper packs being torn open and in five minutes it's dinner. I don't call that dinner.

One of my sons went into the army and stayed in it for twenty-eight years. He's got a tidy old head on him. He came out of the army with a lump sum and bought a little business, but he got too big and he fell. Now he has to work for a farmer. It doesn't matter how well off you become, you can overdo it. Then you will fall. But I fancy he isn't the only one who has done something wrong.

My youngest son looks after me now. He is nigh on forty but he doesn't think about getting married. He's not the marrying sort, I think. His best friend is an older man – well, he takes the pension, so you know how old he is! Been taking the pension a twelve-month. My son works on the next farm. He has looked after me well since his mother died. He went to Burma during the war. Just before he went, he said to his mother, 'Mother, if I ever get out of this alive, I'll never leave you again'. He kept his word. He was her baby and they stayed very close. He did all her housework when she got old, ironing and all. The mawthers say, 'A woman couldn't do it better'. But he's too tidy, too straight. I get in the wrong if I leave ash in the fender. And I mustn't sit in the dark. I mustn't do this, I mustn't do that. Take my advice, don't get old.

My son has a car but he doesn't take me for a drive. I've been out with him once, that's all. He took me to the Horse Show at Framlingham – me and my neighbour. And that is the only ride I ever had in his car. I never ask him for another one, although I'd love to go. He must offer. I daresay if I said, 'I would like to go for a ride', he'd take me. But I won't ask. You would think that he would take me for a ride without being asked, wouldn't you? I don't worry too much about it. I have my chair. There is some comfort in the world now. More comfort and less talk. My son doesn't talk to me. He'll wash, change, cook the tea and be out by seven. I don't know where he goes. He doesn't tell me. I'm pleased to think that I've lived to see such nice times.

Samuel Gissing · aged eighty · retired farm-worker

I just went when they called me; I didn't mind. A lot of us went from the village but we soon got split up. I never saw most of them again. All the time I was in France I only saw three boys I knew. It was a funny thing, but when I came home on leave the women would say, 'Did you meet my George out there? My John? He's in the Artillery, you know. You must have seen him.' They thought we were all fighting in one big old meadow, I suppose.

The war changed me – it changed us all. You could call it experience. It broadened your mind and one thing and another. Everybody ought to have this military training. It would do them good and make them obedient. Some of the young men now, they need obedience. They don't know what it is. Our lives were all obedience.

I was home on leave when the Armistice was signed. I came to the village on the Friday and the Armistice was signed on the Monday. I went back to France but now it was like a holiday. I was now in a Scottish regiment – the glorious 51st. The officer tried to persuade me to stay in the army but I said, no, sir! I wanted to get home. We all did. We were fed up, you know. And we had seen terrible things.

It was hard when we got demobbed. And wicked later. You couldn't get any kind of work.

It is really wonderful how the time has gone. It has absolutely faded away. It all goes so fast. It doesn't seem many minutes from the time we sign the pension book to the time we sign again. But a school morning was a whole lifetime. Life fades while it is still yours. I still do all this garden myself but sometimes I stop and think, 'It was *me* who had a half-holiday from school for the relief of Ladysmith!'

SAM'S SONG

It is late on Saturday night, virtually the eleventh hour, and the pub roars its contentment. One or two say they are going to make an early night of it but they don't make a move. In fact, nobody moves. They stand or sit in controlled, cautious clusters, talking their heads off but somehow rooted to the spot. A note of warning wavers in the blare of conversation and when somebody – obviously a drunken fool – shouts, 'Come on, Sammy, let's be hearin' you!' there are nervous pleas of, 'Quiet … quiet …' 'Come on, Sam!' shouts the fool again, but Sam doesn't look up or react in any way whatsoever. He, too, is talking hard and apparently unable to make head or tail of what is going on. His neighbour is turned to stone. Smoke crawls along the beams. A boy reaches towards the one-armed bandit, then controls himself. The landlord takes up the attitude of a priest, hands resting wide apart on the bar, head glorified by the glitter of doilies, mirrors and miniature bottles festooned with fairy lights. Mysteriously, for there is no commotion, a space appears in the middle of the room, a ring of worn flagstones littered with matches, ash and beer spots. Still nobody looks at Sam and he talks steadily on to his friend, who now has the worried expression of a man entrusted with a key role. The uproar now becomes less casual-seeming. Eyes search for 'young' Hickey, who is forty-ish and waiting his cue. He rises.

'Good night, Hickey,' somebody says provocatively.

'Good night to *you*,' Hickey returns in a voice which means, 'If you bugger things up at this stage I'll kill you'.

He then dances. His suede shoes slap lightly on the paving and his tie jumps out of his waistcoat. His hair hangs away from his bald patch in a big flap. He dances with his back to Sam, who at first ignores him and then begins to watch the tripping flutter of Hickey's feet with a kind of pity. Hickey, the enticer, now breaks into a fast soft, clopping step, then breaks down, slaps his thigh and begins again. He does very well but gives up with a 'It's no good. I can't keep it up, you see ...'

'*Hickey!*' shriek the women on the settles in affected outrage.

The landlord holds up a large white hand as though he is going to give a blessing, but it falls on the light-switch panel. Sam stands up, buttoning his jacket, emptying his glass. He could be leaving – even when he reaches the bare floor he could be on his way home. But he stops, stretches like a wiry old cat, makes himself tall – and dances. His eyes blaze in the firelight. Huge polished boots fly. The dance is a kind of kicking stamp, coltish, vigorous. Sam's heel-irons actually produce sparks and this makes everybody laugh. He dances and dances, eventually clasping his hands nonchalantly behind his back with a gesture of, 'Stop me when you've had enough ...' Nobody does and he has to stop himself, which happens in the midst of a crescendo of stamping. His body resumes its old slightly bent position gratefully and heaves with breath. The applause is solemn, a patter of clapping – no shouts. Young Hickey then opens his melodeon with a great yawning chord and Sam sings his song, with difficulty at first because he hasn't got his puff back, then with surprising strength. Like his dance, Sam's song is violent, full of attack. Nobody joins in though 'several' know the words backwards.

There was a man lived in the West,
         Limbo clashmo!
There was a man lived in the West,
He married the woman that he liked best.
With a ricararo, ricararo, milk in the morn
         O' dary mingo.

He married this woman and brought her home,
         Limbo clashmo!
He married this woman and brought her home,
And set her in his best parlour room,
With a ricararo, ricararo, milk in the morn
         O' dary mingo.

My man and I went to the fold,
         Limbo clashmo!
My man and I went to the fold,
And caught the finest wether that we could hold,
With a ricararo, ricararo, milk in the morn
         O' dary mingo.

We fleeced this wether and brought him home,
         Limbo clashmo!
We fleeced this wether and brought him home,
Says I, Wife, now you've begun your doom,
With a ricararo, ricararo, milk in the morn
         O' dary mingo.

I laid this skin on my wife's back,
         Limbo clashmo!
I laid this skin on my wife's back,
And on to it I then did swack,
With a ricararo, ricararo, milk in the morn
         O' dary mingo.

I painted her with ashen oil
         Limbo clashmo!
I painted her with ashen oil,
Till she could both bake, brew, wash and boil,
With a ricararo, ricararo, milk in the morn
         O' dary mingo ... mingo.

John Grout · aged eighty-eight · farmer

Mr Grout has been recently widowed after sixty-seven years of marriage. He was married at eighteen – 'I was a pretty lad' – but had begun work on his father's farm when he was eleven. Both his father and his grandfather had worked this farm of some 150 acres and had lived to a great age, so Mr Grout had often talked with men who knew the Suffolk farmers of the eighteenth century. He is short and sturdy, with a shining brown face and the strange new-looking wide blue eyes of the very old countryman. Day by day he sits in his hilltop house, dressed in thick rough clean clothes and polished buskins, sometimes listening to the clock, sometimes to the radio. [Where is Vietnam, Mr Grout? – 'Far away ...']

The rooms in the house, once the Akenfield miller's home, are sedately brown: brown paint, pale oatmeal brown wallpaper, snuff-brown tablecloth, oily brown lampshade, creamy brown curtains. There are sash windows at a right angle and nothing passes on the road which doesn't offer the chance of a second complete glimpse if one happens to have missed the first. Just outside, and casting a livid reflection on to the ceiling, is the harsh green circle of the miller's pond. At the side of the house rest the millstones, with nettles and honeysuckle sprouting through the shaft-holes.

*

I have farmed in Akenfield since 1926. I had 135 acres and didn't use a tractor until 1952, and then I never got on with the thing. I have been a man without machinery, as you might say. I was born near Campsey Ash and worked for my father as a child. I did the cows. He was a man who didn't like cows, so I did them. Then I went to school. My father had five labourers who got 9s. a week but he always gave them a shilling extra when they got wed.

Nobody really saw money then, though that didn't mean that they didn't want to see it. I wanted to see it so much that I applied for a job on the railway. A 'situation', they called it, and they weren't so far wrong – it was a situation all right. Whatever could I have been thinking about! A relation of mine spoke for me and soon I was working at Broad Street Station near Liverpool Street. There were lots of Suffolk men working there and hardly any mortal one of them ever got home again. They all wanted to get home, they were that sad in London. And their big wages were little there. Some ran away to Canada and were never heard of again. They couldn't write, you see; that is how they got lost. There was a place in Broad Street Station where you can stare through the arches and see the stars, and they were the only things I can remember seeing in London. That is the truth.

I stayed ten months and then I got home. I wouldn't go back to my father's farm, I got a job with Lord Rendlesham. He was a rare big gentleman in the neighbourhood and was famous for his horses. Why, he kept three men who did nothing else but see after the stallions. There were scores of horses – mostly shires and punches. The greatest of these was a punch stallion called Big Boy who had won so many brass medals he couldn't carry them all on his harness. Men came from all over to see these horses but they hardly ever saw Big Boy. He was hid up and not to be looked at.

The head horseman was called the 'lord' – and that's what he was, lord of all the horses. That was me one day, I was the lord of the horses. The place ran like clockwork. All the harnessing was done in strict order, first this, then that. The ploughing teams left and returned to the stable yards according to the rank of the ploughman. If you happened to get back before someone senior to you, you just had to wait in the lane until he had arrived. *Then* you could go, but not before.

The horses were friends and loved like men. Some men would do more for a horse than they would for a wife. The ploughmen talked softly to their teams all day long and you could see the horses listening. Although the teams ploughed twenty yards apart, the men didn't talk much to each other, except sometimes they sang. Each man ploughed in his own fashion and with his own mark. It looked all the same if you didn't know about ploughing, but a farmer could walk on a field ploughed by ten different teams and tell which bit was ploughed by which. Sometimes he would pay a penny an acre extra for perfect ploughing. Or he would make a deal with the ploughman – 'free rent for good work'. That could mean £5 a year. The men worked perfectly to get this, but they also worked perfectly because it was *their* work. It belonged to them. It was theirs.

The plough-teams left for the field at seven sharp in the morning and finished at three in the afternoon. They reckoned a ploughman would walk eleven miles a day on average. It wasn't hard walking in the dirt, not like the rough roads. The horsemen were the big men on the farm. They kept in with each other and had secrets. They were a whispering lot. If someone who wasn't a ploughman came upon them and they happened to be talking, they'd soon change the conversation! And if you disturbed them in a room where the horse medicine was, it was covered up double quick. They made the horses obey with a sniff from a rag which they kept in their pockets. Caraway seeds had something to do with it, I believe, although others say different.

A lot of farmers hid their horses during the Great War, when the officers came round. The officers always gave good money for a horse but sometimes the horses were like brothers and the men couldn't let them go, so they hid them. I wasn't called up. Nothing happened to me and I didn't remind them. We didn't really miss the men who didn't come back. The village stayed the same. If there were changes, I never felt them, so I can't remark on them. There was still no money about. People seemed to live without it. They also lived without the Church. I'm sorry about this but it is true. I hardly ever went when I was young. The holy time was the harvest. Just before it began, the farmer would call his men together and say, 'Tell me your harvest bargain'. So the men chose a harvest lord who told the farmer how much they wanted to get the harvest in, and then master and lord shook hands on the bargain.

We reaped by hand. You could count thirty mowers in the same field, each followed by his partner, who did the sheaving. The mowers used their own scythes and were very particular about them. They cost 7s. 6d. in Wickham Market, but it wasn't the buying of them, it was the keeping them sharp. You would get a man who could never learn to sharpen, no matter how he tried. A mate might help him, but then he might not. Some men mowed so quick they just fled through the corn all the day long. Each mower took eleven rows of corn on his blade, no more and no less. We were allowed seventeen pints of beer a day each and none of this beer might leave the field once it had been brought. What was left each day had to be kept and drunk before eight on a Saturday night. It was all home-brewed beer and was made like this:

You boiled five or six pails of water in a copper. Then you took one pail of the boiling water and one pail of cold water and added them together in a tub big enough to hold eighteen gallons. You then added a bushel of malt to the water in the tub. You then added boiling water from the copper until there was eighteen gallons in all in the tub. Cover up and keep warm and leave standing for at least seven hours, although the longer the better. When it has stood, fill the copper three parts full from the tub, boil for an hour and add half a pound of hops. Then empty into a second tub. Repeat with the rest. All the beer should now be in one tub and covered with a sack and allowed to cool. But before this, take a little of the warm beer in a basin add two ounces of yeast and let it stand for the night. Add this to the main tub in the morning, then cask the beer. You can drink it after a week. And it won't be like anything you can taste at the Crown, either.

The lord sat atop of the last load to leave the field and then the women and children came to glean the stubble. Master would then kill a couple of sheep for the Horkey supper and afterwards we all went shouting home. Shouting in the empty old fields – I don't know why. But that's what we did. We'd shout so loud that the boys in the next village would shout back.

Stacking was the next job, all very handsome they had to be – handsome as a building. Then thrashing. It was always reckoned you had to thrash a stack in a day. There wasn't any rest after the harvest. The year had begun again, you see.

2 · God

If you came this way,
Taking any route, starting from anywhere,
At any time or at any season,
It would always be the same: you would have to put off
Sense and notion. You are not here to verify,
Instruct yourself, or inform curiosity
Or carry report. You are here to kneel
Where prayer has been valid.

T. S. Eliot, *Little Gidding*

High over all
By none observed
A wooden Cross, side-tipped,
At which three darkling birds
With ancient, horny beaks
Pecked everlastingly for food.

James Turner, *The Interior Diagram*

See yonder preacher to his people pass!
Borne up and swell'd by tabernacle-gas:
Much he discourses, and of various points,
All unconnected, void of limbs and joints;
He rails, persuades, explains, and moves the will
By fierce bold words and strong mechanic skill.

George Crabbe, *Religious Sects*

Over a third of Akenfield's population is engaged in a proliferation of Church- or Chapel-based activities, with councils, committees, charities, amusements, social welfare, education, youth work, national organizations and much else, all of it connected with Church membership. This large percentage doesn't include those who write 'C of E' or 'Chapel' on official papers but contains those who worship regularly in the two buildings, one erected soon after the Conquest, the other shortly after the defeat of Napoleon. Besides the two main groups, the village has three Roman Catholics who hear Mass in the neighbouring market towns, a Quaker, two Unitarian families and a few Presbyterian

Scots. Nearly everybody, including many of the chapel folk, uses the Anglican church for their weddings and funerals, and crowd it for harvest festivals, carol services and Armistice Day. The latter is held in particular veneration, whilst Good Friday is barely observed at all, everybody playing football then.

The Christian God of both church and chapel is approached by worship which is low-toned, pragmatic and unemotional. Where the Anglicans are concerned, the national attitude towards religion, seemly, decorous, polite, restrained, sensible, still dominates both the personal and the intellectual. Suffolk farm-workers use the incomparable English of the Book of Common Prayer and the King James Bible with natural-ness and ease. Modern translations and the 1967 new Communion Service do not possess for them the virtue of the immense Elizabethan and Stuart incantations. Simplification is bafflement. So, to a great degree, is the business of moving out of the parish cloister into the broad ecumenical scene.

The Baptists are even more insular. Against their extreme with-drawal and backs-to-the-World attitude, the Anglicans appear quite eagerly outward-looking. Even adventurous. They are Strict Baptists who have descended from part of the fiercely unconforming East Anglians who helped to settle New England, a church which has been constantly paring itself down to scriptural fundamentals. The Akenfield church has been autonomous since 1812, since when it has never abandoned a single strict sentence of its code. It is, strangely enough, a rather cosy and gay church, a church of summer marquees, enormous Sunday-school anniversaries announced by florid posters, vast tea-parties and outings. It is a ceaselessly expository church where country people worry the meaning out of the Word Sabbath by Sabbath, generation by generation. Since all else is rejected – science, learning, art, history – the Bible has to focus all inquiry and all inventiveness. The Strict Baptists are quite logical for, after all, what is Beethoven, Polaris, 400 million Chinese, moon-travel or Picasso when, as they say, 'God had predestinated an innumerable multitude of persons to be con-formed with the image of his Son with all the blessings of eternal life ...' and that God 'is self-sufficient, immutable, eternal, omniscient, holy, almighty and incomprehensible'? The highest human achievements hardly seem worth bothering about in such a context. For such certain folk it can only be, 'Lord Jesus, come quickly!' Nothing else would make sense. There are 2,180 members of the Suffolk and Norfolk Association of Strict Baptist Churches. It is an intimate, inter-married rural minority, an exclusive religious club whose deliberations smell

more of tea and trodden grass, Sunday-best suits and varnished wood
than of brimstone. The World racketing around outside at an ever
madder pace makes the assurance within even more of a relief. Solid
Suffolk caution informs the faithful about Christian unity. 'Hands are
being held out to us ...' warns the Moderator '... there appears to be
a big friendliness. ... We can soon have unity if we make the platform
low enough ...' The chapel doors in all the gentle villages and the great
doors of Ipswich's Doric Bethesda are blocked by implacable texts.

All the same, chapel and church in Akenfield have managed to
practise ecumenicism for years, the occasional union being forced on
them by the fact that the war memorial is in the church. Nor are chapel–
church social divisions at all extreme. In fact, it must have been the
rigid entrance terms demanded by the Strict Baptists which forced
working-class people to remain Anglicans during the latter half of the
nineteenth century when so many parish churches became a middle-
class preserve.

The parish church itself retains the mysterious quality of an ancient
sacred place which has never been out of the possession of a long line
of simple rural people. It is a steep, light building consisting of nave
and chancel in one, an extravagant tower built of narrow orange-coloured
bricks during the reign of Henry VII and a pinnacled Tudor porch. It
stands near the foot of the hill to the north of the stream. The village
once sat on the crests all around it, but for a hundred years since the
draining of the valley more and more houses have appeared along the
low road. The south side of the church is elaborate, decorated with
flint cameos, stone carvings, rich windows and intricate brickwork, and
it also displays all the important tombs. The north side is an almost
blank rubble wall looking much as the Norman/English left it. Paupers
were buried behind it. Above the main churchyard, in an acre carved
out of Accommodation Meadow, lie the recent dead under a harsh drift
of stone-mason's chippings and white marble kerbs, crosses and books.

The interior of the church preserves the evidence of almost a
millennium of national religious history. Two windows not much later
than Domesday, stairs to the vanished rood, the Host and Mariolatry
incised deep in the flushwork, decapitated evangelists huddled under
the font, table silver (valued at £10,000 by Sotheby's) lent by a Renais-
sance squire for the altar after the King had taken the chalice, a table
made for the divine Suppers of 1630, the mutilations of 1650, a great
Jacobite bell named for Dr Sacheverell, the pomp and Latin of the
Augustans, an Oxford Movement reredos, Empire glory banners and
now, on Laud's oak table, the flood of booklets about Vietnam,

Marriage, Unity, the New English Bible and well-printed signs of
expert publicist talents being employed to disseminate the new *caritas*.
'You must see our church,' they say in the village, 'it is a pretty little
place.' A long roster of servants arrange its flowers, polish its brasses,
oil and wind the clock, tend the bells, hoover the carpets, launder the
linen, mow the grass, heat, dust, trim. Gargoyles shoot the rain from
the roof through screaming mouths. On its patronal day, the keys of
St Peter whip from the flagstaff, and in winter gulls sit in the louvres
of the bell-chamber. The sea is near, yet, by Akenfield, quite unfelt.
The tower is like a finger held up to test its existence. 'No, I've never
been up it,' said the ditcher born in the village in 1908. 'I might'n fancy
what I'd find.'

The chapel is a pleasant square building made of red bricks and has
a pyramidal 'Roman' or pantiled roof. There is a burial ground behind
it. The windows have the blankness of an injured retina, a bloomy
sightlessness. Texts in glass cases hang outside on the front wall and
can be read by passengers in the village bus, which stops just there.
Inside, there is a high rostrum for preaching, galleries and more texts. A
trap-door in the centre of the large pale room covers a tank – the
baptistry. The chapel says little – it doesn't intend to. It is no more
than a sounding-box for all those words describing the Word. Above it
there is the spring from which the deacons, carrying pails on a shoulder
harness, fetched water for the immersions before the mains were laid.
By the side of it is the field in which their huge June rallies are held, in
a tent which seats a thousand. It is a famous chapel and people once
walked twenty miles to hear the Word in it. 'Of course,' said the
deacon, 'you'll get those who can't stop, as you might say. I remember
a man who went on for over an hour and so someone got up and said,
"Excuse me, but, with all respect, I think you have said enough" –
"And with all respect to you," answered the preacher, "I'd like you to
know that God is still putting words into my mouth, so where do we
go from here?" And so we had to let him go on. He used up five people's
preaching time. I wouldn't call that Christian.'

Extracts from the Rules of the Akenfield Strict Baptist Church:

That persons wishing to join the Church ... shall be requested to relate the
dealings of the Lord with their souls ...

That any member knowing ought against the moral conduct ... of any fellow
member, shall not make public the statement ... but shall communicate the
same properly authenticated to the pastor and Deacons ...

Should any inconsistency of life and conduct be brought to the Pastor's notice

... and there should be no amendment ... he shall bring the matter before the Church.

That every member shall keep the business of the Church to themselves, it being unseemly to carry the solemn deliberations into the World.

That any member absenting himself from the Table of the Lord for three consecutive Ordinance Sabbaths without justifiable reason, shall be deemed to have forfeited their membership ...

That the majority shall rule all matters ...

The Church has 31 members (including 5 deacons) but the congregations are usually double this number. There are 40 pupils in the Sunday School and 9 teachers, and there is also a Fellowship of Youth (12 members).

Except for £6 2s. contributed to the Association's central funds, the Church manages its own financial affairs.

Its worship is led by visiting itinerate preachers, of which there are 56 in Suffolk, or by the deacons.

The whole Strict Baptist movement in East Anglia has been severely shaken by the rapid change of events precipitated by Vatican II and the liberalization of sexual behaviour, and a well-written *Affirmation of Faith* has been issued (1966). It is the doctrine of Cromwell's Saints set in Baskerville 11 point.

The parish church involves more people in more activity than any other institution in the village. The living is worth £1,175 and is held by the incumbent in plurality with two other livings. There is no centralization; the three villages each have their church and parochial church council, and operate separately. Akenfield church is governed by fifteen councillors, two of whom are church-wardens. The council sends representatives to deanery meetings and to the annual diocesan conference. The vicar and his wife use their elegant Victorian vicarage for Sunday schools, meetings and countless interviews, and the village tennis club uses the courts made in the grounds by a previous vicar in 1927.

The following is an analysis of the events connected with St Peter's Parish Church, Akenfield in 1967.

Number of services:	Holy Communion	46
	Matins	27
	Evensong	6
	Litany	2

Attendances:		
	Average, Sunday Morning	31
	Carol Service	110
	Harvest Festival	102
	Armistice Day	94
	Easter Day	44
	Christmas Eve	55

Prayer and Bible study evenings in private houses 38.

Lectures on 'Why Chapel?' and 'Why Church?' 2.

Visiting preachers 12.

Talks: 'The Ipswich Telephone Samaritans'; 'The Wycliffe Translation'; 'The Race for Tomorrow'; 'Christian Aid'; 'The Challenge of England'.

Cantata: From Olivet to Calvary (Maunder).

Billy Graham All Britain Crusade: The church was one of 2,000 which was linked with the mission.

Whit Sunday: the congregation worshipped with the Strict Baptists as an act of unity.

October: Church and Chapel worked together to revive the 'Horkey' – the great harvest feast which was traditional in Suffolk up until about 1900. It was held in a decorated barn and was attended by almost the entire village.

Charities: Some £70 is given away annually to various charities and the congregation helps to support, with money and clothes, a shelter for destitutes and meth-drinkers in the East End. It also, sends regular gifts to the local mental hospital, the Red Cross missionaries in Persia and old people.

Finance: Collections for 1967 £316 0s. 1d.

Complete church funds amount to £896 6s. 7d. of which £600 is invested in the Rural District Council.

Diocesan Quota: £75 0s. 0d.

Total expenses for year (including donations to charities) £427 13s. 6d.

Among the almost endless list of involvements was a house-to-house collection for the East Suffolk blind and visits to the local Borstal (twelve miles).

Publication: The Parish News, monthly, price 4d. and delivered to nearly every house.

Societies connected with the church: The Over-Sixty Club; Mothers' Union; Caleb Club (teenagers); Friday Fellowship; The Saplings (under-tens).

The Village Doctor

I've *thought* of following Christ – many, many times. But it would have to be the real thing – not this business going on in the church. St Paul altered it, spoilt it all at the very start, didn't he? Yes, I'd certainly have a go at the original idea if I had the nerve, but I wouldn't waste my time on the rest of it.

The Brigadier (rtd)

The church is going to pot because of all these young inexperienced parsons. Servicemen make the best parsons. They are men of the world who are used to handling people. You take these chaps getting ordained in their twenties – what do they know about life? What you need is the padre type, somebody who will have a drink with you in the bar and who has the right to say to you, 'Now look here, old boy. You've been grizzling away about your Ethel and her shortcomings, but do you ever think about how she feels being left alone all the evening while you are lining them up here? I mean, fair's fair ....' A man shouldn't be a parson until he's in his forties; he can't know about life till then. The best advice I ever had was given me by a padre, you know. Changed my life, you know. 'Think of the other fellow,' he said – something like that. Made me a different person, you know.

The Teacher at the Agricultural Training Centre

There are a couple of hundred village boys taking the courses and on the whole I'd say that Christianity isn't relative to their lives. Most of them have little real knowledge of it. They're all in the book as baptized Christians but you watch them in church on their wedding day! The vicar will be saying, 'Stand here, kneel, rise, find page 22, do this, do that ...'. They'll be all at sea. They'll have about as much notion of what to do as if they were being married in a Buddhist temple. I can quite understand this because I don't believe either. It isn't just their generation, is it? It is mine – their parents' generation, too. We doubted – they ignore.

The old village people communed with nature but the youngsters don't do this either. The old people think deeply. They are great

observers. They will walk and see everything. They didn't move far so
their eyes are trained to see the fine detail of a small place. They'll say,
'The beans are a bit higher on the stalk this year ...'. I help to run the
school farm but I'd never notice things like that. The old men can
describe exactly how the ploughing turns over in a particular field.
They recognize a beauty and it is this which they really worship. Not
with words – with their eyes. Will these boys be like this when they are
old? I'm just not sure. Nobody is trying to bring it out in them. Nobody
says to them, 'This is heritage'. Somebody should be saying to them,
'Let's go and *look* ...'.

Orchard worker

When we had our son, my wife wouldn't leave the house until she
could take him to the chapel and thank God for him. She wouldn't step
outside the door until she could do this. We went down there and we
said to the minister, 'We want to give thanks for the birth', and the
minister said a prayer for our boy before the church, and said his name
to them. He didn't make a song about it, it was just a passing word.

The Deacon

I was baptized into the Strict Baptists after the Caravan Mission to
Village Children visited Akenfield in 1950. The evangelist travels
across Suffolk in the summer-time with his tent and caravan, and when
he arrives in a village the church parson and the chapel pastor go out
to welcome him. He stays for a fortnight and holds two meetings in the
tent every evening, one at six for the children and one at seven for the
grown-ups. The evangelist is a strict time-keeper and if he says his
meeting starts at seven, it starts at seven – and not at five past. So you
know where you are. On the last evening, at the end of the meeting, he
said, 'I don't want to force anybody but if there are those present who
would like to come forward and make a confession of the Lord Jesus,
they would be very welcome'. Well, funnily enough, there were seven
of us went forward. We were nearly all teenagers. I was nineteen, my
wife-to-be was seventeen, there were two college girls of sixteen and
three lads round about eighteen. One of the college girls became a
missionary and went out to Africa, I became a deacon when I was
twenty-one, my wife became a Sunday-school teacher and not one of

us who accepted Christ that night has fallen away from Him. I mention this because you hear a lot of mention of the falling away after Billy Graham and not a lot of the staying. Five of the converted went to the Strict Baptist chapel and two to the parish church. And there they are still. This is because the evangelist is a man who is well-equipped with the Word and can more or less explain himself to everyday people in church or chapel. He created a wonderful spirit in his tent and all the village felt it.

This making an open confession of Christ is our chief difficulty where getting Strict Baptist Church membership is concerned. We've got about seven families who count themselves chapel and attend the services but they don't belong. They are held back by the witnessing. They are that bit shy of making this open confession, you see. You have to be very careful with cases like this because of the Serious Step. It is a free-will choice. You could, with a little persuasion, make some of these people come out to be baptized, but in a year or two they'd resent being pushed. So, while a general invitation is made and the *hint* is dropped, we don't make a straightforward approach. I think that immersion is some of it. But the witnessing could be worse. If you want to become a member of our church, first of all you must tell the pastor and he will tell you that you must be baptized by total immersion in our pool. You've got to have courage to face this. But before this happens, the pastor tells the full church that you want to join it and the church then says that two 'Messengers' are to be sent to you. The Messengers are chosen from among the members and are as near as possible the same sex, age and status as the applicant. So they can get into the person. These Messengers are very responsible. They see you in your home and hear why you want to join the church and listen to you make your confession of Christ as Saviour. They then report back to the church and give an account of their Visitation, as we call it. The whole church listens and then asks the Messengers, 'Is this a true report?', and whether they think you are a suitable person to join the church. If the Messengers say yes, then you come into the church and take up a position in front of all the members and give an account of yourself. A lot of folk can't face this, so they just come to the services. They don't belong and they can't take the Supper. They can't face two people from the village calling on them and wanting to know all the whys and where-fores. But we are the Strict Baptists – so it can't really be any different, can it? The thing of it is, you see, we don't want any impostors. Well, after you have come before the church and have been accepted, the pastor says, 'When would you like to be baptized?'

The baptism usually takes place a fortnight later at the close of the Sunday evening service. You'll get people coming just out of curiosity and there'll be plenty of children present just because of the novelty. And you'll get the regular old diehard Baptists from all round, as this is a great solemn occasion for them. They live for this sort of thing. So the church is packed. Well now, just imagine yourself. You've confided to the Messengers, you've stood in front of about forty village people and given your testimony, and now you've got to step out in front of everybody you know for miles around, and dressed in a white cricket outfit, and again be asked if you own the Lord. You say yes, so the pastor will say, 'Then do you want to be buried with the Lord?' Again you say yes. Then he says, 'Shall we go down on to the water together?' And you are taken under. It is hard and we never make it easy. We say we will never make the Lord's Table an easy factor. This Table was strictly instituted by the Lord for His disciples and it must never be that any Tom, Dick or Harry can lightly eat the Supper. The Sunday following the baptism, the new member is given a set of the church rules and told that he must help run and pay for the church.

We have no pastor at present: the church is run by five deacons and nine Sunday-school teachers. We have about fifty members and twelve of them are aged between fifteen and twenty-five. Seven of the teachers are under twenty-seven. There are more than forty children. We are a young church. Fifty per cent of the children belong to parents who aren't chapel folk; we pick them up in a van every Sunday morning from five surrounding villages. But nearly all the adult congregation lives in Akenfield. Each Strict Baptist church likes to choose its pastor from away and has to pay his wages when he comes. We paid our part-time pastor £5 a week but we would have to give a full-time man £10. We also have to pay for the upkeep of the chapel and the manse, so the money side is quite a problem. Twenty-five years ago, when money was short, we had a full-time pastor and ran the buildings all on £3 a week! We could do this because the pastor was, well, a saint you might say. He *was* Akenfield. Ask anybody. Nobody ever did so much good or was so kind. A rich friend from Ipswich, a rare big businessman who wasn't one of us, gave him a car – this was when cars were rare in the village – and he never used it for his pleasure. Only for others. It was known as the 'hospital motor' because he used it to take patients and family visitors to Ipswich and Melton hospitals. It never mattered what time of day or night it was. We don't quite know where this man came from. He arrived soon after the First War – out of work, I think they said he was. Anyway, he stayed and cared for us, and none better. He stayed thirty years and was one of us.

We meet twice every Sunday. You get the cream of the people in the morning who know it is right to worship the Lord first thing, and the skim of an evening. We worship, eat our Sunday dinner, take a walk and have a piece of tea, and worship again. It is reasonable. The Strict Baptists don't change with the changes, you might say, it is very much the same. The biggest thing which is upsetting us is this Ecumenical Movement. It is getting the Roman Catholics in. If it does this, we must stay at loggerheads because with us the Roman Catholics are completely *out*. We stay at peace in the chapel. With your own denomination you have to live together and tolerate one another as best you can.

If you think we're strict, you should see the Brethren at Wickham Market! They are well-to-do people and the strictest Christians you can get in Suffolk. You have to hand it to them. They are farmers and smallholders and they do a lot of good but never say a word about it. They are *really* out of the World.

As a deacon I have to be like Timothy, sober and a ruler of my own house ...

The Rev. Gethyn Owen · aged sixty-three · Rural Dean

I arrived in the village immediately after the last war and so I have seen the 'revolution' – I think you can call it that. I came from the Welsh valleys, where my father was also a clergyman, and where the industrial dereliction of the 1930s sprawled for as far as one could see, to a part of Suffolk where the old feudal system was dying hard. The men had not as yet come back from fighting and those who remained in the village seemed to be as they had been for all time. Many were still drinking the pond-water and were goitrous because of it. The old dialect was pretty much undisturbed, horses worked the land and the 'big people', as the landowners were called, still ruled it.

I have been very happy here and what I have to say about the people mustn't be taken for negative criticism. I am a Celt and different to them. They are the children of dissent; Unitarianism, radicalism, anabaptism, these are the forces which have moulded them. I came to them when they had, for several generations, been literally worked to death. There was scarcely a moment they could call their own, a time when they could stop toiling and ask, 'Who am I?' Yet so were the miners in my father's parish – I mean it was even worse for them – yet nothing made them indifferent to colour and beauty. If you can measure the spiritual nature of men by these things, then the nature of the people of Akenfield strikes me as being uncultivated and neglected. The church was abysmally dull when I came and there was no parish communion. No warmth or feeling. It was very noticeable after Wales.

I came to live in friendship and understanding with most of the inhabitants but I found that to talk on any deep level about their Christianity was intensely difficult – even when death was round the corner! It could have been me, of course! I don't think that the ordinary villager, who is linked to deeper propitiatory practices in the fields than he is aware of, has either the energy or feels the need to inquire what the Church is all about. Where it might have touched him – at the imaginative or creative level – all this side of his personality has been blunted and crushed by toil. I am talking about the older folk now, although a man doesn't have to be much over forty to have the results of the bad times marked on his heart.

I have sometimes dared to question the incredible perfection attached to certain tasks – this is heresy, if you like! Take ploughing or ricking, why should these jobs have had such a tremendous finesse attached to them? The harvest would not have been the less if the furrows wavered a little. But, of course, a straight furrow was all that a man was left with. It was his signature, not only on the field but on life. Yet it seems wrong to me that a man's achievement should be reduced to this. It was a form of bondage if he did but know it. Their wives had their part to play in this; a woman was admired if she scrubbed and polished until she dropped. In my father's Welsh parish it was the doorsteps.

One of my most difficult tasks has been to persuade little groups of people to get together and, in a very simple and friendly way, to discuss the meaning of the Faith. But no one would come to a meeting if he thought he had to say something. When they have said something, one often finds that it is something quite irrelevant to what is being discussed. Religion has a lot to do with where their families and ancestors are buried. They spend hours tending graves and they are also very concerned about the state of the churchyard. Television is now breaking down their silences. They are getting accustomed to the idea of dialogue. The older villager was very different: he accepted or rejected but he said nothing. There was no debate, or argument, as he called it. One discovered saints, of course, people of prayer and worship, men of a profound simplicity and to whose natural conception of the divine one could neither add nor subtract a thing. But generally speaking, the God of the Suffolk countryman tended to live outside the church, which was a building near the graves, and thus holy. It was all very vague. One could never get really near to them where such matters were concerned, as one could get near to the Celt.

I remember an example of the importance attached to church burial. When old Thrussel died, his widow came to me and said that he wished to be buried in the churchyard. I was very surprised to hear this because he'd been a Strict Baptist all his life and had been far from friendly towards the church. The Baptists, of course, have got their own burial ground behind the chapel. Why couldn't he be buried there? 'He fancied the churchyard,' stated his wife – 'that bit up by the top there.' The penny now dropped. I recalled great battles with Mr Thrussel about a scrap of his land which we had had to take in order to extend the churchyard. He had fought us all along the line but lost. Now he was getting his own back by being buried, as he believed, on his own farm! I always liked this old man. He and his family were all out of the common run, vital and clever. In the early days they had to struggle in a way you never see now. It made him tough and acquisitive. Whatever he gained he held. Bitterly. He was like the rest of the working farmers here. They didn't see this attitude as meanness but as strength. Life had taught Mr Thrussel to hang on tight!

I am not really close to them. When I first came they said, 'You'll have to winter us and summer us, sir', and twenty years later I'm still doing this, if the truth be known. Newcomers have broken down many of the old community ideas and people have become sentimental about the passing of ways and customs, although many of them were narrow, limiting and bad. The church has been improved out of all recognition by the new inhabitants, who have brought fresh life and leadership to it. All the young people are mobile-minded, and that is a good thing. But men are still leaving the land and the land itself has less and less place in the mind and emotions. The power of the gentry has gone. Nobody takes any notice of such people nowadays. But behind the progress there lies the great imponderable of the East Anglian character, something to which I now know I shall never have the key. I have spent most of my time searching for the point of contact. They are hard people. Their lives at the higher level – and make no mistake, there *is* a higher level: I have seen it, a fugitive glimpse into a country where I cannot belong – present an imponderable. It is the only word I have for it. Fatalism is the real controlling force, this and the nature gods, the spirits of the trees and water and sky and plants. These beliefs seem to have no language, but they rule.

The more one visited the homes (which are improved out of all recognition since I came here) the less one bridged the gulf. No one likes to think that after so many years of genuine love and caring one is defeated, so I don't think of defeat. They have been awfully welcoming … helpful. Yet I don't know. It makes one wonder. The young are different. They have common communications with the world. The old look inward at things we cannot see. The young have a common image. The past is boring and shabby to them. They don't want to know about it.

There is another thing which is better now – morality. There were people living in the cottages near here who were like – well, I hardly like to say it – like animals. They had a sort of code but all the natural human relations were covered by cruel and ugly taboos which obsessed some of them. They loved children. Every child was 'the little dear' except if it was born out of wedlock. This was regarded as a terrible thing and never forgiven. The village would remember such a thing for ever.

The people who do best are those who leave the village for a spell and then return. Such people are quite astonishing. They have usually lowered their defences and the effect on their friends and family is extraordinary.

3 · The Ringing Men ...

Ardua molimur: sed nulla nisi ardua virtus – We
attempt the difficult, but there is no virtue in
what is easy.

Written in the Ipswich Senior Society's records after it had attempted
a peal of 6144 Treble Bob Major at Woodbridge Church, March 1851.

Robert Palgrave · aged fifty-five · bellringer, tower captain

Handel called the bell the English national instrument and still, in a
great loud web of percussion, there are the hundreds of bellringing
societies, guilds and associations which unite town with village from
one end of the country to the other. The societies are ancient but those
belonging to them are invariably called 'youths', and there is something
in the tensely permutating atmosphere of the ringing chamber, the dozen
or so reaching out figures, the leaping ropes and the blindingly passion-
ate clamour above, which suggests the climatic ascension of young blood.
The ringers are utterly absorbed. Such a total absorption takes over
their mortgaged, class-bound, year-measured lives that these conditions
of existence are temporarily cancelled and the Self revels in noise, logic,
arithmetic and a kind of intoxicating joy which accompanies the striking
of one's own particular bell in the deafening harmony.

The ringing men must reach stages of exultation which are on a par
with those of cannabis, but if this is so there is no outward evidence to
prove it. The less extreme degrees of pleasure derived from the art of
campanology are similar to those derived from chess. Yet, perhaps
because all bells are feminine and are 'raised' or 'turned over' by the
neat strength of the bellmen to 'speak' their Pleasures, Tittums,
Superlatives and Surprises, something less entirely cerebral than chess
causes the contentment. The towers literally rock and the peals can be
so overwhelming for those living near the church that the belfry windows
are louvred so that the sound can be cast out at the highest level.

Ringing is an addiction from which few escape once they have
ventured into the small fortress-like room beneath the bells, and the

sally – the soft tufted grip at the end of the rope – leaps to life against the palm of the hand like an animal. There then begins a lifetime of concentration, of perfect striking and a co-ordination of body and mind so destructive to anxieties and worries of all kinds that one wonders why campanology isn't high on the therapy list.

The bells tumble through their paces with hypnotic precision. They are incredibly old and vast, with the names of saints, princes, squires, parsons and merchants, as well as rhymes and prayers, engraved on their sides. The ringing men know them both by parish and individually, and will travel from tower to tower across the county in pursuit of a particular sound. The world to them is a vision of belfries. Some part of the general fretfulness of humanity seems to be soothed by this vision. Theology is put to the count. Lost in an art-pastime-worship based on blocks of circulating figures which look like one of those numismatic keys to the Great Pyramid's secret, the ringing men are out on their own in a crashing sphere of golden decibels. The great changes are mesmeric and at half-way through the 'attempt' the ringers are drugged by sound and arithmetic. Their shirt-sleeved arms fly with the ropes and, because their whole personality bends to the careening mass of metal above, they often look as if they had lost their will, and as if the bells were in charge of them. They are famous for avoiding church services. They keep in touch by means of a weekly magazine called *The Ringing World* which, to the outsider, presents a scene of extraordinary fantasy. The ringing men are indifferent to all the usual 'craft' or ancient art talk and are a different race altogether to Morris Dancers, say. They just walk or drive to a given tower – the fact that the building is a church is always a secondary consideration – and ring. The curious thing is that the sweet uproar of change-ringing is so integral a part of the village sound that it is often not consciously heard. When listened to by the non-ringer, the general effect is soothing, bland, a restoration of God to his heaven and rightness to the world. The reality of what is occurring is known only to another ringer.

Bellringing is one of the most claiming activities imaginable. The magnificent noise and belfry drill took John Bunyan over completely and his description of his efforts to abandon the obsession has the desperation of a man longing for drink or sex:

Now you must know that before this, I had taken much delight in ringing, but my conscience beginning to be tender, I thought such practice was but vain, and therefore forced myself to leave it, yet my mind hankered. Wherefore I should go to the steeple house and look on though I durst not ring. But I thought this did not become religion either, yet I forced myself and would look on still. But quickly after I began to think, how if one of the bells should fall? Then I chose to stand under a main beam that lay overthwart the steeple, from side to side, thinking there I might stand sure. But then I should think again, should the bell fall with a swing it might first hit the wall and then re-bounding upon me, might kill me for all this beam. This made me stand in the steeple door; and now, thought I, I am safe enough for if a bell should fall then I can slip out behind these thick walls, and so be preserved notwith-standing.

So after this, I would yet go to see them ring but would not go further than the steeple door, but then it came into my head, how if the steeple itself should fall? and this thought, it may fall for ought I know, when I stood and looked on did continually so shake my mind that I durst not stand at the steeple door any longer, but was forced to flee for fear the steeple should fall on my head. Another thing was my dancing ...

The modern passion for change-ringing began in the seventeenth century with the publication of Fabian Stedman's *Tintinnalogia* in 1668. But half a century before this someone had carved on the tower door-post of Buxhall church the following cipher:

12345

21345

23145

23415

23451

2 . .

Buxhall is only seventeen miles from Akenfield, home of one of England's greatest tower captains, Robert Palgrave. A tall, handsome man, he has carried the change-ringing virus to Australia, New Zealand, the United States and to Europe, but with little hope of it raging with anything like the fervour it possesses in Suffolk.

*

During the war, in 1916, the parson here had two daughters who did a bit of ringing. I once saw them what they call 'raise the bell', that is bring it full circle. So one day I went into the church and climbed the belfry, wound a sack round the clapper, went downstairs – and pulled! To my amazement I got the bell up, so then I started practising. That is how I first came to ring. I then brought other boys to the tower and taught them how to do it, and then one day we all walked to Burgh and rang the six bells there. After this we hurried off to Hasketon and rang the bells there – we couldn't stop. A ringer is first attracted by the sound of the bells, then he comes to see how it is done and something quite different gets a hold of him. Some people say it is the science of the thing.

What a ringer needs most is not strength but the ability to keep time. Everybody must be dead-on with their pulls. Nobody must be uneven. You must bring these two things together in your mind and let them rest there for ever – bells and time, bells and time. When I first started the young men were so keen to ring that they would be lucky to get five minutes' practice each – so many of them wanted to have a go. We would think nothing of walking six or more miles just to have a five-minute practice ring in a good tower. And I have walked between twenty and thirty miles in a day to ring a peal of 5,000 changes. All the ringers were great walkers and you would meet them in bands strolling across Suffolk from tower to tower. Many of the old ringers couldn't read or write, yet they turned out to be really famous bell-composers and conductors. They could get hundreds of rows of figures into their heads and put them all into practice when they reached the belfry. They could set all the bells ringing wherever they went and bring them all back to 1–2–3 4–5–6–7–8.

The bells tolled for death when I was a boy. It was three times three for a man and three times two for a woman. People would look up and say, 'Hullo, a death?' Then the years of the dead person's age would be tolled and if the bell went on speaking, 'seventy-one, seventy-two ...' people would say, 'Well, they had a good innings!' But when the bell stopped at eighteen or twenty a hush would come over the fields. People were supposed to pray for the departed soul, and some of them may have done. This practice was continued up until the Second World War, when all the bells of England were silenced. It was never revived. The sexton got a shilling for ringing the death-bell.

I left the village when I was eighteen and went into the guards, which meant Windsor and London. I met the ringers in these places and became very accomplished. I think I can say this without being boastful. I have been a regular ringer ever since. It is such a fascinating art, you see. I know all the bells in Suffolk – and other counties, too, for that matter. I think I have just passed my two thousandth tower. Cathedrals, minsters, priories, abbeys, churches and the secular bells at Windsor Castle, I have rung them all.

Ringing requires a lot more mental than physical application, particularly now when the modern bell-composers create such wonderful changes and the bells are hung so beautifully they don't need great strength to move them. But of course you have to be fit to be able to swing a bell for two or three hours at a stretch and 'put it in its place', as we say. You also have to be bitten by the bug. You have to be smitten. If you are a real ringer you think about bells morning, noon and night, and you only live for the next time you can have a go at them. You have your ringing books and a lot of study at home. An old ringer at Hasketon told me, 'You must learn it at home and ring it in the tower'.

One of the fascinating things about ringing is that there are about 5,500 peals of bells in the British Isles, ranging from rings of five to peals of twelve. So, you see, you can travel to the towers all your life and still find something new. The towers have a great effect on the sound of the bells which hang in them. The tower here is soft red brick and it absorbs the strike notes, whereas in a modern tower made of concrete and steel you would get a harsh bell note. The old bricks soak up the sound and sweeten it. The taller the tower, the quieter the bells in the village itself. The shorter, the louder. Nowadays, the tendency is to hang the bells about twelve feet lower than the louvres in the belfry windows, so that the noise can come up and then go out across the land. The notes of the bells are distributed evenly. Some towers 'burl out', as we say, and it can be most unpleasant. If you want to stop burling you have to board or brick the windows up until only a small opening is left at the top.

The average weight of a bell in Suffolk is about eleven hundredweight – as against the tenor bell in St Paul's Cathedral, which is sixty-two hundredweight. When we say 'ring of bells' we mean towers where there are peals of five, six, eight, ten and twelve bells. An eleven-hundredweight bell would be the largest of these. People are very attached to old bells because they have spoken for the village so long and are its angel voices, or because they listened to them when they were courting and were young and happy. But I have to reluctantly say that, for those who understand bells, modern bells are best because they have been scientifically tuned. Much of the old bell-making was a hit-or-miss affair. The bell-makers were like a woman with a cake who could turn out four or five passable efforts to every one which was perfect. It was just the same with the bell metal. If it was poured too hot it would split the bell, and if it was too cold it would spoil it. But with a thermometer the modern bellman knows exactly when to pour his metal. He also has instruments to tune his bell 100 per cent perfect. A new bell today is in tune with itself as well as with the other bells in its peal. A bell can be in the key of D but it will still contain many other tones and a bell-founder of today will know how to get rid of these other tones. In the old days a man would cast many bells of the same dimension and yet no two would be alike. It was rule of thumb. And it is just a myth that a silver coin was put in the bell metal because all bell metal, now as then, is about two-thirds copper and one-third tin – and nothing more. Tuning was then done by chipping at the inside of the bell to flatten the tone and chipping at the edge to sharpen it. But it was all very hit and miss. Too many chips might come off – or not enough – and the bell-founder had only his ear to guide him. Now we trim the bell to agree with a tuning machine. The old bellfounders were itinerate workers. When a village wanted bells they would bring their tools to the church-yard, dig a pit and make a furnace. The bell core was baked whole and then the outer cope was made. More metal was poured into the space between the inner core and the cope. When it was cool, the top was either lifted off or broken off, and there was your bell in its crude state. Then came the tuning and the hanging. It was a great business. One of the finest bells in the world is in Suffolk. It is the Lavenham tenor which Miles Gray made in 1625. It is known to be the sweetest bell in England.

Most of the bell-frames round here are between four and five hundred years old but if they are replaced iron and steel is used, not wood. A bell-frame must be absolutely rigid otherwise it will affect the swinging of the bell and hurt the ringer. The towers sway a lot during the peals. Most of the Suffolk towers sway tremendously, particularly St Mary's at Woodbridge. The vibration of the bells is said to fracture the towers but architects will laugh at this and say it is rubbish.

Before change-ringing came in, bells were used just to make great grave sounds on important occasions, or simply jangled. Then Fabian Stedman evolved a system by which they could be used to make real music. His method is still the most popular today. It is one which is rung on odd numbers of bells – on five, seven, nine or eleven bells. But there has to be an even number of bells to ring it, which sounds rather paradoxical. In other words, you ring 'Stedman' on the front five bells with the largest bell, called the tenor, covering. It would be 2–1–4–3–5 with the tenor bell coming in behind. It produces the best music. After Stedman died, the country people amused themselves by making variations on his method until, all over England, there was a great rage for ringing. The names of men who made important attempts to ring Grandsire Triples, Bob Major, Stedman Caters, Tittum Bob Royal, etc. were painted on boards and hung up in the towers. The great Suffolk ringers were the Chenerys from Wilby, the Banisters from Woolpit and the Baileys from Leiston. The Baileys were eleven brothers and they were ringing in the towers round here just before the Great War. Six other brothers, the Wightmans from Framsden, were ringing at the same time. They rang a seven method Minor peal at Monewdon on March 18th 1914. They had to take their father with them to do this, of course.

The maximum number of changes which can be rung on eight bells is 40,320. This is called 'accomplishing the extent' and it was accomplished on the foundry bells at Loughborough. It took seventeen hours, fifty-nine minutes. It presented a challenge, you see, just as Everest presented a challenge to our friend Hillary. If you are the conductor of a peal you have in your mind a picture of how those bells have to be kept going without one single change repeating itself. And so at intervals the conductor has to make a call which changes the work of the bells.

The ringers are now able to do far more than what was possible forty years ago or more. Some of their sons have been to the university and have applied their mathematical brain power to the art. My youngest son is a most brilliant ringer and probably one of the greatest ringers in the world. He is a mathematician and he was getting things out on paper when he was five years old. He went to the village school, then to the grammar school and then to the university. Nothing ever came difficult to him. He conducts and composes. Where bells are concerned there is nothing he cannot do.

There are new ringing methods composed all the time but people who are not ringers do not hear the tunes. I should say that ninety-nine per cent of the people just hear 'bells ringing'. That is all. Many first-class ringers are tone-deaf and the bells to them are just a noise. It is all figures to them. But when I hear the bells I think, my goodness, how beautiful! How wonderful! The combinations of sounds delight me. If you read the peal boards in the Suffolk towers you will be reading the names of many happy men.

Sammy Whitelaw · aged fifty-eight · farrier

I started ringing when I was fifteen – and walking too! Ringing and walking went together. The ringers from Cretingham would walk to Eye and those from Brandeston would walk to Woodbridge, and you'd get some ringers who would damn-near walk across England. That's a fact. You would meet them walking about all over Suffolk, looking for a good tower. Bell-mad, we were. I wasn't all that good. I could manage about 720 changes and that is about as far as I could go. Stedman started all this, you know. Most of the ringers I knew are dead and gone. I watched them, I did what they did, but it's a funny thing I couldn't ever do more than the 720 changes. I remember ringing one harvest time and the bell flew clean off the frame. Imagine that! Bell-tongues and our tongues stopped together then! 'That's a masterpiece!' old Charlie said. I can hear him saying it. The expert ringers used to call ringers like me 'turkey-drivers'. I didn't want to be a turkey-driver but you can't always choose what you want to be in this mortal life. I knew a ringer who could ring the bell up once, make it wait, and catch a second toll as it came down. True. I wanted to do that but I couldn't.

I remember one cold November – I couldn't tell you how long ago – and a woman came to me and said, 'My Billy has passed, Sam. Ring the bell.' I said, 'How can I do that, Ma'am? The tower has all been scaffolded for the repairs.' So off she went sorrowful. Then I had an idea. I climbed up into the bell-chamber, sat on the frame and banged the passing-bell with my hammer! I thought, old Billy won't mind. It was that bloody cold. But all could hear of the passing and take note.

Billy was one of the old people. The old people have gone and have taken a lot of truth out of the world with them. When Billy died, his wife walked down the garden and told the bees, and hung black crêpe on the hive. My grandfather did this, too. He said that if you didn't, the bees would die as well. Bees are dangerous to some folk and a gift to others. You'll get someone who'll get stung once and perish and another who'll get stung all over and get cured of all manner of things. There were a rare lot of bees in the village in those days. When they swarmed we used to all rush out into the garden with the fire-irons and scuttle and bang away; that brought them down.

I hope you like this village. I have lived here all my days and have been happy enough.

4 · To be a Farmer's Boy?

That is the land of lost content,
I see it shining plain,
The happy highways where I went
And cannot come again.

A. E. Housman

The drift from agriculture intensifies. Only ten per cent of the boys leaving rural schools in 1967 wanted to do farm work although it offered a beginner's wage which was often considerably more than that offered by most other jobs in the neighbourhood. But the young people from the village cannot be enticed by this or by the famous perks of the industry – a practically rent-free cottage when they marry, free milk, wood and potatoes, and being able to have dinner at home every day. Two things, the first imprecise and emotional, the second a hard blunt fact, decide the issue. They are that young men in the 1960s prefer the more impersonal contract between a firm and its employees to the farm's 'special relationship' and that they know that after they are twenty-one they are likely to be earning half or even twice as much again in any job other than farming.

The present abandonment of the farms is on the same scale as that of the decade 1871–81, when 200,000 labourers fled their villages for Australia and Canada. Between 1962–7 men have left the land at the rate of 20,000 a year and the figure is now approaching 30,000. The great difference between the two emigrations is that in the 1870s the farms were at their worst, choking in a depression which lasted until the Second World War, when the nation's food needs broke it, and that in 1968 England's farms are incomparable and one of the wonders of the agricultural world. Yet only a fraction of the ten per cent of young people going into farming really recognize the excitements of what in essence is a second agricultural revolution. The remainder take to farm work because, perhaps, they have inherited the small residual static quality in all village life, that thing which is either condemned as apathy or praised and envied as contentment, but yet which is really neither of these. The attitude contains something determined and enduring, and also incorporates some kind of duty or loyalty to the village fields.

Questioned as to why he hasn't joined his friends on some £20-a-week development scheme in Ipswich, works-bus waiting to carry him from door to site, or why he hasn't followed a brother to New South Wales, the farm loyalist is unable to find words to explain the actual meaning of his life and falls back on sentimental clichés about 'peace' and the 'open air'. One senses some more ancient pull for which there is no adequate sociological heading. It is the nucleus of these 'opportunity'-resistant farm-minders which becomes the village proper. They are rooted-in deep and before they are middle-aged their lives have become entirely circumscribed by the parish boundaries. A car will carry them to events within a fifty-mile radius and television will open up the world nightly, but neither will extend them. The question confronting many employers, with their highly sophisticated new farming, is, are the undoubted qualities of these acceptance villagers those needed for the mechanized and scientific agricultural industry? Should it not be attracting the restless, imaginative, creative, questioning countryman? Should it not be attracting, as one critic has suggested, not 'workers' entirely but a new kind of professional who can earn £1,000 a year? The present position is getting dangerous. British agriculture, rescued by the war and made to flower as it never did before, is being avoided like the plague by the more intelligent rural worker.

The dilemma is not being ignored. Both the Government and the National Farmers' Union recognize it. The latter has accepted a levy of £6 a year per member to create a fund for setting up a re-training scheme. As the output for each worker is reckoned to be worth £2,000 a year to the farmer, even if it only goes up by one per cent it will increase the man's worth by £20 annually, which is more than three times the levy. But the National Union of Agricultural Workers view this and many other 'farm attraction' ideas put forward by both Government and employers alike as irrelevant to the real issue – wages.

The wage (1967) for an often highly experienced man in charge of complicated and valuable machines, and livestock, is £11 11s. for a forty-four-hour week. Average overtime brings this up to between £12 and £14 12s. for fifty hours. This, placed against industry's average wage of £20 6s. for forty-four hours makes agriculture the largest concentration of low-paid skilled workers in Britain. The N.U.A.W.'s claim for a basic £14 for a forty-hour week is unlikely to be settled for a long time to come. And behind the present injustice, and menacing the prosperous scene – woven into the very fabric of the farming pattern, in fact – is the grim old tradition of labour without money. A few shillings up until 1940 and the fewest pounds since. Although wages *in kind*, of course.

This is instantly pointed out whenever the subject is raised. But when these traditional perks were assessed in 1967 it was found that they were worth 7s. 3d. a week, which was almost the exact amount which the bushel of malt, etc., given by the Victorian farmer to his man after the harvest, was worth. Before the war, farmer and worker shared the slump and were plunged into common hardships – 'There worn't no money about', and that was that. But since 1956 farm profits have increased forty-three per cent – by £113 million in eleven years – and evidence of this new wealth can be seen in every village. Old farmhouses are beautifully restored and made luxurious with fitted carpets and oil-fired central heating, deep-freezes for game and fruit, and new furniture. Rovers and Jaguars fill the garages, also the son's new sports car. This prosperity is more wondered at than resented by the worker who, if he is middle-aged, might remark, 'When I went to work along o' him afore the war, he hadn't got two ha'pennies to rub together'. What has happened in the purely social sense is that the financial position of the ordinary 'working' farmer and that of the two or three men he employs has become as extreme as that which existed between landowner and labourer before 1914. Little of this utterly transformed scene can be obtained by the ordinary village man. The farm doesn't offer him a 'career', with the word's sense of advancement and real rewards, it offers him a mid-twentieth-century version of the old hireling position. With land at over £300 an acre, it is useless to dream of a place of his own. With the social structure of English village life proving to be more or less impervious to real change and constantly attracting a retired element which clings to all the old attitudes as to a lifebelt, he will never have the same sense of freedom as a worker in one of the new towns. It is all this, an inescapable *status quo* maintained by a poor wage and the social pressures exerted by a small community, which decide the bright boys against farm work. The work itself has never been despised and those that leave it know that they will never find anything else which is so entirely satisfying.

183,200 of England and Wales's farms employ no workers at all; they are cultivated entirely by the farmer and his family. 24,600 employ only part-time help. And of the 116,000 which employ whole-time workers, over ninety per cent employ less than five. With the methods of culture having undergone complicated technological changes which involve heavy fertilizer and machine bills, nearly all the young workers are bound to have lives of swiftly increasing responsibility. But those village men most needed to cope with the second agricultural revolution are the very ones likely to reject farming altogether, not because they hate it or because it doesn't have a natural draw for them, but because, where they are concerned, its ideas are primitive or moribund.

The N.U.A.W. acknowledges the threat 'from the increased difficulties experienced in maintaining a high level of recruitment from an ever-reducing pool of agricultural workers ...'. The Union has 3,406 branches, 361 less than ten years ago. Suffolk, one of the centres of its founding struggles, has 160 branches. Sales of its magazine *Land Worker* are declining and giving anxiety, and the Agricultural Apprenticeship Council, on which the Union is represented and in which it places great hopes for the future, shows a poor response.

The N.U.A.W. arbitrated, nearly always with success, for some forty of its Suffolk members during the past year. The chief claims, as always, concerned the tied-cottage (twenty cases in Suffolk in 1966). The tied-cottage provides both farmers and their employees with their most emotional grouse, evoking all the traditional melodrama of the wicked squire and the rustic tenant being pushed out into the storm, and requires some kind of final solution. All the prejudices, myths and indignations of the past rise up when a man changes his job but can't leave the house which went with his old job because of the shortage of accommodation. The farmer can't get a new man because the near-free – approximately 6s. a week – cottage is the carrot which makes him accept his low wage and local politicians are quick to pounce on any trouble created by the situation to add fuel to the class war. No less than 413 tied-cottage cases were tried in 1966, an increase of 203 over 1964, although only one farmer dared to take the law into his own hands by evicting a tenant. He was heavily fined. Although the legal position for both worker and employer is now as fair as reasonableness and the law can make it, the tied-cottage idea is one of the chief dislikes of the young-farm-worker who wants to keep himself free from farmer-paternalism. It belongs to the wages 'in kind' system and the intelligent countryman would prefer £14–15 a week as a straight return for his work – no house, firewood, milk, potatoes or the odd gallon of petrol.

Union membership is far from 100 per cent but there has been a considerable East Anglian upsurge of interest in its policies during the last five years. It was in these clay-land villages that the first effective agricultural trade unions were formed during the late nineteenth century to fight the wage cuts brought about by the great farming slump. Wages in Suffolk – 10s. 6d. a week – were then the lowest in England. They crept up to 36s. 6d. in 1919 and back to 25s. in 1924. In 1938 they were 34s. and in 1947 £4 10s. It wasn't until the end of the 1950s that the great disparity with the rest of industry began to show itself and reminded people that, as a previous secretary of the Suffolk N.U.A.W. wrote,

despite all that has been done, the farm-workers remain a class isolated and apart. Low paid, living in many cases in tied-cottages which made the worker dependent on his employer not only for his livelihood, but also for his home, his children often getting scrimped schooling and with local life and local justice still largely in the hands of the farmers and the landowners, it was small wonder that the young men went away at the first chance ...

The following was written sixty years ago by a Wickham Market farmer to Sir Henry Rider Haggard, who was making an inventory of England's then wrecked rural scene.

The labourers 'back to the land'. That is the cry of the press and the fancy of the people. Well, I do not think that they will ever come back; certainly no legislation will ever bring them. Some of the rising generation may be induced to stay, but it will be by training them to the use of machinery and paying them higher wages. It should be remembered that the most intelligent men have gone: these will never come back, but the rising generation may stay as competition in the town increases, and the young men of the country are better paid. It should be remembered too that as many men as formerly are not required to till the land. During the last three years by the use of the self-binder I have seen five men gather in the harvest on this farm instead of seven. Other labour-saving machinery will be introduced. Uniformity of wages should also be discontinued, and the best men must be best paid: this will help them become farmers themselves better than any other means ... the fashion of the present day is the worship of money, and from this the labourer is no more exempt than the townsman.... It is not a question of rent or labour, or the farm, it is the *man* and, let me add, his wife.

Change 'self-binder' for combine harvester and 'labourer' for worker and the letter is uncannily similar to *The Times* first leader of 5 January 1967.

In modernizing and mechanizing their businesses, British farmers have easily led Europe. They have, in the past twenty years, gone on producing more and more food with fewer and fewer men. Now they are beginning to ask how much further the process can go without something breaking down.... The planners have assumed that they can afford to part with about 12,000 men a year to industry, but over the past five years the rate for the United Kingdom seems to have been about 20,000 a year and there is no sign that the drain from the land is slackening.

Recession or not, factory buses still stream out into the countryside from the cities to collect new workers and it is all too often the energetic and the ambitious who are the first to take advantage of them. They do it even if it means changing a job which is skilled and interesting for one that is mechanical and unrewarding in all except cash.

It is becoming harder to recruit likely youngsters for the farms ... and harder still to keep them. Investment in new machines may fill the gap for some operations, but there are many jobs on the farm to which the machine provides no real answer. Better buildings and better management may enable one man to milk more cows or look after more meat animals, but each move of this kind puts a greater premium on his skill ...

Clearly, the main reason for the exodus is the disparity between the agricultural and industrial wage rates, which has markedly widened in the past few years.... New skills have been developed but, like some of the old ones, they have not yet been fully recompensed in terms of status as well as cash. The recently constituted training board may do something to change this and dispel old suspicions, though these die hard.

The trend that has set in will not be quickly reversed.... It is not only the boys themselves who need to be convinced that there is a sound future in farming but their parents and their teachers as well. Unless they are, we may have the paradoxical situation ... of an undermanned agriculture losing its workers permanently to industries which find themselves periodically over-manned ...

George Kirkland · aged forty-five · farm-worker and Secretary of the Akenfield branch of the National Union of Agricultural Workers

I went from school to work as a shepherd boy on this farm and the only time I have been away from it was during the war. It is one of the big farms – about 700 acres – and mostly arable, although we've got everything, two herds of cows, grassland, sugar-beet, potatoes, rye, barley, wheat, oats, fruit – just everything.

As regards to money, when I first started work I got 10s. a week for seven days a week. It was 8s. for the ordinary week's work and about half a crown more for Saturdays and Sundays. If you were a man you got 5s. extra for Saturdays and Sundays.

In those days, son followed father. That was the usual thing. So all of us boys followed father. Nearly all the village boys did this. We just had to watch and carry on. One or two broke away but it didn't seem a natural thing to do. People didn't need to ask a lad what he wanted to do when he grew up if they knew what his father did. You hear that farming was unpopular then, but it wasn't deep down. We began watching at an early age; that was our training. I watched the shepherd and did what he did. He didn't have to speak very often, which was just as well as he was a man who liked to keep words to himself. They used to call him Old Silence.

We had 250 ewes and when they all lambed we had something like a 500 flock all told. Shepherding was a very boring job for a boy. You just sat around and watched the sheep. It was most boring and after about two years with the shepherd I was allowed to go along with the farm's rough carpenter and help him fence, thatch, gate-hang, and make hurdles. We were actually thatching when the war broke out. The aerodrome was near and I was young. I could see all the village boys going off and the R.A.F. boys in their blue, and I thought, 'If they are all going to the war, so am I'. The farmer tried to stop me. This was actually in 1938, the crisis year, so I didn't join up until 1940 in the end. I went up to Euston House in London but I hadn't the education for air-crew. Also I was in a reserved occupation and they said, 'You must go back to your work, it is just as useful as flying'. But I wasn't going to have that. 'I am going to fight,' I said. And I did. I was in the Air Force for five and a half years, and that was the only time in my entire life that I was off this farm.

My father used to say that farm-working was bad pay but a good life. In those days there wasn't all that much difference between the farm-worker and the bricklayer or any other kind of workman. Since then there has been a great drift between the wages in what they now call the agricultural industry and every other industry. Last year (1966) we lost five per cent of our farm labour in Suffolk alone. The National Plan estimated a loss of only two and a half per cent. It is the bad money which makes men leave the land; they are quite proud enough of their jobs. The tied-cottage is another thing. The Labour Government said that they were going to do this and do that about the tied-cottage but so far they have done nothing, or very little, and things are still difficult. The tied-cottage isn't such a problem in Suffolk as it is in Cambridge-shire and the Isle of Ely, where things are very bad. The agricultural worker, just as soon as he becomes redundant or leaves his job at a particular farm, is given two months' notice to quit his house. Even the new law doesn't help him much and he's lucky if he can stay on for three months. Who can find a new house in three months? Our journal, the *Land Worker*, publishes a list of every tied-cottage case which comes before the courts. They are listed under the various counties and they give the name of the farmers involved. We publish up to fifty tied-cottage court cases each month, so you can see what a disgraceful problem it is.

We are not 100 per cent members of the Agricultural Workers' Union in the village – I wish we were. The trouble is that television and that sort of thing is keeping men away from the meetings. We get a head-office speaker, we send out information, or we might just have somebody giving a good talk on agriculture generally – anything you like – but hardly anyone comes. We don't get the people like we used to. I've been in the Union for twenty-three years and there were some great meetings twenty years ago. But they've all dwindled away. There are thirty-odd members in the Akenfield branch but I bet if you called a meeting to-morrow you'd be lucky if you saw six. We are out for a £14–forty-hour week. This is our policy at the moment. It is very important. But when we had our annual County Conference no more than half the branches were represented. It was terrible. A lot of farm-workers don't take any interest in politics at all.

If there is any political talk, it is usually at breakfast time. The whole crowd of us is in the workshop having breakfast and perhaps some political thing has happened, and then we talk. Of course, I think nearly all agricultural workers are with the Labour Party and that is that. We are mostly Socialists vote-wise, and that's about all. My father was a Liberal. Most of the old men are Liberals. He's often told me that if his employer had known that he voted Liberal years ago he would have got the sack. It could be because of stories like this that the young men are so secretive. Why, they'll tell you more about their sex than about their politics. Politics makes them very shy.

Things were bad in my father's day. He's still alive, so you can't say it was so very long ago. The farmers owned us then – or thought they did. Father said there would be dreadful dos if the farmer found out that his men were going to a political meeting or a liberal talk. This was in the 1920s. Father was in the trenches during the First War but since then he has hardly left the village. He may have gone to Norfolk occasionally but mostly he's stayed put. He was classed as a head-labourer, a time-keeper, and after the gamekeeper John Daniel died, father put in for his job. He could do this because, as well as being head-labourer, he was the keeper's handyman. If the keeper was after poachers by night he always called on father to help him. There were between fourteen and fifteen keepers on this estate then which took up all the land between the rivers. In my father's day a poacher was nearly always just a farm labourer who simply had to go out and get a bird or rabbit for the family dinner then – back! This kind of poacher was a job to catch, which was just as well, I thought. I once told my father about this. 'Father,' I said, 'if you take into account what the good book says, that every beast on this earth is for the good of mankind, why should Colonel Hawtry have the bloody lot?' My father couldn't see this. He was brought up in the old ways and the game laws were the holiest laws where he was concerned.

My mother died in 1945. She was like all the old folk, she did every-thing in strict rotation. That is how they all thought and lived. It was always washing on a Monday and baking on a Wednesday. It could be raining cats and dogs on a Monday but she'd still wash – sheets, flannel shirts and all. Like as not, Tuesday would be hot and she would have burnt half the coal up Monday night getting it all dry. I've heard her say time and time again, 'If I get out of my routine I'm finished!' She had seven children and she had to work – there was no doubt about it. Doing great old piles of knitting and darning half into the night she reckoned was her 'rest'.

We all lived out our lives entirely on the farm. It was much more than just a job or a wage. Before I married and us brothers were all at home with father, many's the time our sisters used to say, 'Finish talking farming do! It's all we hear, farm, farm, farm!' We were at it morning, noon and night. Nowadays it is different; the young men have motor-bikes and they're away, off, out of the village after tea. They don't care *all* the time. They've learned how to make a break between five at night and seven in the morning, and so they are different to us.

I don't want to see the old days back. Every bad thing gets to sound pleasant enough when time has passed. But it wasn't pleasant then, and that's a fact. Everywhere you looked there was this graft to keep things going. Working at the graft sapped people of their strength to live their lives decently. The farm labourer used to be looked down on – 'You're an old farm labourer!' – that sort of thing. And the girls would look at a boy in Ipswich on a Saturday night, find out that he was a farm labourer, and then stop looking sharp!

It was often rough on the farm then. It was hell-fire and water for a young boy then when he started work. The older men made it a point to be rough with the lads because that was how it was, that was the tradition. I remember one man as though it were only yesterday. I was about seventeen and we were working on cattle-beet. I had to pick the beet up, top them, put them in the cart, take them to the clamp and cover them up with old bracken from the heath. We didn't earth the clumps up until later in the year, after they had dried out a bit. We got 20s. an acre for this work. I was just the boy but I turned and turned about with the men, doing exactly what they did because I was very strong and because, well, if the truth be told, that was the way I liked it. I'd pull half a day, fill half a day and draw-off half a day. It was piece-work and I did exactly what the men did, but at the end of the week the foreman said, 'He's only a boy so he only needs to take half-money!' Only one man stood up for me and he was jeered. Fancy standing up for a boy – it was thought very funny. If a youngster does piece-work today, you chop out the money equally. The difference between a boy and a man at work is that although the boy is strong, he hasn't got the kind of strength to allow him to keep up all the day. It was this which the men used to mock when I was young. No one liked being young then as they do now; they wanted to get it over with.

Much of the farm was all waste and ruin then. We used to graze sheep on the fields where the corn is now. When I was a shepherd lad I lay in these fields when they were all rough bracken and ling, so high that you could hardly see the sheep. Now it is corn. I helped to clear it of heather and birch trees and now we get twenty tons an acre of potatoes off it! Who ever would have thought that?

I'm definitely happier than I was years ago and I'm sure most farm-workers are. We had depressing jobs which lasted so long. Sugar-beeting was very depressing. You'd start it in September and it would go on till January. It made life seem worthless. Now you just sit on the harvester! The farmers have changed for the better too. I work for an exceptionally good boss, although he's a Tory. I pull his leg about the Tories and he pulls mine about the Labour. You wouldn't have got this before the war. He's an altered man, particularly these last ten years. It used to be 'Get here' or 'Get there' – that is how farmers spoke to their workmen. There were forty men and boys working here then, now there are eight. The boys can go to relief classes if they want to; no-body would dream of stopping them. We have a boy on the farm who went to the Framlingham agricultural engineers for six weeks on a Fordson Major course. He learnt tractor maintenance and all manner of things. The very idea of such a thing would have been unthinkable when I was a shepherd lad, and I am only forty-five. The Secretary of the N.U.A.W. is on the committee which arranges these classes for boys and thinks that they are very important.

I enjoy working for the N.U.A.W. The members are getting very worried about the present Government. We all feel that we are being let down because of what they said they were going to do and haven't done. We are also worried about the farm students who go to agricultural colleges. They get their training free through Government grants and then they won't do the job for which they have been trained. They go into the business side of things, agricultural contracting, fertilizers, that kind of thing. I only know one student who does what I would call proper work on a farm and he's a foreman. Although that doesn't mean much. A farmer will make a man foreman by giving him a couple of pounds extra a week but the job isn't usually as grand as it sounds. It isn't good enough for a young man who has been educated.

The students soon learn that they can't do everything by the book. I tell them, 'Look at the land'. On this farm, for example, we've got very light land and then, down by the swale, it's suddenly heavy grey soil. Get past this and it goes light again. That field, if you go by the book, would lead you into the devil of a muddle. If you started ploughing there in a bit of rain, you'd never get through it. All the same, the students who come here are willing boys and I tell them all I know and what we have been through.

You don't get as much bickering on a farm as you do in most jobs. The men stay close friends. None of us are looking for wonderful changes. My opinion is that a farm-worker is as important a man as a skilled man in any other industry. The only thing I can't fathom is why they are subsidizing the farmer to keep the cost of living down and aren't helping his workers at all. Country people have to pay through the nose for their goods. All the things you buy in the village shop are more expensive than they would be in Ipswich or any town. It has always cost more to shop in a village, and when the village shopkeeper sends things to out-of-the-way cottages, you can be sure he's going to charge you something for the service. And there's no choice; there is one kind of cheese, one kind of bacon, take it or leave it. The truth of the matter is that everything a countryman buys in a village is brought to him by little men who sell mostly inferior things. The town worker has more money and cheaper goods.

Men like myself, who have followed father's footsteps, we're a finished race. Boys today won't take their fathers' footsteps – that is exactly where they refuse to tread. So the town boys are being told about work on the farms. My boss goes to Ipswich schools and tells the boys about jobs on the land and the town boys come out here on their motorbikes to work. It is just a job to them. They're not involved, you understand. They just see new machinery. They haven't heard what happened here or if they have it doesn't sadden them because it is history. They are glad when you stop talking about it because they want to listen to their transistors.

I'm very interested in birds – I'm a true ornithologist! I go about with an expert who rings for the British Museum. This year we are ringing reed warblers and sedge warblers and we're down in the reed-bed just as soon as work and tea are over. I do this every moment I have to spare, so does my brother. We saw a rare sight last Saturday – a grasshopper warbler. I've lived here all my life and it is something I've never seen or heard before. It is a very rare bird indeed. You might find three or four pairs on Minsmere, and now we've got a pair here. They're usually found in the West Country.

We've had some marvellous recoveries from the birds which we have ringed. A blackbird was ringed in the wood here in 1963, was caught again here in 1964 and was eventually shot in Russia in 1965. A blackbird! I was down at Shingle Street last year and there were oyster-catchers all around. One bird kept swooping so close to me that I knew there was a youngster near by and then I heard a twittering right under my foot. I was covering a bullock's footprint and there inside it, safe and sound, was the oyster-catcher chick. I picked it out and ringed it. It was the latter week of July 1966 and it was shot in Spain in October.

There used to be a lot of sheer killing of birds and creatures when I was young. The men all did it, ferreting, breaking necks, stoning. ... But not now. And there were all the gin traps. The early morning was full of little screams – very exciting and strange. The boys used to blow up frogs. They stuck the end of a straw through the frog's skin and blew through it. It is different now. People like to look at animals and birds. All the same, I still like my gun sport. I like pheasant- and pigeon-shooting, also wildfowl. I always carry a gun. When I was a boy I'd sooner go out with a gun than watch a football match and in fact I'd really have liked to have taken my father's footsteps and been a gamekeeper. He kept game for twenty-seven years and it is in my blood. So some things remain and some things pass.

David Collyer · aged twenty-nine · forester and Labour Party organizer

David Collyer is married with two sons. His wife belongs to the village and is a very pretty girl with a sharp intelligence and, even at this early stage of her husband's rural political career, an easy way of crossing difficult social frontiers. They live some way out of Akenfield in a small modern house with central heating and a neat garden, an official car and a telephone. Their attitude towards these things is apologetic. A similar reaction is sometimes seen when an ascetic socialist clergyman is landed with a mansion-size rectory. With the Collyers, the devoted priest analogy can be taken further; he is the custodian of the old village truths and the remembrancer of the sufferings out of which much of the contemporary character of Akenfield has emerged. His job is to organize Labour support in the area. Meeting him, it is impossible to conceive him finding any kind of footing on the slippery Wilsonian platform, and strange that such an innocent man should be able to contribute anything which the sophisticated scene at Westminster finds necessary. Support for socialism in the East Anglian countryside remains cryptic. The scene is one in which only the insider can touch on the realities. David Collyer is such an insider. He comes to the little meetings with a complete understanding of the confused mixture of old-fashioned idealism, secrecy and emotional brotherliness with which they remain informed. He has another advantage. He belongs by birth to the *élite* of the political field men. His grandfather helped Joseph Arch, the Warwickshire hedger and founder of the modern agricultural trade-union movement, to enter Parliament in 1885, and his father worked staunchly for Arch's successor, George Edwards. Although David Collyer drives a Triumph Herald along the lanes walked or bicycled by his father and grandfather in their search for union members, his message is very little different to theirs. The world beyond the village roars away. But in the cottages and council houses near the farms primitive problems resist the smart answers. Like mining, agriculture creates its own mysterious climate for those engaged in it. David Collyer's role in a district threatened by the Common Market revolution, Greater London expansion, wholesale desertion by those who have lost all patience with the way-of-life argument (workers are leaving the land in Britain at the rate of some 30,000 a year) and a void left by rejected skills and beliefs is one of conscience, is partly to reassure.

He is slight, round-faced and dark. His mildness is of the undefeatable sort. That sweet smile has out-lived the blusterings of history, a subject which Collyer confines to Suffolk and Norfolk village people during the first half of the twentieth century.

*

I have been interested in village politics for as long as I can remember. My grandfather was one of the founders of the Agricultural Workers' Union and spoke on the same platform as Joseph Arch. So in fact trade-union life and political life – socialist life, I should say – is part of my family background.

I hardly left the village all my schooldays – once a month at the most, and then it would be to go on the bus to the nearest town to buy a pair of shoes. You hear of ordinary boys like me who have got on because someone has seen that they could be extraordinary, with a little help, and who have been lent books and given a start, but no one took any interest in me as a child. You also hear people saying, as the nun did on television the other evening, that God called them. Well, I feel that I was picked out for this work which I am doing while I was still very young. I won't call it 'vocation'. Not yet. I must see what happens.

I went to the village school and had a poor education. I never took the 11-plus exam and I've always wondered why. Nobody seems to know and I was never asked about it. I want to know whether, when I was eleven, did everyone have the chance to take this exam? Or was there some selective thing which deprived me of my chance? One misses a lot by going to a village school. I never learned to swim, for instance. It doesn't sound much but when everything is added up the average village schoolboy is left with a mass of disadvantages. I still cannot mix easily and I am instantly ill at ease when I come into contact with people who have had a university education. Or even for that matter a grammar school. I have an inferiority complex about such things. When I am worried I think of George Edwards, who couldn't read at eighteen; his wife had to teach him. He became a member of Parliament. I felt that if he could do it, I could do it.

Although I do not like towns, I think they are very necessary when one is young. A town boy can drift into an art gallery – if it is only to get warm – and then see a picture, and then begin to feel and think about art. Or he might go to a concert, just to see what it was like, or hang around in a big public library. From the minute he does these things he begins to be a different person, even if he doesn't realize it. He has started to be fulfilled. For an ordinary village boy everything to do with these things is somehow unnatural. The village people live almost entirely without culture. I was over twenty before I realized that classical music was just 'music', and therefore all one had to do was to listen to it. I listened and at first believed that I had no right to listen. I felt affected. But when I began to enjoy it I stopped worrying. Everything I do begins with doubt and insecurity. It is as though I am using a language which I haven't a right to use. I used to read a lot, although I don't get much time for books now. But I would still sooner read than watch television. I am not conceited about my achievement but I am spurred on by it – parish councillor, urban district councillor, assistant area secretary and now divisional secretary at twenty-nine – it is an achievement. At each stage I reached a point where I thought I would have to stop because of lack of education, then I thought of George Edwards and passed the point.

The thing which I believe I have got in my blood is this: our grandparents fought their whole lives to improve the terrible conditions in Norfolk and Suffolk but, although much has been gained, we mustn't rest. We must go on striving for the farm men. Things are so much better that it is easy to imagine that there is nothing left to do. This is a deception. When I was fifteen my father took out my first year's subscription to the National Union of Agricultural Workers but he said that the next year I would have to pay the money from my own wages. I soon became very interested and very active in the Union and at seventeen I suddenly became involved in the Labour Party itself, probably because the Union had brought me into close contact with village poverty, tied-cottages and the low status of the farm men. It seemed astonishing to me that these things should still exist. They were a personal challenge to me to use my socialism for my own village. I did voluntary work as the local Labour Party secretary until I was twenty, when I became a full-time official in the Movement.

All this time I worked as a forester for the Forestry Commission. I had no intention of working on a farm after seeing what my father had to put up with and when I was about to leave school, and my father's employer implied that he would take me on – for that is the East Anglian way, father-son, father-son, all down the years – I said that I would rather work in the forest. I didn't know much about it but knew a lot about my father's situation and I had seen enough to put me off the whole concept of farm work. There were good prospects in the forest. The furthest you can get on a farm is foreman and you won't be this until it's nearly time to retire. You see, I am talking of only a few years ago, before the farm-apprenticeship schemes and farm schools got really going. I liked the forestry work and obtained my woodman's certificate when I was eighteen, which is young for this qualification. If I had stayed in this work I would have become a Forestry Commission fore-man while I was still very young.

The state forests near Akenfield are mostly soft woods – Scotch pine, Corsican pine, larches, etc. – which grow quickly. Oaks take too long to grow. You can collect saleable branches from soft wood trees in eight to ten years of planting. These branches are used for rustic work. There is still a great demand for mining timber and they have discovered that metal is no real substitute for the old wooden pit-props. And these are best when they are soft wood. A pit-prop is thrown away after it has been used once. They use so many that they want the cheapest thing they can possibly get – and also the safest, of course. All the trees are grown from seed. We had to climb the trees and gather it, rear it in a nursery and plant it out. I liked this part of the work very much. When we were felling we moved through the forest in gangs, for safety's sake. A woodman never works in the forest on his own. He could wound himself and lie in some lonely place for hours before he was found.

An agricultural worker and a forestry worker have a similar character. The Commission employs hundreds of men who have left the farms. It pays just that fraction more and offers a clear-cut career of exams, promotions and a kind of goal ahead. This goal isn't visible on the farm; it is all vague. Also, the Forestry Commission gives good housing accommodation. They are tied-houses, of course, but in a quite different way to the farm's tied-cottage. Men living in these can lose their homes for a quite frivolous reason. There should be greater security. Everybody understands that a farmer must have a cottage back after a man has left his employment but much more common-sense and sympathy is needed during the change-over. It should never come to an eviction.

You will think that because I rejected the farm I look down on the farm-worker. I do not. The farm-worker has no position, no status, yet he is really the greatest worker in the village. But he has this low social standing. A member of the Union of Agricultural Workers is still thought of as a low-class person by stupid people. But he is the country-man with all the skills. The old men had thatching and ploughing skills and the young men have mechanical skills. Such men should not be classed as common labourers. The shepherds and cowmen know a lot about scientific feeding and breeding methods, and are almost vets. Such men are more than hands. My father was a horse-team man and gave his whole life up to looking after valuable animals, although he received very little in the way of wages. This happens all the time today; great responsibility, not much money.

There is one good thing. The hostility between the farmer and his men has either disappeared or is on the way out. It definitely is. The young farmers and the young workers are closer together. I don't really know why there was all this bad feeling. I am not old enough to give a judgement on it. My grandfather was called by his surname – '*Collyer!*' the farmer would shout – and he had to run. The farmers call their men by their Christian names now and aren't interested in humiliating them.

I have a slight guilt about not working on the land but I felt I had to resist getting caught up in a bad system. I also felt that I had my work to do and that I needed all my strength to do it. Politics plays a large part in village life, although you won't hear much about it. You get it on the Parish Council and in the personality of anyone you talk to. Only it never comes out and proclaims itself. I – my party – try and educate the country people, not about Westminster things but in the political things which concern them at the village level. It is all changing. The young people are becoming educated. They go to Ipswich Tec. or even to the university and they learn to talk about anything. They aren't a bit intimidated. My greatest job as a political organizer is to persuade people to participate in Labour Party work. It goes against the grain of their secrecy. So many people have been taught to be 'loyal' to their employer's politics that it makes them feel deceitful to vote in another way. But quite a few of the employers are beginning to realize that a man can hold different beliefs and still do his work well. Yet there is still a lot of assumption – kind but firm assumption. A lady near here, for instance, kept her two 'dailies' and her gardener tremendously busy during the last general election while she organized transport and re-freshments for the local Tories. These people voted socialist but they were expected to work like blacks for the Conservatives on polling day! What could they do? It was an ordinary working day for them, yet they were helping their employer to muster more votes for the other party. I think that the lady should not have assumed that her servants thought as she did. But like so many people of her type in East Anglia, I suppose that she simply believed that anybody who was nice just couldn't vote Labour. And these people were nice. They had worked for the lady for years and they were all fond of each other. This is a common situation in Suffolk – loving feudalism, is what I call it. There is plenty of it about. And on the other side of the county, during an election about five years ago, a Conservative vicar arranged the Mothers' Union outing to coincide with polling day and took a bus-load of people to Yarmouth. Some managed to vote but most of them didn't. This was a case where it was assumed that all the ordinary women were socialists. These assumptions! But what else have you got in village politics, when everything a person believes in is guarded and mysterious? It would be funny if it wasn't so sad.

I find great caginess when I am canvassing. If I ask outright I get nowhere. People will tell you what they wish you to know about themselves but it is usually something different to what you want to know about them. They are strict about this and cannot be persuaded to add any fact which they think better withheld.

The women play a great part in village politics. They do a lot of the organizing and if their men hold trade-union offices or party positions, they will do all the writing for them. The women are political because it is they who spend the wages. A man will take his wage and think it fair enough but his wife will have a weekly experience of how inadequate it is. She soon comes to understand that it is this constant just-too-little money which must always keep the family static. The Women's Institute has educated the village women. Women like organizations. They like committees for this and sub-committees for that. They don't care what they say to each other when they are on a committee and when they come to a unanimous resolution about something – it has to be done! The women never lost their independence during the bad days as the men did. The men were beaten because the farms took every ounce of their physical strength and, as they had no great mental strength because of lack of education, they were left with nothing. Their physical strength was their pride and as soon as it was gone they became timid. It was the farm versus their bodies, and the farm always won. The farms used to swallow up men as they swallowed up muck and the men realized this quite early on in their lives. Things are different now, of course, but there is a legacy of beaten men in the Suffolk villages. Some of these men are surprisingly young. You don't find women in this condition, no matter how hard their lives have been.

It is a good thing in this village that the women are able to find so much part-time work. The money helps to off-set their husbands' low farm wages. The £14 basic wage for farm-workers should have happened long, long ago. To think that men in one of the country's greatest industries have to work a forty-five-hour week for £10 12s. – and such skilled work, believe me! And in all weathers. In a factory it could be as much as £20 a week with a roof over your head, music playing and plenty of tea. I have a friend who left a Suffolk farm to work on a farm just outside Northampton, where there is a great shortage of agricultural men because people have left the land to earn better money in the shoe factories. So he got £12 14s. a week. All the farm men were getting this wage in the Northampton district. So my argument is that if farms can pay better wages when they have to – and still make a good profit – then there is no reason to continue paying such a bad one. And the profits of an East Anglian farm are probably as great as they are anywhere because the land is so good. A good-sized village like Akenfield should have a small factory so that the farms have to compete for the good men. It is only when this kind of thing happens that you will be able to push up the earnings of the farm-workers. It is something which must come.

Money is the primary reason for a young man's leaving the village, but there are other pressures. When you are young you want the amenities of the town. I have lived in both town and village, and I know. You don't feel free when you are young if you live in a village. Everybody you meet knows you. It is 'Where are you off to?' and 'Where have you been?' It is in their eyes even if it is not on their tongues. So the village boys hurry away on their motor-bikes. Ipswich is full of country boys drifting up and down and thinking things out.

They belong to a generation who have learned to live partly outside the village. They are good with machines and the farmers with modern farms will always prefer them to the labourer-craftsmen of forty-five and over. But there are still many people who cannot bring themselves to travel and London can remain a foreign country, although it is only ninety miles away.

East Anglia is a nation, which makes it different. They talk their heads off in the West Country and Wales but the only kind of East Anglian who will talk freely are the fishermen. You will always notice that when a village boy joins the navy he begins to talk easily. It is because the sea is free and people catch the freedom. The inland country people do not have this sense of freedom.

It is not so much to promote the Labour Party that I work among the village people. It is because I have to serve them. I am one of them. They don't need to explain to me. I understand their quietness. I am uneducated like them but I know enough to help them. They accept me. They won't call me David – it is always Mr Collyer – I don't know why.

Brian Newton · aged nineteen · farm-worker and day-release student at the Agricultural Training Centre

I don't belong to Suffolk at all. I was born in Lancashire, I live in Ipswich, I work in this village ... I am a bit of a mixture! And now I might leave. I like it well enough but I'm thinking of the future, you see. I can't see a lot of hope in it. In fact, I can't see any hope in it. Yet I like it, but who can stay where there's no hope? A farm of my own is out; it is impossible to think of starting one, and now I think that farm work is out because I think that there is something unreasonable about its conditions. The modern machine methods and the old-fashioned wages ideas are all mixed up in a funny kind of mess. I am sorry that I have almost decided to leave the farm and join the police force because I shall be leaving something that I always wanted to do. When I was a boy I stayed on farms in Wales and in the Midlands, and helped with the work. There was never any doubt about what I should do when I left school. Having done it, I think that I made the wrong decision.

You are all right if you specialize, perhaps. If you work only with animals or become really skilled on the machinery side, and not just a tractor man. The Agricultural Education Centre would then be only the beginning of the training and I would go on to Kesteven. But how could I be sure that, after all this, I wouldn't come back to the farm and find myself no better off than I was? There are so many trying to get the few really good jobs and so many bad jobs. The opportunity isn't there. You work for a farmer and one day he will make you his farm foreman, but what is that? Yet it is a pity because although my parents have always lived in towns, I feel like a countryman. I like it here! Although I live in Ipswich and travel twenty miles a day to and from the farm, I know many more country people than I do town people. We live on the main road and, except for our immediate neighbours, Ipswich is really quite strange to me. I met most of my country friends at a Young Farmers' Club and I have come to think of myself, quite naturally, as a countryman. But I am getting on for twenty and I have become engaged, and suddenly there is all this question of the future. I hope I am not proud, but I can't think of myself just as a worker – a labourer – for ever. I like reading – I read very much. I study a lot. I listen to good music – and pop, although I am not one for the Big Beat. I mean that although I work on a farm I can't pretend to be all that simple. I am at the cross-roads and I must think about what I shall be doing when I am thirty – or even forty! The men who work with me on the farm say they didn't think at all. Perhaps they couldn't when they were nineteen. I mean that it would have been no use. But I must. At the moment I can't see any climb or development however hard I work. If I stay I am already where I shall always be.

The older farm-workers aren't all that keen on boys like me. They don't appreciate your running about. There are three men who have been on the farm all their lives and I know they resent me. Two of them have never learned to drive and have nothing to do with the machinery at all, and each year there are more and more jobs they can't do. It is embarrassing for them, I suppose. They'll talk all day about what they did years ago. You'll occasionally meet men who'll say, 'Thank God – those days have gone!' but you'll still meet quite a few who, if they had their way, would be back with the horses tomorrow. They'll fiddle about with some ditch or other miles away, making such a rare fuss of it. It is all quite unnecessary but nobody dare say so, of course. They are so slow. They have to touch everything with their hands – they dislike the idea of not touching things. They must handle, touch.... They would do the sugar-beeting perfectly – the worst damn job on the farm – even if their fingers were half-dropping off with the cold. If they saw one on the heap with a bit of green left on they'd be scrambling up to get it. All unnecessary. These men are in their early fifties and they hold the idea that theirs is the right way and that we shall have to come round to it. There is another 'stranger' on the farm – a boy from the South. Our ideas are different, we speak different and we even look different – to these village men who have never left their village, unless perhaps for the war. The worst thing about these older workers is that they really do believe that we shall have to come round to their way of thinking. They have some sort of fear of the boss. The boss used to expect them to be hard at it all day, although I don't know that he can expect it these days. What they can't understand is that work is just work – something to be done and paid for. Of course we know that the old men had art – because they had damn-all else! It kept them from despairing. And we young men have efficiency, and I'm not saying that efficiency is enough either. This tractor is efficient. A man is more than a tractor, isn't he?

Most of the older men would find it very difficult to get a job if they left this farm. The jobs they are best at are no longer being done. Each week, after I have been to the Agricultural Education Centre, I come back to the farm and I think how I would run it. I know I shouldn't say that I would get rid of those three for a start – yet that would be the start. They are not there because they are necessary but because of the farmer's good-will – and he will have to show them his good-will for another ten or fifteen years. But he knows and I know that another young tractor-driver could do all their tasks.

The day-release course has been a great help. More and more boys are doing them. They are equivalent to one year at an agricultural college. The farmer who allows me to attend the classes thinks that I should stay at least three years on his farm so that he can get the benefit of my training. I don't agree with this. The farmers still have this habit of trying to hold a man by some kind of obligation to them. It has all got to change. There should be a good wage–work contract between employer and skilled worker, and nothing else. The farmers aren't used to their men being free. My farmer gives me little things – petrol for my car sometimes – things like that. He wants more than my work, which he agrees I do well. He needs me to be beholden to him in some way. Loyal. He is emotional and patronizing. He should pay me for what I do and not expect my whole life to be his. He wants me to throw my life into his farm. He wants to own me.

I have a sense of division but I don't want it. I really like the Suffolk people and I really don't want to leave the land. And yet if somebody really made it worth my while I don't think that I would stay. There is talk that I can have a cottage on the farm when I marry and that my wages will rise, but what is ahead? The basic situation between farmer and farm-worker just isn't going to change, so there will always be a little wage, a lot of trust and little presents like the petrol.

One of the drawbacks to working on a farm when you are young is that you are kept away from people and when, as I am, you spend day after day with middle-aged men who never read, who never go any-where outside the village itself and who cannot understand what makes any modern gadget work, you begin to lose touch yourself. I went to the pub to meet the young men. They never talk ideas, it is always people with them. The church is the vicar – that kind of thing. They seem, well, hemmed-in by the village itself.

You wouldn't think that working – and *wanting* to work – on a farm would be so worrying, would you?

5 · Good Service

*'As to all that,' rejoined Sir Walter coolly, 'supposing I were induced
to let my house, I have by no means made up my mind as to the
privileges to be annexed to it. I am not particularly disposed to favour
a tenant. The park would be open to him of course ... but what
restrictions I might impose on the use of the pleasure-grounds is
another thing. I am not fond of the idea of my shrubberies being always
approachable....'*

Jane Austen, *Persuasion*

Christopher Falconer ·
aged thirty-nine · gardener

Feudalism is a kind of game, set and match with partners at both the
serving and receiving ends knowing exactly what is expected of them
and abiding unquestionably by the rules. Questioning, in fact, is point-
less; it breaks rule one which is accept the lot of the draw. The last of
the old acceptors – on both sides – are now in their sixties or more and
prefer not to see any difference between working for 'Lordship' and
working for one of the North Sea Gas projects, or 'him that grows the
peas for Birdseye'. It's all work, they will untruthfully insist. But
'Lordship' and what went with him was far from being all work. A
good deal of worship and now lost and forgotten mystery managed to
interpose themselves in the ritual toil of the manor or 'big house'.
Wasn't this where the god lived? And certainly the goddess. 'He was
a real gentleman,' said Chris the gardener, 'but Ladyship was *frightening.*' The note of awe and wonder in his voice was familiar enough; one
heard it often from aged people either in Akenfield or in any of the
neighbouring villages as they tried to describe the particular menace
and unpredictability of certain landowners and their wives. It was the
duty of a squire to be meaner, odder and richer than any of his equals
in the locality. The feudalists on the serving end seemed to demand
this. They also liked to have 'big people' in their particular 'big house'.
The Duke of Hamilton and Brandon who lived in the big house at
Easton surrounded by the biggest crinkle-crankle wall in East Anglia,
and probably in the world, was the Zeus of the neighbourhood. The

villagers maintain that it was in the cock-pit in his garden that the Jameson Raid was planned. His coronet, picked out in gloss paint and cheerfully snowcemmed round, remains fixed to many of the cottages. Lord Covehithe was not quite up to this, being but a baron, but he possessed one mystic card which trumped the county – he was a close friend of King George V. His house lay just outside Akenfield, which had supplied it with servants for centuries. The supply gushed until 1939, trickled dutifully until about 1950, then abruptly dried up. Casual people arrived, at times to suit themselves, and 'kept the garden down' with park-size mowers and other machines, and on the face of it everything looked as neat as before. Inside, a Maltese butler wearing suede shoes served dinner at seven and drove off to Ipswich in his Fiat at eight sharp. On fine days, Lordship and Ladyship sat on the terrace to a different silence. 'We always had to work as if we weren't there,' said Chris. Now, more likely than not, nobody was there. 'I felt sorry for them,' he added.

He is an easy, loquacious man who seems to be both ashamed of holding the key feudalistic ideas and at the same time anxious to put in a good word for them. He uses the word 'calibre' as a euphemism for the word 'class' – 'people of my calibre ... people of their calibre' – stocking Suffolk like an arsenal in which the light modern weapon has taken over from the great crested field-piece. He is married with three children and now works in one of those small, wall-secluded gardens of incredible perfection which lie behind the streets of Woodbridge. He has the rather natty good looks of a tail-gunner advertising Jif or Brylcreem during the last war which, however, he is young enough to have missed. His manner is quick and anticipatory. There is in him a kind of craving to give, to assist, to smooth the path. At less than forty, he feels slightly ill at ease in a world which has turned turtle and encumbered him with a new bungalow, car, television and foreign holidays. He is one of the last generation of initiates of a social faith whose claims (to use his own staunch ballistic metaphor) have been exploded. Father, grandfather and great-grandfather were in service at the big house. Their lives were dedicated to Lordship and Ladyship as totally as other lives have been dedicated to an altar. Chris followed them at fourteen in 1942. The war was on and the big house with its flagpole and royal memories focused the local patriotism. Lordship and Ladyship, both very old, made the most of it. Their refusal to allow 'that dreadful man' to change a thing in their lives was the talk of the village and one tale of how Ball the butler had been immediately called to restore the vast precision of the dining table after a bomb had disturbed it was much admired. In such a climate it did not seem odd that Chris should be taken on as trainee under-gardener while civilization rocked. He described it with a kind of apologetic amazement. It was 'all wrong' yet, for him, 'somehow right'.

*

I went to Lordship's when I was fourteen and stayed for fourteen years. There were seven gardeners and goodness knows how many servants in the house. It was a frightening experience for a boy. Lord and Ladyship were very, very Victorian and very domineering. It was 'swing your arms' every time they saw us. Ladyship would appear suddenly from nowhere when one of us boys were walking off to fetch something. 'Swing your arms!' she would shout. We wore green baize aprons and collars and ties, no matter how hot it was, and whatever we had to do had to be done on the dot. Nobody was allowed to smoke. A gardener was immediately sacked if he was caught smoking, no matter how long he had worked there.

We must never be seen from the house; it was forbidden. And if people were sitting on the terrace or on the lawn, and you had a great barrow-load of weeds, you might have to push it as much as a mile to keep out of view. If you were seen you were always told about it and warned, and as you walked away Ladyship would call after you, 'Swing your arms!' It was terrible. You felt like somebody with a disease.

The boy under-gardeners had to help arrange the flowers in the house. These were done every day. We had to creep in early in the morning before breakfast and replace great banks of flowers in the main rooms. Lordship and Ladyship must never hear or see you doing it; fresh flowers had to just be there, that was all there was to it. There was never a dead flower. It was as if flowers, for them, lived for ever. It was part of the magic in their lives. But the arrangements were how they wanted them and if one of the gardeners had used his imagination, Ladyship noticed at once and soon put a stop to it! The guests always complimented her on the flowers and she always accepted the praise as though she had grown, picked and arranged them herself. It was logical because servants were just part of the machinery of the big house and people don't thank machines, they just keep them trim and working. Or that's how I look at it.

As the years went by, we young men found ourselves being able to talk to Lordship and Ladyship. 'Never speak to them – not one word and no matter how urgent – until they speak to you,' the head-gardener told me on my first day. Ladyship drove about the grounds in a motor-chair and would have run us over rather than have to say, 'get out the way'. We must never look at her and she never looked at us. It was the same in the house. If a maid was in a passage and Lordship or Ladyship happened to come along, she would have to face the wall and stand perfectly still until they had passed. I wouldn't think that they felt anything about their servants. We were just there because we were necessary, like water from the tap. We had to listen for voices. If we heard them in a certain walk, we had to make a detour, if not it was, 'But why weren't you listening?' and 'Be alert, boy!' and, when you had been dismissed, 'Swing your arms!'

The garden was huge. The pleasure grounds alone, and not including the park, covered seven acres. The kind of gardening we did there is not seen nowadays. It was a perfect art. Topiary, there was a lot of that. It was a very responsible job. You had only to make one bad clip and a pheasant became a duck. The gardeners usually made up these creatures themselves. We were tempted to cut out something terrible sometimes, so that it grew and grew ... but of course we never did. Even when we went on to mechanical hedge-trimmers we still kept on topiary. There was a great pride in it, and in hedge-cutting of every sort. It was the hedge which set the garden off and all the big houses competed with each other. Fences were marvellous things, too; there were more than two miles of them round Lordship's and not a pale which wasn't exact. The hedges had tops like billiard-tables. It was get down and have a look, and stand back and have a look. No hedge was left until it was marvellous. There were so many things which really had no need to be done but which we did out of a kind of obstinate pleasure. The asparagus beds in winter were an example. We'd spend hours getting the sides of the clamps absolutely flat and absolutely at a 45° angle, although an ordinary heap of earth would have done just as well.

None of the village people were allowed into the garden. Definitely not. Trades-people came to their door and never saw the main gardens. Work in front of the house had to be done secretly. About seven in the morning we would tiptoe about the terrace, sweeping the leaves, tying things up, never making a sound, so that nobody in the bedrooms could hear the work being done. This is what luxury means – perfect consideration. We gave, they took. It was the complete arrangement. This is luxury.

Of course, they spent a terrific amount of money on the house and garden. It was the machinery they had to have in order to live. So they kept it going, as you might say. A bad servant was just a bad part and was exchanged for a good part as soon as possible. I thought of this when I was doing my National Service as a fitter in the Tank Corps. It made sense. Yet I got so that I didn't know quite what to think about it all. It was obviously wrong, yet because Lordship and Ladyship were old and had never known any other kind of life, I suppose I felt sorry for them. I always had to give more than was necessary. I couldn't resist it. It was exciting somehow. But when I got home I would be angry with myself. The butler would sometimes come to the pub and imitate them. Laugh – you should have heard us! But I would feel strange inside, pitying and hating at the same time. His favourite joke was:

Ladyship: 'Shall we ask the So-and-Sos to luncheon, Bertie?'
Silence, then, 'Can they play bridge? Will they like my garden?'
Ladyship: 'No, I don't think so.'
Lordship: 'Then don't have 'em.'

Lordship was a friend of King George V. He was a terribly nice man – a real gentleman. A lot of royalty came down from time to time and Lordship and Ladyship were sometimes at Sandringham. The Queen (Queen Elizabeth the Queen Mother) came. She treated us very well and loved the garden. She would tell us boys what they ate for luncheon and then we'd all laugh. The Princess Royal was just the same – easy. But Members of Parliament always imitated Lordship and Ladyship and treated us like fittings. I was amazed by the Royalty. I imagined a bigger kind of Ladyship, but definitely not.

It was strange coming back to the big house after the Tank Corps. I was married now and we had an estate cottage without inside water, a bath or electricity, although it was very pretty and we were very happy. At first, that is. Until Ladyship said that my wife must work in the big house. My wife didn't understand what it would mean. She came from Ilford and had never seen anything like it. She got worried and then she got migraine. The doctor told her that she must leave her work at the big house because it was making her anxious and ill. I told Ladyship, who said, 'But she must come'. I told her what the doctor had said but she just drove to the cottage and told my wife, 'You must come back to the kitchen – do you understand? You *must*.' So that is why we went away. I felt sorry for my wife and for Ladyship; they had no way of knowing each other.

The big house helped me in my life and changed me. Being in private service has educated me. I can talk to anybody. There is one thing about Suffolk folk and that is that they find talk terribly difficult. I don't. I have learned to talk. But working for Lordship made me a foreigner in the village. Those who remain with their own calibre in the village stay in the village family. I belonged to the big-house family and it was hard to leave. I saw the last of the big house while it was self-supporting. Everything, milk, cream, butter, game, fish, flowers, chicory, endive, melons, they were all there behind the hedges. Whatever Lordship and Ladyship wished for, they asked for, and it was brought.

I had a great training as a gardener and acquired all my knowledge completely free. Although I was often horrified by the way we were all treated, I know I got a terrific amount out of it. It is a gardening background which few people now have, and scarcely anybody of my age. In a great garden you grow from the seed and then you see the plant growing where it will always grow, but in a nursery garden it is just produce and sell, produce and sell. Nothing remains. A private gardener like myself would never get on in nursery work because I have had the fine art of tidiness drummed into me. I work privately and could have a choice of twelve or fifteen jobs, all with houses. There is no kind of gardening I can't do. I am not boasting, it is a fact.

How can you describe this anxiety we have about our gardens in Suffolk? I have been to Scotland and they don't have it there. Are gardens our pride? I think so: it is a breeding in the Suffolk people. I have never thought about this before but now I would like to get to the bottom of it. We are all obviously urged to do it as a great necessity in our lives. It is my life. I would die in the attempt to produce a plant, a flower, and bring it to perfection. You take my employer. She never goes abroad. All her holiday imagination is put into her garden. She prefers this to a seven days' wonder. Another thing, I think, which you can put the gardening urge down to is simply ownership. It is wonderful to realize that a beautiful plant is yours. Suffolk people love you to go and boost their gardens. If people want to be polite, the first thing they say is, 'What a beautiful garden'. If a man is clipping a hedge, you must compliment him on it. Hedges have to be praised. This is where the old employers went wrong, they didn't understand about praise. If there had been more praise for gardeners there would still be plenty of good gardeners around. An industrial worker would sooner have a £5 note but a countryman must have praise.

There are a tremendous number of people who garden morning, noon and night and can't begin to be got out of their gardens, but they are a different calibre to myself. They are ex-army officers, ex-naval officers. About seventy per cent of the gardens open to the public in East Anglia belong to ex-military men. I think it must be something to do with time and order. They love complete order and nobody can stop them imposing it on a garden. There must be something in this because I have thought about it a lot. So many of my employer's friends are middle-aged army officers, retired, and they are all fascinated by horticulture. The things which they will do to make a garden is astounding. I've known them to drive all the way to Wiltshire to pick up a stone sink. You see, gardening allows them to go on having routine, order, tidiness, straight edges, upright posts. You can be strict in a garden. They were fantastically strict in the Tank Corps barracks. And tidy! 'If it doesn't move, whitewash it,' they used to say. You look at the names belonging to the National Gardens Scheme and you'll find it's three-quarters officers. And how they work! Although if they're going to have a garden and going to have a good one they have hardly got any alternative. I know a colonel near here who, when he opens his garden for the National Gardens Scheme, has all his machines and tools on display. All the mowers, barrows, spades – everything – are polished and oiled and lined up! You wouldn't have got Lordship doing a daft thing like that – but then you wouldn't have got Lordship letting Tom, Dick and Harry into the park, let alone into the gardens.

The village gardens aren't as good as they used to be for the very simple reason that a man can go to work for an hour or two extra and earn enough money to buy vegetables for a week, whereas, if he grows them, he's got to dig, buy seed, sow, hoe, water, worry, take up and I don't know what – and all for something he can buy for a few bob. There's not time, anyway, because probably he is out to work, fruit-picking and that sort of thing, and so it is easier for them both to have a packet of frozen peas handy. Life now is much less elaborate and, consequently, much less interesting. As a qualified judge of flowers, I would like to say that Akenfield is more horticultural-minded than it used to be, but it is not, and this is the truth. Not the ordinary village worker. But then you have only to go the next step higher, the salesman in his new bungalow, and it's a very different story. Their gardening is a form of ownership and 'getting on'. They garden neatly. They don't know the difference between tidiness and neatness. They buy expensive ugly things. Their gardens look like shopping. These are the new gardeners who are making the nurserymen rich. It is not the young farm-worker – I wish it was.

The young boys in the village won't touch the garden. They earn too much money as far as I can see. They don't pay enough for what they are learning. I had to help my father in the garden when I was a boy; there was nothing else to do. It was expected of me. You wouldn't get a boy to do this now. You just can't reach the boy. I have cousins in the village only just ten years younger than myself and I can't connect or talk to them. I can talk to educated boys, that is different. They are not changing. Supposing I wanted to talk about horticulture, it wouldn't do for me to talk to a village boy of about seventeen from the council houses. I'd be much better if I went over to Framlingham College and talked to a seventeen-year-old there. The boy from the village seems to have no interest in anything. That is why the village garden is in decline. But the gardening industry is booming. You have only to go round the nurseries at the week-end – all the car parks are absolutely full. But not with proper village people. The cars belong to suburban folk. They are intelligent and lively. They are busy with gardens, boats and holidays. They buy very different things to the old country chap who spent no more on his garden than the price of a packet of carrot seed.

I have been judging village flower shows and gardens for nearly ten years, and am one of the officials of the Village Produce Association. There are branches all over the country and Suffolk is actually a very poor one. It is an organization run by the Rural Community Council. Each judge – there are about forty of us in Suffolk – attends about a dozen flower shows during the season. It is very progressive and professional; the old-time amateur judge is out. The shows, and gardening itself, are spoilt by the tendency to try and grow the biggest vegetable or flower. People are not nearly so keen on the professional exhibiting side of things in Suffolk as they are in Yorkshire, for instance. They are more interested in Suffolk in being the first to have peas or potatoes, or whatever it is. The great thing is to produce something before your neighbour does. Real gardening is dying, dying ... dying. There aren't many gardeners of my calibre left. I am a young man who has got caught in the old ways. I am thirty-nine and I am a Victorian gardener, and this is why the world is strange to me.

6 · The Forge

You must either conquer and rule or serve and lose,
suffer or triumph, be the anvil or the hammer.

Goethe

Gregory Gladwell ·
aged forty-four · blacksmith

The blacksmith's shop in most villages is now either a garage, a smart
cottage called The Olde Forge or a forlorn lean-to still redolent of horse
musk and iron, its roof gradually slithering down to the couch-grass mat
which covers the yard. But any smithy which managed to survive the
great transition of horse by machine and the years when, as Gregory
put it, 'nothing was bought and nothing was sold', and which is run by
someone who is able to combine a traditional training with a new
adaptability, is likely to be one of the most prosperous businesses in
the neighbourhood. This is what has happened to Gregory's smithy.
Success is his dilemma. Is he keeping faith with the 'old ones', as he
calls them, the men of his blood who shod the farm horses and made
the ploughs 'in the seventeen-somethings – *and on this very floor*'?
Deeds and apprenticeship articles give a formal assent to Gregory's
claims. They were passed on to him when he was seventeen, a mockery
it seemed at the time. These curly bits of paper, an anvil, some odds and
ends of tools and a lot of trade secrets which had suddenly become a
dead language. He was like an anchorite sticking to his beliefs and bare
cell in a land which no longer had any use for his sort. Now, with not
only the village but every passing car slowing at his door, things are, in
effect, much worse! He has become a great craftsman. Calling on him
has become a must. Rich open-plan farmers have to wait patiently for
the expensive fittings needed in the restoration of their ancient halls and
manors – nobody else can make them, and Gregory has only four pairs
of hands, his own amazing ones and those of the three boys who are
learning the trade. The question he continually asks himself is something like, 'Am I exceeding the terms of my indenture?'

He is lanky and fine-boned – not at all like the classic forge Samson.

Silky black hair fringes out from an old cap and the shirt gapes to reveal an ascetic olive-skinned chest stippled with spark-burns. In some ways Gregory could be a Celt, yet not with those tall gaunt lines of nose and cheek; the eyes piercing their way from their deep sockets. These are East Anglian features, to be traced in the Ipswich and Norwich streets or in stone high up on the church walls. He is married to Nancy, a beautiful woman from 'up London like'. She is educated; a trained artist. She is disciple as well as wife – as are the three apprentices. So is everybody who buys anything.

The furnace blazes away at all hours as Gregory breaks the time barrier. Crucifixes, iron coats of arms, hurdles, harrows, vast abstract light-holders for a West Country cathedral, surgical horseshoes and the primitive templets made by his ancestors rage in the flames. Orders roll in. Gregory views them with misgiving. Sometimes he thinks that it would be better to break faith with the boom than with the Old Ones.

Newcomers to the neighbourhood are good customers. Most of them aren't in search of the old ways but of the original fireplace in the old house which they have bought. If they can tug out a Victorian grate and find the ancient hearth around which centuries of field men have sat, they are moved profoundly. It is the old sacred place and nothing is too good for it. The re-garnishing of this cavern made of small orange-rose bricks, with its stately breast and blackened chimney-beam, has become the most popular tribute paid by the twentieth-century middle-class villager to his ancestors. It will lead him into great expense – copper canopy, huge log basket, firedogs, fireback, brass and pewter ornaments, light brackets – but the money is never grudged. Only the forge can supply these essentials. Gregory's forge contributes as much to the hearth cult – and all its decorative subsidiaries – as does any firm in the area, but with a difference. Everything he makes has to be signed by a signature which is recognizable and acceptable to the 'old trades-men', as he calls them. The nameless ones who built and adorned the village, and whose bolts and horseshoes lie about with the flints in the fields, and none of whom would have laid claim to be 'artists or architects or anything of the like'.

Nancy smiles. She follows her husband, of course, but on an enthusiastic circuit which takes in student journeys to churches, castles and mansions where she sketches anything from a hinge to armour. She reads and checks. The village says that she has made Gregory. He agrees. They say that he must have known that he was on to a good thing when he took on the family business. He agrees. But they aren't thinking of the same good thing. Gregory hankers for the hard past. He is an atavist but his history is all voices, forebodings, notions – hauntings, really. Nancy's are the facts as they are generally known. 'Gregory talks a lot,' says the village. He is a man who is fighting not to be more than he is.

*

I was born in Akenfield. It was in the year 1923. I have spent all my life here. I have the family records back to the eighteenth century and my name is mentioned in Domesday Book. We were at Saxmundham then. Then there was a time when we got lost – right out Dennington way. But we found our path eventually. I have a lot of my grandfather's features, although I'm not so tall as he was. I have his hands. Hands last a long time, you know. A village sees the same hands century after century. It is a marvellous thing but it's true. My grandfather was a most extraordinary man and very headstrong. He'd got a way of his own and I tend to take after him. My father started work when he was ten and I started when I was fourteen.

My family had been Liberal till several years ago, then they changed over to Conservative. I don't know why; it was before my time. They had damn little to conserve so I don't know why they did it. Suffolk people are cagey about politics. It makes me laugh when the Tory women stand outside the voting booths on election day 'just ticking the names off the Electoral Roll', as they say. How on earth do they reckon they'll ever discover a thing about the village politics? All the same, I don't think it should be allowed. It makes people nervous. I have a tendency to be like Charles Bradlaugh, who was a Suffolk man. I am not an atheist but I have strong views about politics and the Church. Bradlaugh wasn't against Church, he was against the set-up. I'm against the set-up. But I think it was an extremely good thing that religion should be accepted as the saviour of civilization. So I think it right that it should be carried on. If you forsake religion, it's back to the savages. This is what is happening now. Whatever you think, this is what makes you. You don't have to tell folk everything you think. I have a lot of personal views about religion, for instance, which I never tell a soul. But I've often been tempted, particularly when I was young. I saw cases of men – grown men – in this village, packing their bait to spend the whole Sunday at chapel. People used to go to chapel at nine in the morning and not come home until eight at night. It is the truth. Most of them behaved shocking during the week. It's a fact. They were nothing but a lot of bloody hypocrites. Suffolk used to worship Sunday, not God. I don't know why they all went to this trouble. Anybody with a mite of common sense could see how useless it was, chapel, chapel,

chapel, Sunday, Sunday, Sunday. Best suits. They were Baptists. *What were they trying to do?* There were so many of them they could have set the whole village on its ear had they followed Jesus. But all you heard them say was Sunday. Bugger Sunday, I say, and praise God when you can. People never think why they go to church or chapel, they just go. It is very strange.

I was born during the bad times. My brothers and myself went to school for part of the day and to work for the rest of it. When we left school at half past three we'd go gleaning, picking up beans and all such things as that. We'd most likely work till eight if it stayed light. We biked to school at Framlingham. It was 1934 time. Things weren't very sharp. Father was making out by killing pigs for Danny Linton at Pettistree so we had to bike from school to home, eat some bread and cheese, or whatever there was – and there wasn't much – get an old sack and then bike on to Danny's farm to collect the pigs' insides. Then we biked home with them and tipped them out on the scullery floor and scraped them. We had to get them as white as a board, scratching out all the filth with the back of an old knife. Then we washed them in salty water and – hey presto! – sausage skins. But it wasn't the end. There were all these pails and pails of muck to be got rid of. We had to bike out of the village and bury it. On Saturdays we used to take a bundle of these skins to old Boot the butcher and he'd give us a three-cornered lump of brisket, all fat and bone, and weighing about a stone, in exchange. But even this is better than what happened in 1930, the big black year. In 1930 we had blackbird pie for Christmas dinner – and we had to catch the blackbirds before we had the pie! It had got to Christmas morning and we were going to make do when my father said, 'Come on, boys, let's try a blackbird!' We knocked a few over quite easy. I could take you to the spot where we did it. We cooked the pie in the brick oven.

This was the year my grandfather had to shut down the forge. He never went back to it. I used to walk by it, eyeing it and thinking. But nothing was rosy wherever you looked. Nearly everybody went out of business. Nothing was sold. People who had left school began to think about the Big House. You realized that it was there, with all the gardeners, grooms and maids and food. You have to face it, the Big House was then an asset to the village. It paid us to raise our hats, which is why we did it. I hear people run the gentry down now but they were better than the farmers in a crisis. Theirs was the only hand which fed us which we could see. So we bowed a bit; it cost nothing, even if it wasn't all courtesy. Nobody left, nobody went away. People were content.

However hard up they were, they stayed content. The boys had the arse out of their trousers, no socks and the toes out of their boots. My brothers and myself were like this, yet so happy. I think other families were the same. The village kept close.

The biggest change which I have seen in Akenfield is the growth of discontent. Greed. Nobody ever said, 'Bugger you, Jack, my head is out!' when I was a boy. When you wanted help it was given. It was 'Thank you very much', and that was that. You mustn't pay. It was good enough for a row if you offered to pay. Payment was a crime. This was how things were when I told my parents that I wanted to go into the family business. My grandfather had died and my grandmother was paying a man to open the forge and try and do some trade. My father couldn't afford to pay the apprenticeship fee of half-a-crown a week, so I had to do another job as well. I worked from eight to five at the forge and then three more hours night and morning for a man who kept 160 pigs. I was paid a-penny-a-pig-a-week to feed and clean them out. They weren't the little old things you get today, they were big pigs. Enormous ... 30–35 stone apiece. The pigman used to pay me when the pigs went to market. It would sometimes come to £5 10s., which was a tidy fortune.

It was all agricultural work at the forge. Mostly shoeing. All the horses were still with us and at seventeen I was shoeing an average of eight horses a day. I remember making my first horseshoe. I started work at the forge on August 2nd and I made this shoe on August 4th. They put you straight into the collar in those days! There was no messing about. When you got a job you began doing it right away. You were expected to catch on quick.

The man my grandmother allowed to run the forge was old and when I was just over seventeen he retired, and I had to carry on alone. I now had to do every mortal thing myself. What I didn't know I had to find out or make up. There was nobody to ask. It was a terrible job, but there, we got over it. It was still all farm work, of course. Mostly shoeing. The horseman would stand at the head while the work was being done, so that was a bit of help. He could hold it like. I was such a thin little lad it was a masterpiece how I could hold anything! There was no thought of what you might call art-and-craft work, only plough counters, harrows, door-hinges and such farm things. There was no money about; everybody was bare-poor. I charged 6s. 8d. to put four shoes on a horse. I reckoned that with a quiet horse with good feet the task would take an hour. I hardly made a profit. There are still plenty of horses round here, of course – hunt horses, pony-club horses – it is most unusual for a village to have so many of them around. And I don't mind shoeing them. The trouble is that people who have these kind of horses reckon on you shoeing them for next to nothing. I won't do that. Not now. If people will pay what I charge and won't grumble, then I'll shoe for them, but not otherwise. I am supposed to have served a five-year apprenticeship, and if work isn't worth a little when you've done that, then blast them. I won't mess after it. I remember how hard it was to make myself free, for that is what I was really up to when I was here all alone before the war. I don't know what it is, I can't explain it, but you see I am the only one out of all my family – and there are five of us brothers – who had any intention of coming to the smithy. My brothers couldn't have cared less about the place. I wanted to come, *had* to come. But it is silly to be sentimental. What I sometimes think is that I am my grandfather, an old one. It is the truth when I say that I can sit in the shop of a Sunday, smoking my pipe, and be as happy as if I were sitting in the house. I wasn't born soon enough, that is the trouble. By rights, I should be dead and gone. I think like the old people. I have a tendency to do what I want to do, if the maggot bites. However pressing matters are, I do what I fancy. I think, probably, my attitude could be wrong. We have our pressures now with bills and bank managers and book-keeping, but I say to myself, this is not the highest thing; this is business. You are a tradesman; this is the highest thing. Making, doing. I feel I should have lived during the 1700s. That would have done me. But I am losing my place, aren't I?

Well, the war came, and one or two German prisoners came to help me out. They were pleasant lads. When they went back I had a boy from the army school, after he had finished his training. He had been an army apprentice farrier and I finished him off. When he left, one or two more arrived and for the first time in my life I had a few minutes to spare, so I began to amuse myself by making ornamental things. I entered one or two competitions and won prizes. And then, after the war, this wonderful thing happened, I married. The business was steady now. I had over a hundred horses on my books which had to be shod three times a year, which meant that I was making 1,200 shoes a year. Of course, the horses were passing, but so slowly that it didn't seem possible that they were soon to disappear off the farms for ever. I still saw the things I sent to the crafts section of the Suffolk Show as a hobby. I couldn't imagine living by such work.

Then new people came and bought up the old houses. They'd spend a mint of money 'putting it all back as it was'. They couldn't buy the things they needed for the restoration; they hadn't been made for donkey's years. So I had to start making them again. My wife went round, keeping her eye open for bolts, latches, handles, grates; drawing them and finding out their dates, and I made more of them as exactly as you're not likely to tell the difference. Mind you, it took time. It took all hours. But it was a fine thing for me to have something lying on the bench before me made by one of the old men, and my hands doing again what his had done. The new business grew and grew. The Trust House people had bought the Suffolk coaching-houses and now they were doing them up regardless. They wanted to do everything in the old-fashioned way, all mortise-and-tenon studs and plaster. And, of course, hand-made nails. I made all the nails they used. They were each forged and hammered from the hot spar. And they were expensive, I can tell you. You can buy a pound of ordinary machine-made nails for 9*d.* but mine cost 4½*d.* each. A strange thing happened while I was hammering these nails. They found a great pile of Roman nails in the Welsh mountains, all as bright as if they had been made yesterday. I could quite understand why this was because these nails would have been made from lowmore which doesn't rust. It is steel which rusts. Do you know what I thought when I heard of these great Roman nails? – those would have been like the nails they would have used for the Crucifixion. They would have been made from iron smelted with charcoal. This is why the Swedish iron is so good because they were using charcoal right up to my day. But you can't buy iron now; it is all steel. They will smelt it especially for you if you order ten tons of it, but charge you a ridiculous price.

We have to make do with mild steel for all our work, and this is why you get all this trouble with agricultural things breaking sudden like. These steels are too strong. They cannot give. They just get fatigue and snap. They are too good for rough purposes – if you can call anything too good. Iron would do the job much better. But then you can't electric-weld iron. It has to be fire-welded. That is why they manufacture mild steel to fit in with modern methods of production. It is not easier to work – oh no! It is simply easier to weld because you are using electricity and not fire. But iron is always better for bending and real forging. The various parts of the new agricultural machines are all profiled out in the gas-flame; they are cut out flat, not bent. All this has happened during the last few years, so everything is different. We've got a profile machine which cuts the pattern out in a piece of tin. You screw it in on top, light the gas – propane and oxygen – and work with a cutting-head with an electric motor and a magnet attached to it. This runs around your plate and carves out its shape in the metal below. Ours will cut two inches thick. Before this method was invented everything at the smithy had to be forged and knocked into shape.

I don't have a catalogue. I don't like making two of anything. I find out what people can either afford or mean to pay and do a design in keeping with the price. We like to think that when a customer gets something from the forge it is their individual thing. But how much longer we can stick it, I don't know. Not long, I fancy. The time must come when we shall have to settle down to a standard line. It will be a terrible pity if this should happen. So many smiths are just copying the old designs. And making a poor job of it. It is abusing the old tradesmen. I believe that we should work as they worked; this isn't copying, it is getting back into their ways, into their skins. We should either do this or we should go right ahead, like the Germans, and do something absolutely new. The Germans are streets and streets ahead of us with metal designing. They wouldn't do this pretty scrollwork which all the English people love; they only do beautiful, genuine 1960 designs. I show some books of these modern German patterns to the customers. They hesitate. I try and push them, they back away. The man with money to spend on a village house in England has got to have everything quaint and curly.

I never employ extra men, no matter how big the job. I stay up late – we all five stay up late – we crowd the hours. You can't bring outsiders into a place like this; they wouldn't fit in. They would upset the whole atmosphere. I have the boys. They were born in the village, they went to the village school and then they came to me, and I have taught them how to work. And soon they became part of it. It would be fatal to bring in an outsider to spoil it all. When we do a big job we have to *work*. This is understood. Eventually, we get through it. A big job is a big experience.

We don't do more repairs to farm machines than we are forced to. The farmers get most of their repairs done by some mechanically-minded youngster who drives the tractor and they resent having to pay money to people like me. But we don't turn anybody away because the old business was built up on farm work and it is our moral duty to stay within the farming band. We haven't told the farmers not to come. We never did make ploughshares. This is cast-iron work and has to be done in a foundry. But we used to do the plough-counters – the cutting knives. It was a swine of a job. You always swear terrible when you are doing it. You'd think you'd welded it on and beaten it out, and then you hadn't. It was best not to come to the forge when the plough-counters were being mended – not if you were squeamish. My father, who was a butcher by trade, said, 'The Lord sent the meat and the devil sent the cooks'. The devil sent the counters too.

I think I am a dedicated man. I won't have financial trouble – I mean, to hell with it! I won't have life all spoilt by money. I don't worry about dying, although I am mid-way through, but I dread being old and unable to work. We are all living in the rat-race, however far out in the wilds we are. The village is so quiet now. Nobody walks about in it. You don't say you saw your neighbour, you say you passed his car. People wave and toot where they used to talk. They're all out for what they can get. Nobody goes to look at what somebody else has done and have a chat about it. If you saw somebody ploughing or clearing the marsh, you used to meet up with a neighbour and say, 'Let's go and see what he's up to'.

I talk to the boys. I train them in 'steps'. The oldest is twenty-two now and doesn't want much supervising. But the others are fifteen and seventeen and you have to watch them. I treat them as individuals. There's young Den, if you said something amiss to him it would upset him so much you wouldn't do nothing with him for a week. Big as an ox and soft as a girl. He is a great tradesman already. But Robin, you have to swear at him regular once a month, or you wouldn't do anything with him. If those two boys had been apprenticed together, you would have made a man of one and offended the other – or vice versa. You must never offend a boy. I always look at the parents before I take an apprentice. If you know the home, you already know the son.

I'm against sport. I hate it. If work and sport changed places, this country wouldn't be in a muddle. Sport and holidays have become a mania, an insanity. If anybody wanted a holiday, I wouldn't stop them from taking one, but I hate holidays as much as I hate sport, and that's saying something. These boys won't be like me; they'll never work as I have worked – and perhaps they shouldn't have to. I've been working two pieces of metal together on the anvil with the sledge-hammer, when my vest caught fire and I daren't pause to put it out! When two men were working, hitting the anvil in turn, they would get each other's sparks. You would be open right down the front and they flew against your nakedness. A blacksmith always rolls his shirtsleeves under, so the sparks don't lodge in the folds. Now, with the emery sparks, we have to watch out for eye-trouble.

I am worried about everything getting too big. I have been learning how to pack things up to go to America – when only ten years ago, if an order had been finished it lay in the corner of the shop until somebody in the village felt like picking it up. I sometimes want to be alone again. I'm fond of the boys, and they work well, but they take the private spell out of my shop. They are not to blame. It is because everything is rushing so. I am still young myself, and yet I worked here for years with just a pair of tongs, a couple of hammers and a four-and-a-half-gallon cask of beer under the bench. And an old drinking horn which had never been washed up. Now I am packing these things for the United States. I think life would be fuller if I wasn't, and that's a fact.

Francis Lambert ·
aged twenty-five · forge-worker

Francis works for Gregory and is disciple as well as employee. He is a great craftsman, a 'natural'. Exhibitions and contact with artists are beginning to bring him fame. He is both pleased and distrustful. He is 'glad that things are going well' but he doesn't want to 'stick out'. He is entirely uncreative in the imaginative sense – a pair of hands to shape metals to another's requirements. No design is too sophisticated for him to realize in iron, brass or copper. Recent commissions for fifty huge lamps for a cathedral, for instance, can make little aesthetic sense to him and their magnificence reveals his absolute submittance to the artist's will. There is a Henry Moore sited on the river bank near Benjamin Britten's new opera house at Snape (twelve miles) – has he seen it? No, it is not his business. To attempt taking an interest in metal from this angle seems a kind of threat. Two people work as one in order to get the best results, he finds – the artist and the artificer. All the same, Francis has all the ruthlessness of the artist. Work time is holy time for him. Nothing and nobody is allowed to break it up. So far there hasn't even been a girl, although he is handsome enough. He takes exercise, drinks Lucozade, breathes deeply – and all for 'work'. An austere young man.

He lives with his parents and brothers in a fine Tudor house on a hill. Inside, the heavy, stately rooms refuse to hide under cheerful wall-papers and tiled grates. Outside, the view is tremendous – a flood of corn and peas all the way to Framlingham with, here and there, tur-quoise streaks of the Deben glinting through the valley pastures. 'You don't have to go far to see a long way,' says Francis.

The village says that Francis is 'all right', meaning that he isn't like anybody else but it doesn't matter.

*

I won the apprentice-class championship of the British Isles at the Suffolk Show and was sent to Germany to represent the country at an international craft festival. The festival was wonderful. My trip was sponsored by the Metal Box Company. Eventually, I took first prize three consecutive years running with a log basket, a firescreen and a flower stand. Mrs Gladwell designed all these and I owe her fifty per cent of the praise. Mr Gladwell was pleased with me winning and gave me all the materials I had used. There is a lot of labour in show-work. Too much really. But as I went to Germany, it was worth it. My life has been very different to what I thought it would be. I'm not blowing my own trumpet, but I do all the top jobs. This is what it amounts to. The new altar-cross was passed to me and I finished it. Sixty working hours went into making it – although the trouble is we don't often get nice straight runs like this on an important job. It is on and off. It is start and pack up, start and pack up. Every man needs to start and work right through ...

What do you think our bread-and-butter is? – weather-vanes! Weather-vanes are good for bread-and-butter, especially when they have horses on them. Door-stops are very good too. And gates. And, at Christmas, firescreens.

I like working in brass; it is the best metal of all. We normally use the brittle type. You can make a good clean cut; nothing binds in it. The old kind of brass used for the twisted candlesticks was inclined to be soft. They will sell brass to you any length you want, but it's sure to be dear – 18s. a square foot! My mother loves copper. She wants me to make her this and make her that – she doesn't realize how much it all costs. But if I'd got the time and a little more money put aside I would make her everything she asked for.

I used to work a ten-hour day, Monday to Friday. I worked from eight to eight with two hours for meals. This was my ordinary work but on top of this I would do two extra hours each day on my show-work. So I used to work eighty hours a week. This was when I was seventeen, eighteen and nineteen. But it gets you down in the end.

My father said, 'Go and work for Mr Gladwell at the forge.' He said, 'I'm not forcing you – you won't be able to say that I forced you – but go and work for Mr Gladwell.' (Gregory, we call him but I will call him Mr Gladwell to you.) So I went and I have never regretted it. I was fifteen and I always thought I would work here. I was as green as they come. I knew nothing. But I had only been here a month when Mr Gladwell was saying that he would like me to go in for show-work. I was very nervous and didn't think that I could do it. I haven't got a lot of faith in myself. I am a shy sort of person really. But I began to pick the work up and after three years I had conquered it. I couldn't hide this fact from myself. There was no proper apprenticeship. I haven't any papers to say that I have been trained – neither has Mr Gladwell himself. He is self-taught and I just learned. And this is how I like to go on. If people just stand and tell me this and tell me that it doesn't mean a thing. I have to find everything out for myself after seeing it done. I can do it eventually.

I'll be quite honest with you; I haven't any faith in myself. I don't expect to be able to do anything. When it is done, I am pleased and surprised. But the faith is beginning to come now, as you might say. Gregory – Mr Gladwell – has brought this faith to me. He tells us all, when we start at the forge, that he will make men of us. I believe he has done so with me. Although he has an extraordinary way of putting it over, it gets there. The one we call the 'middle boy' was always fooling about; he'd got brains but wouldn't use them. But now Mr Gladwell has altered him and he's a damn useful bloke. Mr Gladwell is really a teacher. He likes to think and work things out. He is the best talker in the village – at least, I think so. The business would have closed up if it hadn't been for him. He believed in it. He won't alter the front of the shop because he says that this is the way his family saw it for 300 years. He likes to leave everything just as it was.

I now work fifty-four hours a week. It is no good doing more than this because of the tax, you see. I found this out during the summer when, because I had to visit my father in hospital, I had to give up overtime. When I opened my wage-packet I found that I had more money when I was working ordinary hours than when I was working all hours. I love work. It would be work all the time if I had my way. I have nothing against work. Young men should always look for work which interests them, no matter how long it takes them to find it. No man should go in at morning to wait for the clock at night. And people who want the money without the work spoil everything.

Outside work, I like shooting. In January, my brother and I go ferreting. I call this a hobby. We are the only men in the village who still have ferrets. My father used to trap – he'd be up early in the morning to find rabbits. It was handy money for him and the farmer was glad that he had set the traps. Rabbits were poor man's food. Our family isn't poor any more but we still like a nice rabbit. Only the farmers have spread the myxy about, so you don't always fancy them. It is a pity. There aren't many boys on the ferreting side these days; they're all for football. They are crazy about football, they talk of nothing else. They don't worry much about drinking and neither do I. The big beer-drinking days are gone. They drank because there wasn't any television. Their houses were so boring, they were glad to get to the pub. The boys drink very little – they might have a couple of small bottles and then they'll go on to minerals. Our fathers had to drink to be men. They thought the beer made them strong and fit. But this is wrong. They were rum old boys. We like playing cards in this village – we always have. It is a card-playing place – although you can go to some villages and never see a deck. We'll play for the odd bob – nothing much more. We don't go in for dancing; the boys don't bother with it – they'd much sooner go to the pictures. Myself, I'd sooner walk than do any of these things. I differ from the rest because I haven't got a car. So I walk over the land, or I might fish a pike. The other boys sit in their cars and won't walk a step. If there is another boy walking, I haven't met him. Of course, you want a lot of money to run a car and I know plenty of boys of my age who are nipping and screwing to run theirs. I earn a little more than most people and I couldn't run a car comfortable – so how can they? They smoke, they don't drink much, as I say, but a few of them buy plenty of clothes. So how do they do it?

Most of the boys have long hair. I don't like to see it. It doesn't look very nice in my opinion. Take my brother, for instance, he's terrible. I've never seen anything like my brother's hair, it is all over the place. The more you get on to him about it, the more he lets it grow. So it is best not to say anything – to just ignore it. But it's hard to ignore your brother's hair when it is as long as a girl's. He thinks it is wonderful. His girl thinks it is wonderful. All the village girls like their boys to have long hair.

I don't do a lot of reading but my brother is just the opposite. He lolls upside down on the armchair with his hair all over a book. He loves reading war stories. He likes to know all about the old-fashioned planes they used in 1940. I read the newspaper – that is the most I read. And I'll read any book there happens to be on ornamental metal work and I buy books about wrought iron. But I'd rather do a job than read any day.

My brother is twenty-one and works on the farm. He puts lots of hours in. He does more hours than I do. He ups and out by half past five in the morning, and like as not he won't be back for good until half past seven at night. Saturday is his half-day, when he works from five-thirty on to twelve o'clock. He'll relief milk on the neighbour's farm on a Sunday morning and he never complains. He's got a car but I've never heard him worry about any other kind of luxury. He laughs a lot. My mother, my father and me, we say, 'Look at your hair!' and he smiles and reads, smiles and reads. So what is the use? When he was sixteen, he and another boy about his age cut the entire farm with a combine. Two boys got the whole of the harvest in. He is a good shot. He is a very good brother. We love him. But this hair! And now he is growing a moustache. His name is Robin.

The young men don't hate the land any more – they used to but they don't now. They can do plenty of mechanical things on the farm, a bit of welding – things like that. They used to call you dumb if you worked on a farm but it won't do to be dumb today! The wages are much too low. Farm men aren't paid properly at all. My brother isn't exceptional; there are plenty of youngsters like him who'll damn-near run a farm – but they'll still get this little wage.

We're pretty interested in politics in the village but we don't really understand it. We argue but we're none too sure what we're arguing about. We hear what is going on but we haven't got the brain to stand it – but we'll argue! A dance is the easiest way to sort out who's Labour and who's Tory. Nobody who wasn't a Conservative would think of going to a Conservative dance, and the same with Labour. The young men worry about the Vietnam war to a certain extent. They don't see the point of it and they would stop it if they could. They don't believe in war but they like to read about old wars in stories. Some of them have some very funny ideas about war, I can tell you! The older men believe in war. They say, 'We went all through the last one and we don't want to see another', but they still *believe* in them. I think that being in a war, however awful, makes you believe in war. We all watch the telly news – everybody does. Television has changed the village people. I like the plays. I am always on the look-out for scenes showing ornamental iron-work. You may not have noticed, but telly plays are full of wonderful ornamental ironwork. There was this programme the other day about the fiftieth anniversary of the Russian Revolution which showed a pair of gates. Marvellous, they were. [The gates of the Winter Palace, St Petersburg, in Eisenstein's film, *Battleship Potemkin*.] It is one of my great ambitions to make a tremendous pair of gates, with all their fine railings. But who would buy them now?

I look at everything. I don't open a church door without looking at the hinges. Occasionally, when I've been to London, I'll be walking down a street and see interesting railings, gates and things, and I'll look and think. There are some fine railings in Westminster Abbey, I hear. They stand round a king. I'll give them a look one of these days. I always look to see how the old men did their work. The metal is all perfect still under the paint – as good as the day it was cast. I don't know how they did it. Of course, in those days time was nothing. Now it is everything. Mrs Gladwell can forget time. She can get so carried away making the designs that she forgets to put the dinner on. I am no good at drawing,

I'm afraid. I was hit every Monday morning at school because I couldn't draw. The strange thing is that this teacher who hit me came to see me after I had won all the wrought-iron prizes and said, 'I wish I were in your job ...'. But why did he hit me every week, month in, month out, because I couldn't draw? There wasn't all that much hitting when I was there, I must be fair. And I was only hit by hand – I never had the stick once. I kept out of trouble as best I could but I'm left-handed and teachers don't like that. My mother is left-handed too, and she had no end of trouble at school because of it. They'd hit her hand, they'd tie it up behind her, they'd watch it, they'd force the pen into her right hand, but she couldn't work it. She was done for. Her schooling was a nightmare. But you take my little brother. He is twelve and he loves school. He has all the brains. He is never frightened by school. The school is different now. As for my dad – when he went to school – he could tell you something! But he won't. Best forget it, he says. It's water under the bridge, boy. Other days, other ways, he says. He talks like that.

I enjoyed going to France and Germany but I didn't go much on their food. It's too fancy. I like good plain food, that is how we live. Everybody in Germany eats twice as much as we do in England and the men walk around with great bottoms on them like women. The Germans gave us each a bottle of white wine every day. It was very good. When the English boys drank beer it was so strong that they were soon well away. They weren't drinking any more beer than they did in England but soon they were all laughing – they couldn't stop. I laugh nearly as much now just to think about it. I've never met any of these young blacksmiths since. None of us seem to worry about writing or anything like that. But they were good mates, as the saying goes.

I haven't got any really close friends. I get on with everybody, none is closer than another. I spend most of my time at home, with my family. We get on well. We don't row. You hear of families which row, well here it is just the opposite. We might shout at my brother about his hair but as he just smiles we soon have to stop. There is a family which rows all the time in this village; you can hear them a hundred yards away. They lift the roof. But I think they're quite good friends. They are a family which rows, and that is that.

I haven't got a girl-friend and have never had one. I'll put it like this. As things are today you've got to be careful. There are no end of marriages breaking up. You must pick the right girl, you must know the meaning of marriage. I have seen young boys in this village get married. They think it is all bed, poor fellows. I see it quite different to this. I'm in no hurry at all. I must work. I mustn't be worried or distracted. Not yet. I couldn't spend time on my work if I was married. I've always said that thirty will do very well. I should know myself by then.

I wouldn't like to own my own business. I wouldn't care for the worry of it. When I say 'the worry', I'm only going on what I've seen at Mr Gladwell's. What I should like would be people to teach. I think I have patience. I teach the two apprentices. You have to be understanding with these youngsters. Some are timid, some are pig-headed. I'm timid with the timid and pig-headed with the pig-headed. If you act the same as the person you are teaching he will be at ease with you and will learn better. The apprentices have to pass the Rural Industries Bureau examinations. The examiners look for four skills: in overhead, vertical, down-hand and horizontal welding. People say that the exams are easy but when you realize that the examiners will be searching for thirteen faults in every piece of weld and that you've only got to drop two on each piece to fail, then you know that it is not. They send a man to the forge to watch. I was nervous and a bit shaky when he watched me, I can tell you! You have to get 120 marks or more out of 200 to pass. I got 160.

The village blacksmiths used to have to be great strong men but you don't need that kind of brawn now. I'm not hefty and I wouldn't want to be. The days of the sledge-hammer have gone; the power-hammer has taken its place. I'm reasonably broad across the shoulders, which is good enough. I don't want to be fat. The Americans are fat. My father is fat – he weighs over fifteen stone! I'm eleven, eleven, which is decent, I reckon. There are people in this village whose motto is 'Eat'. *Don't* eat sometimes, I say. Have a day off. I never eat breakfast on Sundays, although my dad creates like anything. I drink a lot of Lucozade – a bottle a day. I keep myself fresh. My hands aren't so good – they can't be – but I don't think that anybody meeting me of an evening would know that I did dirty work. Anyway, I like dirt. I couldn't bear a job where I was clean all day. It wouldn't suit me.

A lot of people remark on the happy kind of feeling at the forge – it is something they notice. Mrs Gladwell has done this. She has great understanding. She considers everybody. Although she knows that I can't draw or design she always listens if I say, 'Couldn't this go like this ...?' Then she will sketch – and there is my idea. It is very important to get on with your employer *and* his wife. A lot of the farmers have trouble with their workmen because the men can't get on with the farmers' wives. A man might be quite happy with a farmer but will have to leave because his wife is awkward.

The visitors go for the churches in Suffolk. People come here just to see them and for no other reason. I might go in ours to look at a lock, a hinge, but for no other reason – I'll be quite honest with you. Some of the people round here who go to church lead bad lives. I know this to be right. I say that if you lead a good clean life it is not necessary for you to go to church. The churches have fallen right out. Sundays have fallen right out. Sunday is now the big gambling day. My father prefers the chapel to the church – most people do. This used to be big chapel country.

What would I like to do? I would like to have a go at a masterpiece. The cathedral lights took us a year to make and we had to work until midnight to finish them off. My hand was in each one of them. I would like to work like that again.

7 · The Wheelwright

Harry Hole came Friday (October 31st 1919). He spoke of the waggon
which has just been repaired at the shop. He himself once fitted new
raves and stays to it. But the original waggon he thought was built
before his time, by my Uncle John, whom I just remember as a cripple.
Harry mentioned, as evidence, that the main 'sides' show Uncle John's
handiwork peculiar to him. That is to say, they are not much shaved,
but are decorated with a beading cut with a router or 'match-bit'
which Harry never knew any one else to own. 'Oblows' was what
Harry said this adornment was called ...

   But apropos of this word Arnold lately told of a miserly Dorset
farmer who, ordering a new waggon required that it shouldn't have
'any of them 'postles'. He meant shavings, which, he properly held,
cost time and therefore money. 'Apostles', Arnold surmised, was a name
derived from the carvings in church ...

George Sturt, *Journals*

Jubal Merton · aged sixty · wheelwright and blacksmith

I've lived in the village all my life. I've never been away. I left school in
1922, when I was thirteen, and was apprenticed to my father and my
uncle, who owned these premises. My father was the wheelwright and
my uncle was the blacksmith. I was the only apprentice and they were
very strict. 'You've got to have a good eye,' they said. 'Everything that's
got to be done in wheelwrighting has got to be done by the eye. You've
got to let your eye be your guide.' They were right, of course. What we
do here isn't like ordinary carpenter's work. When you get the hub of a
wheel it has to be morticed once and only once first go.

   The first job I had to do was to make spokes, and sometimes I was
allowed to saw out the shafts for the tumbrils. All the shafts were cut
out by handsaw from heavy planks of wood about $3\frac{1}{2}$ inches thick and
about two feet wide. We planed these and shaped them up fine. Heaps of
times I did a shaft and I'd think, 'That's lovely!' Then my father would
rub his hand up it and say, 'Why, boy, it ain't *half* done!' He was a
first-class wheelwright and was known all over Suffolk, and my grand-

father and great-grandfather were the same. They all worked in this same shop and the wagons they made lie about in the farmyards. They ain't used but they can't wear out. When I got so that I could use a plane and a wheel-shave, I started to make wheelbarrows. They were a difficult job, a most difficult job indeed. Especially the front pieces which we called the stumps. The stump was another thing you had to cut right first time else it was no good. There was no second chance in so much of what we did. It made us cautious but at the same time it made us willing to take a risk. It was as much in the eye as in the hand. There was a moment when you had to say *now*! Then you could breathe again.

One of the most exacting things was making the fellies [fellows] for the wheel. There would be six fellies and when they were put together they made the rim of the wheel. These were all cut out by an old bow-saw which belonged to my grandfather and the inner part shaped with an adze. They were made of ash and the wheelwright always chose roadside trees for his fellies. He'd never touch a low-meadow ash because that wouldn't do at all. Of course, ash that grew down by the river was lovely timber to use, but a wheelwright would never use it. He went to the hedges, where the wood was tough and hard. He'd walk through the lanes and note the ashes and when he saw a good one, he'd buy it, cut it down and let it lie in the ditch for a couple of years until the bark fell off. Then it was ready. He also looked for shaft wood. If you look at the ash trees you'll find that many of their boughs grow in the shape of shafts. When my father saw a good shaft shape a-growing, he'd keep his eye on it until it was just the right size to cut and plane. Then he'd have it.

For making the hubs we always chose wych-elm. A wych-elm twists in the growth and it is impossible to split it. You cut the hub out of a ring of the trunk and fixed the fellies to it by twelve spokes. The body-work of the wagons was made of oak, although some farmers had a fancy for poplar wood because you couldn't scratch splinters out of poplar with a rake. It was the old English white poplar which they fancied.

When I had helped to make a wagon I had to learn to paint it. We did everything in this shop, you see. The farmers were most particular about the painting. The colours were all bought in Ipswich. There was red lead and vegetable black, white lead, which was like thick distemper, and there was Chinese red and Venetian red, all these were the old colours used by the wagon-makers. The body-work was all painted blue. Always blue. The blue rode well in the corn. The wheels were done in Chinese red and lined-out with Venetian red, which was marvellously expensive – about £1 an ounce. We mixed all the paints here. Paint for small jobs was ground on a little stone but if we had a lot to do we ground it in a paint-mill. Nothing whatever was wasted of anything. You had to grind paint very, very slowly so that the mill didn't warm-up. If it did it would discolour the paint. The farmers were very proud of their wagons and tumbrils and would wash them down every week-end. Some of them had to go to Ipswich two or three times a week and they had to look fine. A tumbril could travel with about two tons a time. They were beautiful and they had to be kept beautiful. They weren't very expensive. My father made tumbrils for £12 a time when he was a young man. When I first started making them they cost £25 – that is a one-horse tumbril. A wagon would cost about £40. Once they were finished they lasted for ever. The village was full of wagons a hundred years old or more when I was a boy, and still perfect.

My father made the first bus ever used in this part of Suffolk. In 1919. He bought the chassis from Ford's of Dagenham and built a tall old thirty-seater top for it. In this very shop. It had straight sides and an oval roof and it ran to Ipswich every Tuesday and Saturday. It went with crates of chickens strapped to the back and it came home with timber for my father tied to the roof.

I went to the village school but left when I was thirteen because I wasn't learning anything. I did my learning in this shop. Two women taught us; one had been a missionary abroad. All they did was keep us silent and keep us caned. Boys and girls were caned every day. It was down with your trousers and up with your shirt for the big boys! Girls were thrashed on the backs of their legs. These teachers taught us nothing, only to sit still. I was glad to leave school and begin learning in the shop.

It was very hard work from seven in the morning until five at night, winter-time and all. It was reckoned a fine job but the money wasn't great. Sometimes I earned half-a-crown a week, sometimes five bob. Sometimes nothing. Imagine that! My apprenticeship lasted four years and I was happy. In my spare time, particularly when it was chill and wet because it was such a cheerful thing to do, I used to help my uncle in the blacksmith's shop. The fire roared and if it was a real bad day so that they couldn't get on to the land, they would bring the horses down for shoeing. The best place in the village on a wet day was the smithy, with about ten horses and us boys crammed together in the cosy heat. When I was strong enough I was allowed to wield the pliers. There were about a hundred horses in Akenfield at that time. All the farm machines were mended in the shop and all the harness repaired there. You couldn't complain then if life hurt you. The sparks would fly into your eyes or between your fingers but if you said anything my uncle would answer, 'Don't fret, there's plenty more where they come from!' We worked until he chimed on the anvil with his hammer, then we stopped.

What I notice most about the village now is the way people no longer want to get together. All through my boyhood it was a regular thing for twenty or more folk to sit on that bank outside the shop and talk of an evening. They sat on the verge if it was fine and on the benches inside the shop if it was wet. The boys would be there too, rollicking and laughing but listening all the same. It was the good time of the day and we all looked forward to it. We told each other about the things that happened to us, only a long time ago. People didn't usually tell each other things that were happening to them at that moment! But if it had happened years ago – no matter how awful it was – you could tell it. We sang songs. We sang the army songs from the war. 'Nellie Dean' and 'Pack up your Troubles'. Also 'The Fakenham Ghost' and 'The Farmer's Boy'. And sometimes we step-danced, although mostly the step-dancing was done at Cretingham 'Bell'. All that is finished now. People are locked in their houses with the television and haven't any more time for talk and the like.

A lot of young men and boys used to bike to Brandeston to talk. I had a bicycle and went too. We used to stand in the road in the middle of the village, as many as thirty of us sometimes. The policeman was there, waiting for us. 'Move on, boys', he used to say. You could see that he couldn't bear the talk. It was a strange thing. We could have talked in the middle of a meadow, I daresay, but somehow we needed to do it in the middle of the village. It was understandable. Of course the best place to talk was the public house. Men hadn't got much money and I don't know where they found what they did have, but find it they did for the pub. It was all they had, you see. They reckoned that if they had enough to 'lift the latch' that gave them the right to stay in the pub all the evening. Or they might play a game of quoits and win some beer. Our pubs were the Cretingham 'Bell', the Brandeston 'Queen' and the Akenfield 'Crown'.

I was a master-hand at quoits when I was a lad. I started playing when I was eleven and only packed up five years ago. It's a great Suffolk game. Every village had its quoit club and everybody played. You had to pitch the quoits eighteen yards in a clay bed. I played in the Akenfield team and won the Woodbridge Cup seven times. You can't buy the quoits now. We each had our own and we treasured them. They're heavy things, $7\frac{1}{2}$ pounds a pair, but you didn't have to be strong to throw them well. The art was in the letting of them go.

I can remember being really hungry – there are not many people who can truthfully say that now, are there? It was during the First War when folk who had the money had the rations. Rations! That was a joke. We never saw sugar at all. We used to have golden syrup in our tea and if we couldn't get that we had black treacle. We had cakes without sugar – and our bread! My grandmother still baked it, as she had always done, but now, when you cut off the top crust you could put your hand in the hole which was left. The farmers' houses were full of food, dairy butter, sweet cakes, meats – everything. They got it off the shop-keepers. They had some kind of mutual arrangement. It was nothing like the rationing during the Second War; that was very fair and most ordinary village people ate better then than they did before rationing arrived. They don't like to believe this but it's true. I can remember when I was about twelve that we boys were so hungry that we used to get together, crouch down in the corn and bark. It distracted people but once we started we couldn't stop. Barking like dogs – imagine!

Things got worse after the war, yet the land didn't suffer. It went on looking pretty good. The houses came to pieces and the people were hungry and keeping themselves warm with bits of old army clobber, but the fields stayed absolutely perfect. The men forgot that they were the farmer's fields when they were ploughing and planting them, and decked and tended them most perfectly. They were art itself. The farmers like to think that the men did this fine work for them, but they did it for themselves. The farmers had got the upper hand now and wherever he could he made his worker a slave. That was what it was coming to. Have no doubt about it. No man dare open his mouth, or out he went! A man had to be silent to stay in the village. The farmers had become too powerful – and mean! It wasn't their talk which separated them from the gentry, it was their meanness. I'll tell a tale about this.

There was a farmer in the village who gave his men a £5 bonus each for getting the harvest in, and which was money the men counted on for buying the winter boots for their big families. These men, they worked for as long as they could see, day and night, for the first week of the harvest. They were mowing barley mostly and they'd be at it from four in the morning until ten at night. Time made no difference so long as they could see. Well, on the Saturday night they'd had enough so they had a wash and went to the Crown for a drink, which they well deserved. And on the Monday the farmer got them all together and said, 'So you all went home early on Saturday, did you, and left the barley. Well, since you seem to like going home early you can bugger off home now – and stop there!' The men were all still and silent. Nobody dared open his mouth, not because he was afraid for himself but because of his tied-house and his family. Nobody moved. The farmer kept them standing dumb like this well-nigh half an hour and then he said, 'Get to work ...' The men didn't hurry their harvest; they made a masterpiece of it. It was their defiance. The farmer didn't understand this and Tom Makin heard him boasting in the Great White Horse at Ipswich to some other farmers about how he had made his men 'hustle up'.

The labourers' children worked in the fields and so did their wives. The women's job was to pull the grass and weeds out of the corn. They also picked up loose beans and were allowed to keep them. The beans were 5s. a combe – about eighteen or nineteen stones. It was surprising how much money the women managed to earn like this. And then, when there were no more beans, they would pull up the blackened stalks for kindling.

Socialist feeling was very strong in the village before Hitler's war because of the poverty. Nobody had a thing. No one knew what to do or where to turn. It was terrible for young men to be so hopeless when all around them there were these perfect fields. They went on doing their work so carefully. But for nothing. No one said, 'Good!' And when at last the farm-workers were able to go forward, they went forward until they went out of sight! They went off the land if they could. The farmers were used to having the same men for a lifetime and they were muddled when the old men retired and the young men went for any job they could rather than a farm job. So you got young men coming from other villages to work on the farms and when the farmer said, 'I want you a-carting hay on Saturday', they simply answered, 'Oh no! Not on Saturday. We're off!' 'I want the hay carted,' he'd say. 'And we don't care what you want,' the young men would answer. These young men, they changed the farmers in Akenfield. It was a good thing. Their power had got too great.

Before this people scarcely ever left the village. I can't remember anyone ever going off to Australia or Canada when I was young. Except the Dr Barnado boys, and they didn't quite count. During the 1930s some of the men would go malting in Burton, Lancashire, for eight months of the year but they always came home to help bring in the harvest. They wouldn't go just to Snape Maltings. Apart from this none of us ever went away and certainly not for holidays. It is a Christian village. The women go to church and the men bow at the holy name if they happen to hear it.

8 · The Craftsmen

The lyf so short, the craft so long to lerne
Th' assay so hard, so sharp the conquering.
Chaucer, *The Parlement of Foules*

(Chaucer's grandfather kept an inn at Ipswich,
ten miles from Akenfield.)

Ernie Bowers · aged fifty-five · thatcher

'A hard man,' they say in the village. They don't mean hard-hearted but resolute and tough. He has a large family of sons – seven altogether. There is a challenging, raw independence about Ernie. Like Gregory at the forge, he has managed to turn an ancient ill-paid craft to profitable use as cottage after cottage falls into the hands of retired or Ipswich- and London-commuting middle-class owners. The new thatch is a crowning glory indeed. When Ernie has finished with a roof, the result is something which nearly stops the traffic. The reeds shine silver and grey, and the deep eaves are cut razor-sharp. A new thatched roof is thought to be something of an extravagance or, although pleasant, something unnervingly costly. 'But, there,' the people say, 'they must have it, or they wouldn't spend it. Stands to reason.'

*

I started thatching along with my dad at the age of fourteen. This would be round about 1929. My dad had been a thatcher ever since his boyhood. He left school when he was eleven and went along with the local thatcher and he picked the trade up off him. There was a great lot of thatching in those days, you can be sure. And there was plenty of straw to do it with, although straw is rare stuff now.

A thatcher then would have two boys to help him through the summer-time but after October he'd just have the one. The other was stood off and had to fend for himself until the summer came round again. That is how it was. In those days it was seasonal work for some. There would be plenty of rick-thatching then, of course. The farmer would come along and say, 'We've got a couple of ricks want doing. You be along early.' And we were along early, I can tell you – five o'clock most likely. And we'd have done two ricks by midday. Then we would go back to our building job.

I was nineteen when I started on my own. My dad said, 'Well, son, it's up to you now'. It was our parting. That was all he said. I had two boys like the others and I was out on my own. That is how we worked it. The farmers didn't let the farm labourers do the thatching, they always came to us. It was different in Norfolk, where they'd let anybody do a stack. But in East Suffolk it was a special job and my father and myself, working apart with our two boys each, would thatch anything up to 600 ricks a year. We charged according to the size of the rick. Some ricks would be nine yards long by five yards wide, some would be ten by eleven, some twelve by six and some thirteen by seven. When the rick-thatching season was on you would go round and measure your work up and make out your accounts.

Every parish had its own thatcher in the 1920s. But in the 1930s things changed. Most of the good thatchers were getting on the old side and beginning to drop out. I can remember five or six great thatchers of the old school dying then. Nobody replaced them. They were men of the old time – of the old life. They didn't teach their craft to apprentices, they would just pick up the odd man who was walking around on the dole and ask him to give them a hand. They wouldn't teach this man anything. It was a bad time and people were losing heart, I suppose. There wasn't the money about and everything was terrible. Those who didn't see it couldn't believe it. I would be cycling more than fifteen miles to do a job, and in all weathers. There was skimping on the food. We didn't have anything and we couldn't get anything. It was impossible. People have quite forgotten what it was like not to be able to get things. I spent 1s. 6d. a week on my pleasures and gave everything else to Mother. But I got to know the things about the thatching trade which only the old men knew. I can remember the first house I thatched on my own and the first rick. I did the rick alone because my dad fell ill. I was seventeen and it was a stack of reeds at the Church Farm, Campsey Ash. The reeds had been cut and brought up from Alde river at Snape. Thatching reeds is a painful job and plays merry hell with your hands. They were thatched at Campsey to keep them dry until they could be used to mend the barn roof. Reeds are like everything else, you just can't cut them and lay them in a heap and leave them. They have to be cared for. We like reeds which grow in brackish water best. We like them to grow in the brack caused by the salt tides meeting the river waters every twelve hours. They're pickled a bit, I suppose.

I never worked on a farm and was glad of it. I was my own man. The farmers round here treated their men shameful before the war and none of us forgets this. I've seen a lad only two minutes late who'd be told to 'take the rest of the day off and come back in the morning'. They had to be so careful. There was always somebody waiting at the gate to take their place. I wasn't on the farm but I saw it all. And now it's, 'Oh dear, oh dear, the poor old farmer! He can't afford nothing but he has a new car every year. Oh dear, oh dear!'

Thatching was very cheap when I was young. Labour was cheap, everything was cheap. My father would re-lay a ten-foot square of roof for £1 and think that he was earning money! Today, a job like that would cost £30 and to thatch the roof of an ordinary cottage will cost between £4–£500. But you must remember that you are getting a sixty-year roof – a marvellous, beautiful roof, warm in winter, cool in summer – for this price. There is nothing like it. A thatch is wind-proof, frost-proof and good to look at. I cock my eye up at thatches I did twenty years past and watch them getting better and better. I strip right down to the rafters before I start – although some won't. They'll pile on and pile on. Eventually, like too much sewing of a pair of shoes which brings a pulling away from the welt, the thatch begins to slip off. We did a job at Bacton last year where so much straw had been piled on to the roof over the years that it just fell into the house and the owner had to put a complete new roof on. Most of the old houses still have their original rafters. All of oak, they are and very, very old. I make a roof thatch fourteen inches thick, whether it is straw or reed. The reeds are driven into position with a legget, which is a flat piece of board covered with horseshoe nails and set on a handle at an angle. Cruel work, it is. You start at the bottom of the roof and move upwards till you reach the crown, driving the bundles of reeds into position and fastening them to hazel rods which you cut in the woods during the winter. We use hazel because it is the best splitting wood there is and the best to get a point on. Then comes the pattern. We all have our own pattern; it is our signature, you might say. A thatcher can look at a roof and tell you who thatched it by the pattern.

There used to be special patterns and decorations for the stacks years ago, particularly for the round stacks. There were three kinds of stacks, the round, the boat-shaped and the gable-end, and the stack-yard was a nice place, I can tell you – very handsome. They were a way of decorating the village when the harvest was over and great pride went into putting them up. They were set where they could be seen from the farmhouse and from the road, so that they could be looked at and enjoyed. My dad always set a great sheaf of fine ears at the top of his round stacks and very nice they looked.

I work as we used to work. I stop thatching about the middle of December and spend the winter bushing-up. These are the four months when I'm not earning a halfpenny. Just collecting material. I have to search for wheat and rye straw from farms where they aren't using a combine. Thatching straw must be drum-thrashed and barley and oat straw is no use at all. I have to search the woods for hazel branches and cut them into lengths and cut the reeds from the marshes. This is the only cut you make on the reed, the one cut when you take it from the river. Thatching is very popular now and I am teaching the craft to my brother's son, who is eighteen. He'll carry on. I shall have to teach one of my boys too.

I get up at half past five of a morning. I work many hours. I get tired, but I will be all right, I suppose. There are all these great boys in the house – they keep you lively. But you can't get into conversation with a young person as you could years ago. They just haven't got the interest. They don't want our kind of talk. They're all strangers – all strangers.

Horry Rose · aged sixty-one · saddler

A happy man. Beginning life with an apprenticeship to a near-moribund trade, Horry has had the wit to follow change. He has worked hard and done well. There are handsome lawn-mower stripes on the big impeccable grass squares in his garden and a large comfortable car in the garage. His bungalow, built in 1938, is called Glamis. He bought it ten years ago. Until then he and his wife lived over the harness shop with the clean acrid climate of the leather store filtering through to them from below.

Horry is the People's Warden at the parish church and a great committee man. He is an executor of the village's two eighteenth-century charities, one of which allows twelve 'respectable poor women' a cloak every Ladyday, the other which donates coal to six widows on the benefactor's birthday (December 14th). The cloaks, under Horry's guidance, have been turned into overcoats from the Ipswich branch of Marks and Spencer.

He is very much at ease in life and is a good talker. His conversation is a trifle mannered yet free; there are no reserved subjects where he is concerned. Village migration for him has been a series of flights from rash conduct in the meadows and a flouncing, randy recollection emerges of young men and girls in situations not unlike those in the tales of H. E. Bates. The stories all have a reckless charm and a glimpse is caught of a state of events which, if multiplied by similar incidents taking place in the rural scene during the last fifty years or so, explains why so many of the country people will either tell one that they have no relations or will be brother or cousin or uncle to someone in London or Australia who is often either well-off or well-known. Horry's talk could provide the plots for dozens of novels.

He is thin and tall with a great deal of pinkish-white waving hair of which he is obviously proud. He looks like an old youth and dresses rather doggishly, tweed hat with pheasant's feather, tweed suit and Hush-puppy suede shoes. His wife is severe and grey, the peacock's mate. Like so many of the Akenfield women, she has wonderful manners. Horry introduces her as, 'My wife, Mrs Rose', and that is all he has to say about his own marriage, which is an obviously successful one. *Passe-partout*-ed photographs of their sons and daughters in their wedding clothes hang on long strings from the picture-rail. The television set sleeps by the fire like a cat. On it lies Horry's diary – Monday, P.C.C., Tuesday, School Governors, Wednesday, R.D.C., Thursday, Over-Sixties club – and so on, all through the week, the months, the years. Nothing can start in the village until he arrives, no decision can be taken after he has left.

Like nearly all the village people, he hardly ever reads. His excuse is the usual one – he never had the time.

*

I lost my father when I was nine, so I had to think about work. In those days families didn't have money and boys hurried to work as early as they could so they could earn something. I thought I would be a harness-maker. There was this saddler's shop, you see, right in front of our cottage and a new plate-glass window had been fixed over the small panes of the old window, so you saw the saddlers at work in the lamp-light behind the double window. The scene took my eye. I used to long to be inside the window and working away there with the men. It all looked so peaceful and secure. When I was $12\frac{1}{2}$ I forced myself to go inside and talk to the owner, Mr Peterson – 'Knacker' Peterson was what this gentleman was called – and I told him how I had watched him at work and how I would like to be like him. He listened and then said, 'Very well, I'll take you on. I will give you sixpence a week.'

I wasn't a bound apprentice. I worked a four-year apprenticeship and then one year as an improver. I worked from seven till seven each day and after I became fourteen I got 1s. a week. The war had just started and there was a lot to do, and soon the old gentleman was giving me eighteen-pence a week. Two saddlers were called up and that left only the foreman and myself, which meant that I had to do man's work. So my wages rose to 5s. – which wasn't man's money. My mother said, 'Well, you can't help it; you've got to honour the arrangement and put up with it.' It was never a very highly paid job for anybody. A journey-man got £1 a week and the foreman a shilling extra. The old gentleman didn't die a rich man but he had his satisfactions. After you had got a job you thought less about what you were paid for it than you did in perfecting what you had to do. No matter how many times a young craftsman did his work wrong or badly, his boss could afford to say, 'Do that again'. Time was money, but such small money as made no difference. We had to 'honour bargains' – it was a religious law amongst the tradesmen. The old gentleman used to say, 'Horry, if you bargain to do a job for a price, do you do it for that price – even if it takes longer than you thought and you lose a little money. You'll get the customer's good-will, and you'll also learn a sharp lesson on under-estimating time when you have to make another deal.' We had our customers for life. I will say this for the Suffolk farmers, that if you gave them a good deal, they'd stay by you for always. We lived by loyalty.

We also said that the farmers were bad payers, but that was because they hadn't got the money. They were having a bad time like everybody else. The Scotch farmers who came here in the 1930s were really good payers. They worked harder, farmed better – and paid. Their wives helped them. Too many of the Suffolk farmers' wives were trying to be ladies.

The saddler's shop has only been in three hands since 1840. The first owner was a Mr Lyon and he sold it to my old gentleman, and I bought it from him. I got it in 1930. I employed three apprentices but it was a dying trade. I could have done with more boys but they wouldn't come to work for me if they could get anything else. Our trade came from what was known as 'heavy work' which we did for the horse farms. I felt things changing as far back as 1920 and was tempted to leave the village and go to work in Newmarket, but it so happened that my mother was ill. So I lost my chance to go away. Whether I should have been any better off or more satisfied I don't know. I should have done racehorse work. I was a craftsman here and I would have been a craftsman there, so perhaps it would not have been so much of a change.

The shop has always been the largest village saddlers and harness-makers in this area. We have had a long run. It used to be from dead horse to live horse, as you might say, because the leather we used to make harness from came from the hides of horses we slaughtered in the knacker's yard behind the shop. That is why the old gentleman was called Knacker Peterson: it was his common name. There is a rope walk behind the shop where ropes for the farms were made from local flax. They laid the strands out along the walk and then twisted them up. The walls of the rope walk are covered with dozens of little marks, about an inch long. These were the tallies made by a boy called the 'scratcher'. Every time a length of rope was laid in the walk, he marked it up. So you see the business has always been changing.

Our leather was bought from a tannery in Ipswich – W. & A. J. Turner's in the Bromford Road. We bought black harness backs for heavy work, light brown backs for brown-work and we had special mule hide for making the great straps for mills, thrashing machines and such like. Our shop had quite a name for making these belts. It was very, very hard work. Some of our material came from a tannery near Stowmarket. Everything we used was bought locally. Horse-hide is harsh stuff. It is used for special jobs such as heavy glove-making. We called cow-hide 'neats' hide. Neats is the old word for cattle. These were very supple and nice to work. The leather was bought once or twice a year and when it arrived from Ipswich it was laid on shelves and big lumps of mutton fat, Russian tallow and grease were rubbed into it. We worked the fat in with a bone, just as a soldier bones his boots. Then we let it lay on the shelf for months and months before using it.

Our harness lasted for ever, as you might say. It was our downfall, wasn't it! We made these things so well that after a while they did us out of a living. We made plough collars for the Suffolk Punches and the great Percheron horses for 12s. 6d. each – fifteen bob if it was extra special. I made hundreds of these collars. Now it is almost impossible to buy one and if you could it would cost about £12. The price of a set of pony harness was five guineas. It was all marvellously hand-stitched with ten or twelve stitches to the inch and beautifully set out with a little iron.

You don't make much money if you work with your hands. You can't make the turnover. But I have no regrets working so slowly. I began in a world without time.

Looking back, I can see that the arrival of the village bus was one of the first nails in the saddler's coffin. One farmer had a motor-plough, it is true, but he was rich. The bus told me that motors wouldn't always be for the rich. During the early part of the Great War some American tractors arrived – huge big things, nearly as vast as traction engines. We didn't worry too much because they couldn't be used in wet weather. When the farmers started buying self-binders I began to take an interest in canvas belts. Each binder would have three of these great belts and I learned how to repair them. After 1929 I concentrated on this canvas work, advertised and got most of the contracts for it in all the surrounding villages. It helped us over the change. Just after the last war the first Massey Harris combine arrived in Akenfield; but, again, it was one of those things you could only use on nice fine days. And you couldn't cut barley with it, only wheat. Now they are everywhere and the horses are quite gone.

My main job now is making big elevator canvasses for the pea-harvesting machines. I also make canvas covers for trollies on which to collect the game at shooting parties and halters for Tattersall's at Newmarket. I don't see that any craftsman has to stop; he has to develop.

9 · The School

Our village school was poor and crowded, but in the end I relished it. It had a lively reek of steaming life: boys' boots, girls' hair, stoves and sweat, blue ink, white chalk and shavings. We learnt nothing abstract or tenuous there – just simple patterns of facts and letters, portable tricks of calculation, no more than was needed to measure a shed, write out a bill, read a swine-disease warning. Through the dead hours of the morning, through the long afternoons, we chanted away at our tables. Passers-by could hear our rising voices in our bottled-up room on the bank: 'Twelve-inches-one-foot. Three-feet-make-a-yard. Fourteen-pounds-make-a-stone. Eight-stone-a-hundred-weight.' We absorbed these figures as primal truths declared by some ultimate power. Unhearing, unquestioning, we rocked to our chanting, hammering the gold nails home. 'Twice-two-are-four. One-God-is-love. One-Lord-is-King. One-King-is-George. One-George-is-Fifth ...' So it was always; had been, would be for ever; we asked no questions; we didn't hear what we said; yet neither did we ever forget it.

Laurie Lee, *Cider With Rosie*

... to be worth one's salt in school one has always to be actively engaged in the process of educating oneself until the day one is presented with a wheel-chair by the old pupils as a mark of merit for long and faithful service; it means an open mind on such subjects as space travel, and humility enough to learn from one's pupils.... How the children of my generation ever sorted from the bushels of verbal chaff under which they were buried for five solid hours a day the few grains of the wheat of knowledge they managed to assimilate, I cannot understand.... Those who regret the wholesale-instruction methods of their own schooldays, no doubt also regret the lack of the bedside manner of the modern physician. They would be better employed if they spent their time thanking God that there is less and less need for either. However, when all is said and done, the day has not yet come when the doctor tells the patient 'I am only here to see that you cure yourself', nor is the teacher in school just to mark the register and to see that the children teach themselves. He is there to see that they *learn*, and the difference, though subtle, is enormous.

Sybil Marshall, *An Experiment in Education*

The school at Akenfield was built immediately after the passing of the 1870 Education Act on land given by the Duke of Hamilton and Brandon, hence the fine entablature of his arms on the east wall. It is a stark, knife-edged building constructed of Suffolk white-brick, slates and plate-glass, and it stands on sloping tarmac which is fenced in by a hooped iron railing. It consists of two tall classrooms, a spiky porch and bell-loft, a lobby, the headmistress's house – now disused – and scattered, trellis-covered lavatories, Boys one end of the playground, Girls the other. It is a building which says a very great deal, perhaps more than it should, about East Anglian austerity, benevolence, hope and apathy. The oldest and the youngest people in the village, just on a century of children, have sat in these two steep rooms and watched the hard local light framed in the pointed windows, the tree-tops and an occasional free uncaring bird. Fresh white emulsion paint has cured the green and cream distemper, and cancelled out the dado. Free expression pictures of ski-ing fill the spaces where meticulously shaded Cubes, Pyramids and Cylinders hung from precious (counted every Friday) drawing-pins. And the great iron snapping desks which trapped sixty acrid children aged between three and fourteen have vanished, along with powdered ink, liquid paraffin (for verminous hair), Readers which guaranteed a hatred of books for life and Silence. Instead, there is the new covenant de-creeing reasonableness between the teachers and the taught. The children play recorders, model Stonehenge out of balsa-wood, do algebra for homework, write poems and stories and like Science best. They all read a comic, seventy-five per cent of them go to chapel or church Sunday-school, sixty per cent have been to London – up the Post Office Tower, down the river on a waterbus, fed and photographed the pigeons in Trafalgar Square; though none had been to Westminster Abbey, the Zoo, the Tower or St Paul's – they all possessed animals and all spoke with restraint, shyness and delicacy. Not communi-cators. Remote children. Children on an island. Their mother's sons? Their father's daughters? Or leaven for a new kind of rural bread?

Stephen has written a story called 'As I Waded Ashore I said, "Never Again."'

Alan is writing, 'I could see the shell hitting the fuselage of the Messer-schmitt. The next moment it burst into flames and plummetted down-wards. "One down, five to go," I murmured between my teeth.' He is ten.

What is your favourite television programme, Gillian? – '*Bewitched.*'

Susan, 'My daddy is the policeman.'

Crispin, 'I read Biggles until I'm interrupted.'

John, 'Gerald and I made Stonehenge but we let the girls make the plasticine men.'

Michael is writing, 'Sailors were shouting for mercy. The wind was blowing a gale ... terror and confusion reigned.... Lost! ... lost!'

Mrs Sullivan, 'That is enough for today, children. Let us pray. Our Father.'

Everybody, 'Our Father ... Kingdom come ... ever and ever ...'

FROM THE LOG BOOK:

1875 – 1 mistress; 62 children. Total Grant: £30 10s.
Average attendance, 31.
List of songs taught: *Sleep, little brother; Come down into the harvest field; Oh the sunny summertime; Through lanes with hedgerows pearly.*

1876 – Attendance very thin.
Elizabeth Wells appointed monitor.
Total Grant: £28 9s.

1878 – Attendance very poor.
Songs taught: *All the day long in the cornfields so weary; I will not hurt my little dog; Cheerful in duty.*
Recitation: *The Destruction of Sennacherib.*
Report of the Diocesan Inspector: 'The children progress on the whole. There is a fair amount of religious knowledge and the mistress appears to be painstaking in her teaching. Many, however, of the children have learnt imperfectly.'

1881 – From the Vicar's Report: 'The instruction is again unsatisfactory, for although there has been a slight improvement in arithmetic, I could not have recommended an undiminished Grant. It is true that 5 standards and an infants' class, with only one Monitress as assistant, constitute an arduous task, but it is difficult to believe that the results need have been so poor.... Animal pictures are wanted for the children and desks for the infants would be useful. An easel, stand and maps are also wanted. My Lords will look for a much more favourable Report next year as the condition of an undeserved Grant.'
Total Grant: £20 1s.

1886 – The children won't come to school. Only one out of the above list [twelve names] attended this week. Such irregularity is very disheartening.
Songs taught: *Make hay while the sun shines; Will you sign the pledge?*

1889 – There is now a Night School for the children who must work in the day-time.

Attendance bad. Picking stones has ended and weeding in the fields still continues. The school has been open 30 times this month [June] and Frederick Walls has attended half a day. Twenty boys hardly ever attend and are seen working. The law is broken here with impunity. It is impossible to obtain a merit grant. Work how you will, it is uphill work in rural schools – the irregularity is something fearful.

1890 – April 23rd. Field-work, gathering stones, cow-keeping and farm-work has reduced the average. 35 out of 61 attended. It is impossible, in my opinion, to teach either Geography or Grammar owing to the bad attendances caused by the farmers sending the children out on the fields. Many children are always ill with coughs and colds and stay at home half the year.

December: Many boys away brushing for the shoots.

Poem taught: *Casabianca*.

1891 – Mr Goodly called and took a list of the absentees with the intention of bringing them before the Magistrates.

November: Most of the boys in the upper standards have been brushing for the sportsmen. Several children are away with ringworms. Sent Mr Goodly the school bill for children who are paid for by the Board of Guardians.

From the Inspector's Report: 'The order is good and the improvement well sustained. Needlework is fair and English may be classed as good with hesitation. The condition of the Infants is unsatisfactory, the Mistress sorely needing help. The books are in a very bad state of repair.' Grant: £48 5s.

From the Vicar's Report: 'There is an improvement in the Scripture Repetition but I should like to see more intelligence shown in the Catechism ... the children do not seem to understand.'

(November) 10 children stayed away to pick up stones.

1896 – (March 31st) I, Dora Jane Berrington, holding 1st Class Certificate, commenced my duties as Head Teacher in Akenfield National School. The children have been most unruly, so I attended to the discipline. Spoke to Infants' Room teacher about being a good disciplinarian on Wednesday. This she evidently

143

resented ... for she sulked for nearly 10 minutes. I gave lesson on The Hedgehog, and taught Standard III the Division of Factors. Cautioned 5 children not to go stone-picking in school hours. Took word-building with upper standards.

(May) The four children who have obtained their Labour Certificate have taken advantage of it and left the school.

1897 – The glorious reign of Queen Victoria, the Year of Jubilee, the 21st of June 1897, was celebrated. The greatest progress in popular education was made during the last half century. Still, it is very defective, especially in this school.

Had cause to speak to Provisional Teacher about her striking and shaking some of the children. Colonel Manvers visited the school and cautioned P.T. Infants simply do as they like in her presence.

1898 –

Education Department,
Whitehall, London, S.W.
10th Jan: 1898

Sir,

... I am directed to inform you ... that a Grant of £10 0s. will be paid as soon as possible. This Grant is made for providing additional apparatus and meeting the deficit which would otherwise necessarily be incurred in maintaining the efficiency of the school, and my Lords will require to be satisfied that it has been so expended. ... It must not be assumed that the school will necessarily receive a similar grant in future years ...

1899 – Attendance improved, upon two occasions every child present. Taught song, *You can't play in our yard*. The Duchess kindly visited the school and gave prizes of pocket-handkerchiefs and sweets, and expressed herself delighted with the singing drill. Taught Shape of Cube and Brick. Allowed children to take their examination books home, that parents may see progress.

Inspector's Report: 'There are points which call for praise here, and the standards' attainments are on the whole sound and satisfactory. The Mistress spares no pains. ... My Lords have consented to the Grant.'

Mistress had occasion to speak to Monitress about striking a child with a slate, whereupon she put out her tongue and made grimaces.

(June) Such floods outside the school that although children came in carts they were unable to land. New pump fixed. Object lesson, 'Water'. Order in upper department all that could be desired.

1900 – I, Florence T. Spurling, this day commenced duties as Head Mistress of the Akenfield Mixed School. I found the children very backward in every respect. No single standard knew their work. Taught the whole school a new song – *The old folks at home.* The average attendance is 43·2. Commenced the Royal Copy Books. Gave special attention to Arithmetic.

(March) Owing to the very cold East winds a large amount of sickness prevails.

The children went to church for Intercession at 11.15 (The Boer War).

Peter and Nellie Whittle were kept at home two days this week to go stone-picking with their mother.

Government Report: 'There has been a change of teachers here and the Managers are setting an example to the county by their sensible policy. A handsome gift for the improvement of classroom accommodation has been made by a lady. Everything has improved here.'

1901 – Government Report: 'The infants have been kindly and conscientiously taught by Miss Spurling but their classroom should be enlarged without delay. I have found it unhealthily crowded several times. An excellent room for entertainments could be produced by partitioning-off a classroom – and villages are generally admitted to be in need of amusements if the exodus to the towns is to be arrested.'

Alice Tilney, being 13, left school on Monday to go into service. Charles Deering was caned (four stripes) for repeated disobedience and the Brown brothers were caned (one stripe each) for stealing apples. All the big boys were caned on Wednesday for throwing stones at men working in the opposite field. John Marriage was expelled (November) for refusing to obey me. But he apologized the next morning, so I allowed him to come to school again. I administered corporal punishment to William Brown (December) for insubordination.

1902 – Eight children are still away with the water-pox.

Average attendance, 72 per cent.

Government Report: 'Sound foundations are being laid here.'

1904 – I have caned James Williams again for misbehaving himself. He is a bad boy and takes easy advantage. His mother refused to send him in the afternoon and sent instead an insolent message. He is the only boy to receive corporal punishment in this school for 3 months.

83 children are present. H.M.I.s have awarded the school the Highest Grant.

It is impossible to teach here as one would like. I have to work Standards III, IV, V and VI in different subjects in the same room.

1906 – 14 children have received notice that they cannot attend this school after Friday next because of its overcrowded state.

1907 – Empire Day (30th May) was celebrated in school today. Her Ladyship kindly lent 20 flags and the children were taught to salute the Union Jack. Lessons were given on the Union Jack and the 'Growth and Extent of the British Empire'. Several patriotic songs were sung, and the afternoon was spent in organised games. Three selected compositions on 'Empire Day' were dispatched to one of the colonies.

1910 – The dimensions of the two classrooms are 32 ft × 22 ft, and 22 ft × 17 ft. There are 72 children and no lavatories.

1911 – The jumble sale raised £5 towards a school piano.

The following Readers have been purchased: *Westward Ho!*, *Among the Bushrangers* and *The World of Ice*.

The structural improvement has amply repaid the long period of waiting. The school is practically a new school, and the alterations have been carried out in a liberal spirit. It is a pleasure to teach in the bright new classroom. The County Trophy presented by the East Suffolk Education Committee is a decoration on the walls which speaks for itself.

1912 – School gardens have been hired and there is a gardening instructor for the boys. The girls are being taught cookery. Mrs Ellis brought her own baby to demonstrate the undressing and bathing of an infant.

From the Annual Report: 'The children are unsteady and talkative ...'

From the Religious Instruction Report: 'The tone and discipline are excellent.'

1914 – September. Economy in paper has now to be practised because of the War. Mr Peacock, the Assistant, has been called up to serve in the Marines.

1915 – The farmers are taking the boys from school for the threshing and have been told of the illegality of such a proceeding. Bertie Anderson (12) is allowed absence from school for Temporary Emergency Employment.
(August) Owing to the late harvest and the scarcity of labour through the War, many children are needed to keep on the farms.

1916 – A War Savings Association was started in the school, the subscriptions for this week amounting to 17s. 6d.
There are 53 children on the register.
The Headmistress wrote to Her Ladyship the Manager to say that it is impossible to raise the temperature in the classrooms above 38 degrees with the existing heating apparatus.
A copy of *Our Sure Shield The Navy* was received to be used in connexion with the teaching of the use of sea power and Britain.
The subscriptions to the War Savings Association now amount to £111 6s. (February).

1917 – Received circular 112/1917 re. sugar for children's cocoa. Cocoa is supplied at dinner-time for a penny a week.
The boys are being kept away from school by the farmers.
A letter from the Ministry of Food states that no sugar can be supplied for the scholars' dinner-time cocoa.
A half-day's holiday was given for blackberrying.

1918 – The War is over. November – only 30 scholars out of 60 are present, all the rest are sick. They have influenza. The total raised by the children, their parents and friends for War Savings is £1,021 6s. 4d.
Many things happened at the school during the War, including a bomb dropped from a zeppelin on a neighbour's field. Standards II and VII were marched out to inspect it in school hours, as an object lesson in science and patriotism.

1919 – Nurse Powell visited the school and examined the scholars' heads. By her instructions Forms 140Aa were forwarded to the parents of Ada Jewkes, Tom Willingdon, Ivy Cribbins and Eric Smith, all of whom were nitty.

Some parents accepted an invitation to come and see their children work, it being hoped that by doing this they will take a more active interest in their education.

1920 – Mr Worlidge visited the school and taught the children country dancing.

The scholars were photographed in groups and individually.

Mrs Legg sent a letter complaining of the rough treatment of her Michael by the other scholars, both in school and in the village. All the evidence so far points in a contrary direction, to the effect that the other children – especially girls – are seldom free from molestation by Michael Legg.

(February) The scarlet fever has broken out and the school was fumigated with Alformant Lamps.

From the Religious Instructor's Report: 'The answers given showed that the children have grasped the meaning of the Acts of the Apostles.'

The four Thompson children have again (fifth time) arrived in a verminous condition and the prosecution form has been made out. Mrs Thompson returned her children to school 40 minutes after receiving the form – and their heads were perfectly clean. Attendance is 99·4.

Kitchener Emery and Belgium Lambert have received corporal punishment for insubordination.

1928 – Diphtheria has broken out in the village.

A picture 'Youth' for hanging on the wall has been received from the East Suffolk Education Committee.

The Inspector called and watched Drawing, Needlework, Singing and Country Dancing.

Two children have died from diphtheria, and Dr Stocks has taken swabs from all the scholars. The school has been closed. The water-supply has been tested and it has been suggested that the children bring their own cups in future, instead of using the one enamel mug by the tap.

On Armistice Day the scholars 'listened-in' to the Cenotaph Service by the kindness of Mr Bulmer, who lent them his portable wireless set.

Mary Ruth Bridge has been appointed Pupil-Teacher at a salary of £10 the first year, £12 the second year and £20 the third year. She is 15 years of age.

55 children on the Register.

1930 – Empire Day celebrated with saluting the flag and singing patriotic hymns, and lessons on citizenship.

7 children have been excluded from school because of impetigo.

1931 – From the Physical Training Report: 'The work throughout the school is very satisfactory. The children are alert and give apt response to commands, and have a keen team spirit. Netball is played by both girls and boys, though sometimes rather mechanically ...'

1933 – His Lordship has arranged that the older boys should be driven to Woodbridge in his car to see the film *Oliver Twist*. The other school managers are also kindly sending cars.

A gallon of milk – the generous gift of his Lordship – is from and including today (September 18th) to be distributed among the infant and junior children during the morning interval.

1938 – The boys took Art Scholarship Test. Best papers forwarded to County Hall, Ipswich. A hand-sewing machine has been purchased. P.T. equipment has arrived.

From the Diocesan Report: 'The teachers are devoted to their work and are doing splendid work for the Church.'

Instructions on the handling of gas-masks given, each child bringing his or her mask, although the parents of John Prescott would not allow him to bring his in case it got spoilt.

A percussion band (instruments for 20 children) has been purchased.

The Sanitary Inspector called to examine pit where pails are emptied.

1939 – (September) Ten evacuees admitted, along with Certificated evacuee teacher. A.R.P. preparations.

1940 – David and Ian Bolt, and George Hansey have gone off to work on Mr Mumble's farm. Mr Mumble said he had obtained permission for this from the Education Committee. The matter has been reported to Ipswich.

1941 – The Committee have given permission for ten senior boys to pick up potatoes in school hours. The school has been closed for the salvage drive, blackberrying, war-time cookery demonstrations and meetings. Twelve skipping ropes were received from Ipswich and the urinals were pitched and lime-washed. The Diocesan Inspector found the singing 'impressive and beautiful'.

Mrs Sullivan · aged fifty-five · headmistress

Bland, kind, untroubled face, gentle manner only just masking steeliness of purpose, Mrs Sullivan couldn't look more like the village schoolmistress if 'Miss Read' had invented her. Marriage and grown-up sons have given her certain advantages in the matter of poise over many a dedicated spinster in her profession. Children are instantly at ease with her. She doesn't need their fear or plead for their affection. The relationship seems casual at first but is later observed to be based upon a series of checks and balances operated by both pupils and herself. The school has existed for almost a century under massive patronage. Aristocrats, gentry and clergy have steered the management boards set up to educate the farm-workers' children. Thoughtfulness and imagination have not been absent but on the whole they have not exceeded the conditions of 'enlightenment' laid down by successive generations. Mrs Sullivan is no revolutionary. Her predecessors were orthodox in their as-humane-as-possible application of a rigid and deadly syllabus, and she is orthodox in her belief of love, free method and no punishments. She knew the old days so the new days have a great brightness for her.

*

I think it is a good thing to have come here from away. None of the village people know me and I feel free. I am old-fashioned enough to believe that one must have a vocation for teaching. I am married and I have sons but I go on teaching because of my vocation.

People have some odd ideas about village children. I don't say 'town child' or 'village child', I say child full-stop. As a matter of fact I had never taught in a village school before I came here, so if there had been all this difference I would most certainly have noticed it. I don't think that children in an area like this are at all deprived. It is true that they aren't influenced by what they call admass. You don't hear them talking about television and that sort of thing. They're not a bit interested. In a town school it is all *Z-Cars* and things like that. You hear the children singing the advertisements as though they were proper songs. Because there are so few of them they have their difficulties, of course. There aren't enough boys to have an eleven-a-side football match, for instance, yet they manage to play good football all the same. They never seem to worry about what they haven't got; they have a way of managing. With football, they count the success of the game by how many kicks they manage to get – not goals. Perhaps they know the goals will come when they are big boys.

They like order. They are very free from emotional troubles. I think the smallness of the school helps. There is no bullying. The children are very keen on their head boy Terence. I had to be careful to introduce him first – the class would have thought it very wrong if I had started with somebody else. Terence is in absolute charge of the playground and takes his responsibility very seriously. The children stay very well and ninety per cent of them never have a thing the matter with them. They are all so clean and fresh, good teeth, pretty hair, no nasty rashes and things – what a change, if they did but know it!

I don't teach with the exams in view. I just base my progress on what a child should know when he leaves the primary school. They are only examined in arithmetic, English and intelligence. I don't think that the 11-plus is at all unfair. I am old-fashioned in this way. I should hate to simply have to recommend a child for the grammar school. I should feel terrible. Think of being with about sixteen children in this room for three years and then saying, 'You go to the grammar school and you don't'. But if their brains sort them out, that is a very different matter. I have to do some recommending, of course, and I may as well admit that I know all along who is going to get through and who isn't. But now and then I do get some surprises. If they don't get through they go to Framlingham Secondary Modern, where they can still stay on until they are sixteen if they have a mind to. It doesn't make all that much difference; they can still get their C.S.E. And you get children who simply wouldn't be happy at a grammar school. It isn't the children who worry about all this, it is the parents. Very anxious, they are.

They're a wonderful set of parents. You can tell that from all the money they have raised for the school. The Parents–Teachers Association have just raised £180 for a swimming pool. The East Suffolk Education authority said we need only raise £120 and that they would give us the rest. The money was raised through a summer fête and with coffee evenings and a Christmas draw. The parents bought a television set for the school. They meet every month and are anxious to provide anything we need.

You could, if you weren't careful, become attached to the children in a school like this. Sentimental. But you don't if you're wise. They must do what they are here to do. Learn enough by eleven so that they are able to go on learning when they leave. It is all experience, really.

Daphne Ellington · aged thirty-two · assistant teacher at Akenfield Primary School

I've lived in the country for a lot of my life but I've never felt that I belonged. I feel I want to spend only part of my life in a village, and particularly this village. It is so strange. Although I have lived in a number of country places and taught in three different village schools, I have never experienced such an atmosphere – in the school itself, I mean – as exists here. I don't know how to explain it, and I'm not really complaining *of* it. I have to talk about it simply because it is so curious. It is the power which the children have to resist everybody and everything outside the village.

At first I thought that the 11-plus selection had quite a lot to do with insularity. That the village children excluded newcomers like the children of American servicemen and of Ipswich business people who have bought houses in Akenfield because these pupils tend to get all the grammar school places. I mean, when you get seven successes and then you find that they are all imported pupils, it makes you think! But I've come to the conclusion that this strangeness I am trying to describe has nothing to do with this. The village children aren't jealous – on the contrary, they are convinced that they have something which none of the newcomers can ever have, some kind of mysterious life which is so perfect that it is a waste of time to search for anything else. I used to wonder at their slowness at absorbing things but now I am beginning to realize that they know from an early age that they don't need to take in what I am teaching them. They are dreadfully polite. They think that if they are polite it excuses everything. They will do anything you tell them but never that little extra original thing. They have solid faces which say, 'We will do what teacher wants us to do all day long, and then we'll do what *we* want to do!'

I have known instances of 'outside' children being beaten up or ridiculed but usually they are simply left on the perimeter of all the playground groups and when school is over, nobody walks home with them. There is just one game from which nobody is ever turned away. This is 'Peep-behind-the-curtain'. A child stands facing the wall while all the others creep up on him. Every now and then he turns round quickly and whoever he catches moving has to leave the game. It is the only game which everybody is allowed to play. The last person left among those creeping up takes the place of the child facing the wall. It is a game which is played with great intensity. The 'outside' child can win this game but it won't make any difference to his status. He will just have to go on watching when other games are played or, if he tries to join in, he will be ignored.

The school building is seventy-five years old and it was built on land given to Akenfield by a Victorian duke. It used to hold over ninety children but we don't have enough space with only forty-five. There are photographs of the old classes, with boys and girls packed together in tiers. They had to be absolutely still and absolutely silent, and absolutely obedient. Before the First World War, the farmers used to descend on a class now and then and demand the sons of their labourers to help them in the fields, and the teachers would let them go. Most of the parents and farmers thought that education simply interrupted work, and it is a bit like this still. The children are very involved with their parents' work and with adult gossip. Quite little boys will know the technical names of tractor attachments and what is going on in the fields at a particular time of the year and the girls talk together like grown women. Neither seem to want their childhood.

They are never imaginative because, again, they don't need to be. They find it impossible to want anything which they can't actually see in the village or which isn't theirs already. Adolescence makes them a bit restless, of course, but by then they are in such control of themselves that they rarely do anything unusual or exciting. They are very balanced but really it is only because they are so heavy! They never have any desire to explore an unknown area. They resist any pressure to make them inquisitive about things which lie beyond the scope of the village and should there be a boy or girl with initiative and a bright intelligence, he or she is soon frustrated. With most of them it is, 'We know quite enough for what we have to do, thank you very much'.

The mothers are only interested if their children can perform something, recite a poem by heart, strum a piece on the piano. They are proud then. They don't appreciate the need to ask why a thing is done. They say that they don't like their children to ask questions all the time; they think it is rude. There is something treasonable about a child who does well. A market gardener I know, who is now about twenty, is a lonely person because he went to the grammar school and the village women say, 'Didn't get him far, did it? All that schooling and he's still on the land!' Perhaps they know that there is nothing like education for breaking up an ordinary country family. Or perhaps theirs is a different wisdom.

The Cook's Tale

The dialect of the area has a gentle sing-song intonation which is allied with a pithy toughness. The following story, told before radio and other language-changing agencies arrived, gives some indication of the vigorous Suffolk speech and shows many old English words which are still in common use in the village. It also displays the somewhat laconic wit of the people. The story itself is Suffolk's claim – one of many – to the Rumpelstiltskin legend. It was told by a servant at the Big House many years ago.

TOM TIT TOT

Well, once upon a time there were a woman, and she baked five pies. And when they come out of the oven they was that overbaked, the crust were too hard to eat. So she says to her darter:

'Maw'r,' says she, 'put you them there pies on the shelf an' leave them a little, an' they'll come agin.' – She meant, you know, the crust 'ud get soft.

But the gal, she says to herself, 'Well, if they'll come agin, I'll ate 'em now.' And she set to work and ate 'em all, first and last.

Well, come supper time the woman she said: 'Goo you and git one o' them there pies. I dare say they've come agin now.'

The gal she went an' she looked, an' there warn't nothin' but the dishes. So back she come, an' says she, 'Noo, they ain't come agin.'

'Not none o' them?' says the mother.

'Not none o' them,' says she.

'Well, come agin, or not come agin,' says the woman, 'I'll ha' one for supper.'

'But you can't if they ain't come,' says the gal.

'But I can,' says she. 'Goo you and bring the best of 'em.'

'Best or worst,' says the gal, 'I've ate 'em all, an' you can't ha' one till that's come agin.'

Well, the woman she were wholly bate, an' she took her spinnin' to the door to spin, and as she spun she sang:

'*My darter ha' ate five, five pies to-day.*
My darter ha' ate five, five pies to-day.'

The King, he were a' comin' down the street an' he hard her sing, but what she sang he couldn't hear, so he stopped and said,

'What were that you was a singin' of, maw'r?'

The woman, she were ashamed to let him hare what her darter had been a doin', so she sang, 'stids o' that:

'*My darter ha' spun five, five skeins to-day.*
My darter ha' spun five, five skeins to-day.'

'S'ars o' mine!' says the King, 'I never heerd tell o' anyone as could do that.'

Then he said: 'Look you here, I want a wife and I'll marry your darter. But look you here,' says he, ' 'leven months out o' the year she shall have all the vittles she likes to eat, and all the gownds she likes to git, an' all the cump'ny she likes to hev; but the last month o' the year she'll ha' to spin five skeins ev'ry day, an' if she doon't, I shall kill her.'

'All right,' says the woman, for she thowt what a grand marriage there was. And as for them five skeins, when te come tew, there'd be plenty o' ways o' gettin' out of it, and likeliest, he'd ha' forgot about it.

Well, so they was married. An' for 'leven months the gal had all the vittles she liked to ate, and all the gownds she liked to git, and all the cump'ny she liked to hev. But when the time was over she began to think about them there skeins an' to wonder if he had 'em in mind. But not one word did he say about 'em, an' she whoolly thowt he'd forgot 'em.

Howsivir, the last day o' the last month, he takes her to a room she'd niver set eyes on afore. There worn't nothin' in it but a spinnin' wheel an' a stool. An', say he, 'Now me dear, hare you'll be shut in tomorrow with some vittles and some flax, and if you hain't spun five skeins by the night, yar hid'll goo off.'

An' away he went about his business. Well, she were that frightened. She'd allus been such a gatless mawther, that she didn't so much as know how to spin, an' what were she to dew tomorrer, with no one to come nigh to help her? She sat down on a stool in the kitchen, an' lork! how she did cry!

Howsivir, all on a sudden she hard a sort o' knockin' low down on the door. She upped and oped it, an' what should she see but a small little black thing with a long tail. That looked up at her right kewrious, an' that said:

'What are yew cryin' for?'

'What's that to yew?' says she.

'Nivir yew mind,' that said. 'But tell me what you're a cryin' for?'

'That oon't dew me noo good if I dew,' says she.

'You doon't know that,' that said, an' twirled that's tail round.

'Well,' says she, 'that oon't dew no harm, if that doon't dew no good,' and she upped an' she told about the pies an' the skeins an' everything.

'This is what I'll do,' says the little black thing. 'I'll come to yar winder iv'ry mornin' an' take the flax an' bring it spun at night.'

'What's your pay?' says she.

That looked out o' the corners o' that's eyes an' said: 'I'll give you three guesses every night to guess my name, an' if you hain't guessed it afore the month's up, yew shall be mine.'

Well, she thowt she'd be sure to guess that's name afore the month was up. 'All right,' says she, 'I agree.'

'All right,' says that, an' lork! how that twirled that's tail!

Well, the next day, har husband he took har into the room, an' there was the flax an' the day's vittles.

'Now there's the flax,' says he, 'an' if that ain't spun up this night off goo yar hid!' An' then he went out an' locked the door.

He'd hardly gone, when there was a knockin' agin the winder. She upped and she oped it, an' there sure enough was the little oo'd thing a settin' on the ledge.

'Where's the flax?' says he.

'Here te be,' says she. And she gonned it to him.

Well, come the evenin', a knockin' come agin to the winder. She upped and she oped it and there was the little oo'd thing with five skeins of flax on his arm.

'Here to be,' says he, and he gonned it to her. 'Now what's my name?' says he.

'What, is that Bill?' says she.

'Noo, that ain't,' says he. An' he twirled his tail.

'Well, is that Ned?' says she.

'Noo, that ain't,' says he. An' he twirled his tail.

'Well, is that Mark?' says she.

'Noo, that ain't,' says he. And he twirled harder, an' awa' he flew.

Well, har husband he come in, there was the five skeins riddy for him. 'I see I shan't hev for to kill you to-night, me dare,' says he. 'Yew'll hev yar vittles and yar flax in the mornin',' says he, an' awa' he goes.

Well, ivery day the flax and the vittles, they was brought, an' ivery day that there little black impet used to come mornins and evenins. An' all the day the mawther she set a tryin' fur to think o' names to say to it when te come at night. But she niver hit on the right one. An' as that got to-warts the ind o' the month, the impet that began to look soo maliceful, an' that twirled that's tail faster an' faster each time she gave a guess.

At last te come to the last day but one. The impet that come along o' the five skeins an' that said:

'What, hain't yew got my name yet?'

'Is that Nicodemus?' says she.

'Noo, t'ain't,' that says.

'Is that Sammle?' says she.

'Noo, t'ain't,' that says.

'A-well, is that Methusalem?' says she.

'Noo, t'ain't that norther,' he says.

Then that looks at her with that's eyes like a cool o' fire, an' that says: 'Woman, there's only tomorrer night, and then yar'll be mine!' An' away that flew.

Well, she felt that horrud. Howsomediver, she hard the King a comin' along the passage. In he came, an' when he see the five skeins, he says, says he:

'Well my dare,' says he, 'I don't see but what you'll ha' your skeins riddy tomorrer night as well, an' as I reckon I shan't ha' to kill you, I'll ha' supper in here tonight.' So they brought supper, an' another stool for him, and down the tew they set.

Well, he hadn't eat but a mouthful or so, when he stops an' begins to laugh.

'What is it?' says she.

'A-why,' says he, 'I was out a huntin' to-day, an' I got awa' to a place in the wood I'd never seen afore. An' there was an' ol' chalk pit. An' I heerd a sort o' a hummin', kind o'. So I got off my hobby, and went right quiet to the pit, an' I looked down. Well, what should be there but the funniest little black thing yew iver set eyes on. An' what was that dewin' on, but that had a little spinnin' wheel, an' that were spinnin' wonnerful fast, an' twirlin' that's tail. An' as that span that sang:

> *'Nimmy nimmy not*
> *My name's Tom Tit Tot.'*

Well, when the mawther heerd this, she fared as if she could ha' jumped outer her skin for joy, but she didn't say a word.

Next day, that there little thing looked soo maliceful when he come for the flax. An' when night come, she heerd that a knockin' agin the winder panes. She oped the winder, an' that came right in on the ledge. That were grinnin' from are to are, an' Oo! that's tail were twirlin' round that fast!

'What's my name?' that says, as that gonned har the skeins.

'Is that Solomon?' she says, pretendin' to be afeared.

'Noo, t'ain't,' that says, an' that come fudder into the room.

'Well, is that Zebedee?' says she again.

'Noo, t'ain't,' says the impet. An' then that laughed an' twirled that's tail till yew cou'n't hardly see it.

'Take time, woman,' that says; 'next guess an' you'll be mine.' An' that stretched out that's black hands at her.

Well, she backed a step or two, an' she looked at it, and then she laughed out, and says she, a pointin' of her finger at it,

> *'Nimmy nimmy not,*
> *Yar name's Tom Tit Tot!'*

Well, when that hard her, that shruck awful, an' awa' that flew into the dark, an' she niver saw it noo more.

Robert Munro · aged twenty-five · schoolmaster

Did I always want to teach? Although I didn't know it – yes. It was one of those odd things. I started off to be a quantity surveyor, becoming a trainee when I was $17\frac{1}{2}$. I had five O-levels – fantastic! But after a year at this I was in a complete mental vacuum – don't ask me why. I thought, what am I doing ... ? What *am* I doing! Nothing. That Saturday morning, for all this happened literally 'one day', I spent with the old village schoolmaster. We had coffee in his kitchen and he said, 'Boy, I've never mentioned it before, but aren't you ready for teaching?' And I said, 'God, I think I am!' That's how it started. There and then. So I got a place at a teachers' training college near by and started on an art course. I never enjoyed the college, it was just a means to an end. No one was encouraged to be anything there. Dead, all dead. All the same, I managed to become the best male practical teacher on the course. I think it was because the stars were in the right place or something. I did a study of boats for my course – I love boats. I did some sculpture and some design but I wasn't terribly good at these things. The art course stimulated me, woke me up, but taught me little in itself. It was because the college had acquired a stigma for me, so that anything to do with it seemed bad – a bind. But I'd got my qualifications and now I could do what I had always wanted to do, which was to live in Suffolk.

I didn't belong to Suffolk. I came here because I had a kind of dream of it when I was twenty. I am an only child and I knew that I had to go somewhere. I had to leave home, but not for London. So where? Well, when I was twenty I suddenly found this very old British Railways Guide with a photograph of Southwold in it – Southwold lighthouse. I remember thinking to myself, 'I don't know...'. Then I read Julian Tennyson's *Suffolk Scene* – wonderful. I bought an old car and I remember driving away from my parents' house and thinking, 'I'm off to Suffolk'. I had never been away on my own before and now I was taking things into my own hands. When I got to Walberswick I saw Southwold across the River Blyth. I drove down to Aldeburgh, somehow not wanting to get there too quickly. I was thinking, it may be all wrong, then what will I do? I talked to a fisherman at Aldeburgh and took his photograph. Then I went to Southwold and pitched my tent. It was nearly dark. The next day I drove round the town and by the sea, and I thought, 'Two more years teacher-training and this is where I'll come – Suffolk. This is where I will live.' The following year, my father gave me a fairly ancient caravan for my twenty-first birthday and I spent the summer holidays in it at Southwold with Buster my dog. I photographed boats, sketched and talked to the people. I was feeling my way into Suffolk. The strange thing is that I had this tremendous sense of affinity with the place. There was no question about teaching anywhere else. This was it. Suffolk pulled me.

You have to apply to an Education authority for a job when you are still at college and I applied to the East Suffolk authority. All the other students were thinking of exotic places like Birmingham and Coventry. 'Everything's happening there,' they said. 'It's all happening – it's on the scene' – and all that kind of talk. 'It is *bright*, boy.' They looked at me oddly when I told them that I had applied to Suffolk. I was lucky and was offered jobs all over Suffolk – the stars were with me again. I arrived two years ago to teach in the big Primary just outside Akenfield and I am settled. I will move eventually, but not from Suffolk. Because of this hold.

I've got a twenty-two-footer caravan now and the farmer lets me live in it behind his barn. It has a coke stove and a calor gas cooker and is very pleasant. It has a bedroom, a lounge and a little kitchen. It is easy to keep clean, easy to heat. I found the idea of going into a modern house very boring. Modern houses are sterile. The caravan needs ingenuity all the time. I can never understand people who pay all this money for convenience. Convenience has become a drug to them. Easy this, easy that. If I could afford it I would buy a boat and live on that. It would need even more ingenuity to do this. I was terribly lonely at the start but I told myself, 'This is good for you. It won't last for ever, so bear it. It will be good in the end.' And it is turning out this way. I mean that, without being smug, I now have the existence which I designed for myself years ago. Fair enough. Essentially, it has been marvellous.

I like teaching but what I'd really like to do would be to make documentary films about East Anglia for regional television. They need some of these every day on both channels of the local news. At the moment, the level is very poor. I think that of all my ambitions, the greatest is to make good country documentary. It is not an entirely hopeless ambition. I would like to be a Hugh Barrett* kind of chap. I would still be teaching but I would be a personality.

Hugh Hambling · aged thirty · schoolmaster

I am really a foreigner. I come from Norfolk. I got married when I was twenty and the only reason I am in Akenfield now is that there was a cottage here at the right price then, if you know what I mean. We didn't move here at once because I was still a student, although from the very beginning Mary and I thought that this is how we should live. Or try to. We are village people two generations town-removed. Town for us would have been an estate and a biggish rent; village, a cottage and a car at the same price. That was the basic choice. Apart from this advantage, it was hard to decide when we first came here why we did it. We sat in these little rooms and didn't know quite what we felt. We have got almost an acre of orchard. The grass is so high and the trees so bent that it isn't much really. But it meant something when I was twenty-three to plunge into it and shout, 'My trees!' It was marvellous – it still is at times. I've never felt possessive about anything else, except the orchard. I notice that the village men have the same kind of possessiveness about their gardens. They don't garden competitively like suburban men but in a claiming way, like lovers. I hardly touch our garden and I think they find this cold.

I talk to people whenever I can. I am very unguarded. You've only to put a few pennies into some chaps and you get some wonderfully

* The Suffolk writer and television personality.

unexpected talk. But it has to be the right moment. In Suffolk you won't get a thing back if you choose the wrong moment. They won't talk politics in the pub. Their attitude is puritan in such matters. Politics to them is a kind of necessary function which stinks. They stare straight back into Wilson's eyes on the pub telly with that hard blue gaze of theirs, and God knows what they are thinking! They have a passion for telling you what they used to do and not what they are doing now. What they used to do always seems more important to them, so you get old Charlie going on about being R.S.M. in India. They hate to forget a scrap of the past. It is all hoarded up and, if they live long enough, some of the ordinary things that have happened to them this week will end up as epics. Experiences have to turn into tales, and this process takes a long time. If passion or emotion is the criterion of involvement, then the village men never seem to have been involved. They can't get very heated about anything. They show a lot of indignation when they have been let down. They tell everybody and demand sympathy. It strikes me that they always keep personal relationships fundamentally simple. As long as they can 'get on' with somebody, that is enough. 'He gets on with everybody', they say, and it is a great compliment. They are so *private*. They talk about beet, holidays and telly, never about personal hopes or worries. And there is sport, of course – but sport-talk is a kind of sport in itself, with the speakers obeying the rules. They will pass and re-pass football opinions although you can often see that the subject bores them stiff. I chat to everybody in the pub and my wife to anyone she happens to meet on the bus, but we often feel that we are doing all the talking. Mary feels cut off from the central life of the village although she doesn't want to be. We both know that however long we stay we shall never be as near to them as they are near to each other. It is a pity. When I return from studying in London or teaching in Ipswich, it is this small cottage I come home to, not Akenfield. I have no sense of community and the people who live next door aren't real neighbours. I wish they were. The man works on a farm and his wife helped Mary when she was pregnant, and we liked her very much. After the baby was born she just 'withdrew' – that is the only word for it. Mrs Ford, our neighbour, is about forty but looks much older. Her wedding photo shows the perfect English country girl – marvellous. So many of the village women change in this way – a quick switch from prettiness to shapeless comfort – that the men look as if they had married their mothers when they are about forty-five. Men treat one another's wives with extreme respect and call them 'Ma'am'.

My own life isn't at all impaired by what one might call 'village restriction' but I'm beginning to wonder if it is all that good for the children. We have four and it is obvious that they need more than fresh air. The local children are a pretty slow lot. They mature early, physically not mentally. The boys are often men at thirteen and as strong as little oxen. The town children mature in a more subtle way. I teach in a co-ed secondary modern school in Ipswich. There are about a thousand children and they nearly all come from the new estates. They like the idea of being town children; they think it is better, although they come from a kind of no-man's-land of concrete and official grass. Most of them have to make quite a journey to get into the town or country proper. They're rough but bright.

I'm on the committee of the local film society – and here we come to that old business about so-called village culture. Most of the cultural life of the village – of all villages – takes place collectively in Ipswich. People used to go to a talk or social once or twice a year in the village hall, now they're likely to attend some society or club in Ipswich once or twice a month. Or more. They like to belong to things. There is hardly a death notice in the local paper which doesn't tell you that so-and-so was a life-long member of the bellringers or the W.I., or the Traction Engine Society – usually half a dozen things. A good half of the membership of all the Ipswich music, art and scientific societies are village people. It's easy transport, of course. They all have transport now; it has changed everything.

And talking of joining, there's this Civil Defence lark and all these old major-this and wing-commander-thats. My wife and I joined for a bit, I don't quite know why. Certainly not to set an example. I wouldn't want to set an example to anybody. But there we were, with this ginger-freckled major, building toys on the table with bits of stick and stones. 'That,' they say – you should hear their voices – 'is a mark 2 field kitchen. It will be easy to make after the bomb because there are bound to be lots of loose bricks around....' These C.D.s – they're all so worried about each other, that is what we noticed. About who is important, who counts. We sat around and they rapped away at us. We didn't count. You could see our major often wasn't thinking about the Bomb; he was thinking, 'Bloody pansy hair ... *look* at them!' He had a ballpoint pen which he continually dropped on its press-stud between his fingers, making it jump like a nerve.

I was in the army. It's no good, I can't take this type any more. I try and see it their way, but I can't. I see them – scores of them – when I'm on Ipswich station, on the way to London to do this film course. They're all upright and the rest of us look floppier than ever because of it. 'Oh-ho!' they shout when they see somebody they know, somebody who counts. You should hear them, it's fantastic! A charade. They all do it – Oh-ho! The neat minds and the big gestures. I sit on a bench and watch because it's all wonderfully mad, wonderfully English. Big black shoes, umbrellas, the *Telegraph* and Oh-ho! The smile just right, not too little and not too much. It kills me. They are doing all this for me, showing me their Important Things. In the village where they live they are just a small scrap of the pattern: On Ipswich Station they can see a reassuring bit of the full design. So oh-ho!

I'm all for breaking patterns in order to make fresh ones. Life must stay fresh, every day of it if possible. Only how do you do it? Don't ask me. These Oh-hos don't know and don't want to know. They're in Suffolk to be country gentlemen, which is plainly what they are not. There's an O.B.E. at the end of their rainbow. I think they are frightened men. The world is different for them and the nice people fewer. My wife used to baby-sit for an Oh-ho and when he drove her home she had to sit in the back of the car. I mean, sitting in the back of a big car and the door shut behind you! It's incredible. This man writes letters to *The East Anglian Daily Times* about lapwings, Harold Wilson, Rhodesia, churchyard grass, caning boys, West Indians in Ipswich ... I think of the chaps on my film course and then I think of him. We are in another country. The Oh-hos would say it was class because East Anglia has always been classy, but it isn't. Anyway, they aren't class, so how would they know? They are ourselves taking shelter in worn-out moulds.

Looking back on my life, I can't ever recall ever making a decision. One thing leads to another with me and if anything happens it's just because of this. I imagine I choose but in fact it is external pressures which force the choice. Look at this present film-course business which I'm doing at the moment. Could anything have been more accidental? I buy an ancient cine-camera for seven quid to make some home movies. Then I take it to school and let the boys use it. They are fifteen-year-olds, so great excitement. I teach art but I have never had such a response. It must be developed, this school film thing. So here I am back in class again myself, learning about Eisenstein and Huston. People look to education now in the same way as they once looked to religion. Are you saved? Have you got your O-levels? It's the same thing – salvation. I think I am an innocent man. Not in bed, I don't mean that! And not by choice. I teach but I don't know that I believe in education. I am interested, presumably, in showing people how to preserve the valuable part of themselves; only, as this profound thought

163

has only just this minute occurred to me, I can't enlarge on it! Innocent Hambling ... that would make the lads sit up.

We read *The Observer* and *The Guardian*. A group of us also share a *Telegraph* because it has the best cycling coverage and cycling is the new trendy thing. It is going to be like France. Football has become international and intellectual, and cycling is going to be the same. It is going to halve the coronaries! It is interesting to note that the village boys haven't started cycling yet. Our crowd all comes from Ipswich. The thing is to get perfectly physically tired – it is the most tremendous sensation. I can't describe it. One feels nicely hurt. Animal weariness. What people think of as we hurtle through the lanes I can't imagine. The cycling reminds me really why I came here – to paint. I first started painting when I was fifteen. I wasn't a bit sporting then. I wandered about seeing the land joining the sky in the huge way it does in Suffolk. I thought of Constable. I did national service but I still thought of the Suffolk land and sky, and the training lay all in the background unimportantly. I used to say to myself, I'll go there. I meant, I'll stay there. This sounds sentimental, doesn't it? I went to an art school but nothing I learned hit me as this landscape does. The truth of the matter is that I don't see the village, I see the sky touching the land and nothing ever interrupting. This is what I think about during these trendy bike rides. I'm in it, I think, right in it. Up to here. In London I stare at the people and wonder to myself, how do you do it? But I shall have to move. I must get on in my job because of the children. The cottage – Suffolk – has come to my wife and myself too early, that's the truth of the matter. We are concerned with roots when we should be spreading. But it will be an almighty wrench. I've been around and I know I don't all-function anywhere else. I'm an East Anglian and if it has a sign it is on me. Should things like this matter in 1967? I don't know. Perhaps I'm too easily contented. Perhaps I lack a demon. Life just charms me – how daft can you get? I worry about this.

10 · The Agricultural Training Centre

*To be sixteen years old and spend the first
week of paid employment alone in a beet field as
vast as that ninety-two acres was, may be a rough
baptism, but it spelled out in unmistakable terms
two facts. First, that my pupilage was a working
one, and second, that even a chosen and desired
occupation or profession is heavily compounded
with elements of drudgery.*

Hugh Barrett, *Early To Rise*

Raynor Creighton · aged forty-four · master at the Agricultural Training Centre

I was brought up to farm in Suffolk in spite of the fact that my father
had to carry his farm right through the Depression and made no living
out of it at all. He was so stunned that he had no strength left to take
all the opportunities offered to farming during the war. This has influenced my whole outlook. Yet in spite of everything, my father was
the most contented man I ever met. Not placid, contented. Grateful,
even! These boys I teach don't have this contentment; they are restless.

Agriculture is about the last industry to have technical training at the
operative level. The farmer and the farm-manager have been trained at
institutes, colleges and universities for over fifty years, now we are just
beginning, these last ten years, to train the workers themselves. Those
who go through the agricultural institutes have very generous support
from the authorities and they will come out and be – skilled stockmen.
Never much more than this, never farmers or managers. The cost is
high – £8–£900 per student a year. I have a thing about this. I say, give
me £900 for my village school and see how much more I will do with it.
You could have another teacher at the school, or a new classroom, or
some wonderful visual equipment which would transform the whole
dreary feeling of the place – for the money it takes to keep one lad on
this course. The money should be invested in these village children's

education at its beginning, not at the end of it. A boy has only to pass his Stage One, City and Guilds, and he's in, and I'm sorry to say that in many cases the country isn't going to see much of a return for its £900 investment. All the same, the courses are very popular and they do give the young village worker an extraordinary psychological lift. He feels in where he used to feel out.

A lot of the boys would never dream of going away for residential courses, even if they could. These part-time classes sort the seed from the chaff at an early age. Some will eventually go on to full-time agricultural institute studies because they have done their basic stuff with us. Every county is taking care of its farm-workers' education now. It is a phenomenon which we have only seen these past few years. The centres are handsomely equipped and teaching in them is still something of a novelty. They are proving that if you give an operator a good training in a short time you waste far less resources than if he were simply left to pick up what facts he could while working on the farm. Most of them come to us for about four years and are aged between sixteen and twenty-two. The course is regarded simply as a technical education although it could, and should, be a seed-bed in which to plant real ideas about life. These village boys are going to see massive changes and they may have to be re-trained before their working lives are over. They don't think about this. Nobody thinks about it. We're not like Holland, say. Holland is one of those countries which think ahead, which are in good time. We don't do things until it is past time. The education of the village boys has been forced onto us and for the first time we are seeing what these people are really like.

Well, they have a strong sense of *belonging* to a farm, which is a funny thing in 1968 because it is very much in the old tradition. The farmer's son will still feel that he must follow his father on the farm and be apologetic and guilty if he breaks from it. And the farmer will feel more responsible towards his workers and their families than the village grocer will to his, say. Paternalism is a strong factor and you will sometimes get a young worker fighting off a farmer's protective interest in him with the same trapped kind of anger he feels towards his parent. There are farms where the employer is 'good' to his men, which generally means that the paternalism works, or is accepted. I know of one farm not far from here where £50 is added to a man's wages each time his wife has a child. And I have actually heard one farmer say to another, 'If ever you take one of my men, I'll never speak to you again!' He was smiling but he meant it. A worker is made to feel ashamed and disloyal if he leaves a place to get more money on another farm in the district. The simple fact that the man was earning less never comes into it when the farmer bemoans his loss. It is always, 'How well I treated him', and 'Fancy So-and-So taking my cowman – that's a *neighbourly* thing to do, if you like!' If, as often happens, the man returns to his original employer after a year or two, there is quite a prodigal son atmosphere on both sides. A lot of the more independent young men, particularly if they are properly trained agricultural technicians, can't bear all this business. All these men want is a straight contract – so much work for so much money – and to be left alone. This detachment cannot last, of course. The land, as these chaps find out in time, is quite an emotional business. Also there must be some good in this sense of being tied to a particular farm when you think of how well the agricultural workers have adapted themselves to the huge changes in their industry during the last fifteen years. Almost no strife. Factory farming, mechanization, everything his father understood turned upside-down – a man and his employer couldn't take such a revolution if there wasn't something more than just a pay-packet between them, could he?

But the best village men are trickling away to Ipswich and other near-by towns. They have all got cars and motor-bikes, and it is just as convenient to drive off to a factory five or ten miles away as it used to be to bike a couple of miles to the farm. When they get to the factory they will work in a way your ordinary conventional industrial worker will never work – really hard. The factory won't change their country natures. I once taught a young cowman – a head cowman who was doing a regular sixty-hour week for a low wage – and he left his farm for a job in the I.C.I. works. This was about ten years ago. I see him now and then and I always think how little he has been changed by the factory. He is a villager still. A wonderful worker. You will find that nearly every man in the village likes to be considered part of the atmosphere on a farm where hard work is the thing – the good thing! He never really gets used to the kind of 'average' day's work which has to be put in in a factory and he can't understand the kind of bargaining which goes on in industry between the workers and their employers. Having got the job, he likes to really slog away at it and he's bewildered when the town workers say, 'Look at that fool!' A lot of the tough slogging in the farm-worker's life really isn't necessary any more but you can't stop it. It is an East Anglian thing. They're all a lot of little puritans, you know! They used to be proud of how they did a task, now they are proud of the sheer quantity of the work they can shift in a day. You can't blame them. The employers don't want quality work any more. They want young men who will stay with their tractors until the moon is up. Most of these farm-machine operators can't hedge, ditch, stack, use a scythe, thatch or do a fraction of the things which went into 'labouring'. It is the skill needed to control the machine rather than doing good agricultural work which motivates them. To be perched on the top of a 130-h.p. tractor is to be perched on the top of their tree.

Everything isn't rosy. There are plenty of the really *lumpen* ones. They plod on the land because they simply haven't got the gumption or enterprise to try anything else. We don't see many of these at the Centre. This kind of worker just isn't concerned with getting any kind of farm education. He has no ambition. I interview at the village schools and I meet these people. It is 'no answer' to most of the questions. The village just absorbs these boys. They'll hardly ever leave it. They'll be 'old Tom So-and-So'. They'll never marry – the girls know their type and won't look at them. They'll live with their mothers, and then with an old sister, and then on their own. They'll do all the odd jobs. They'll be on the go until they die but they seem to take real care not to arrive anywhere! They are sly, private sort of people. Set apart. You get quite an element of this stolidity in the bright ones. They have what you might call a low enterprise horizon. They mostly don't want to emigrate, for instance. When I was teaching in Norfolk we had people going out to Australia and New Zealand regularly. It was almost a tradition. So was joining the Police Force, strangely enough. But what is really happening is that the young village men are beginning to doubt whether they are duty-bound to work on the land. It is not logical, is it, that just because a man is born among the farms he should be expected to spend his life working them? It might have been once but it isn't now. But what else is he going to do? This is the difficulty, because having come to this conclusion that he has a job-choice like everybody else, these youngsters still find their feet stuck solid in the Suffolk clay. They long in many ways to move out, to meet new people, but somehow they can't. Their characters seem fully formed very early in life and they are able to resist acting on many of the normal youthful impulses. They are quite unadventurous in every way. They are also sceptical and cynical for their age. I wasn't half as doubting – I believed that politicians would do as they say. These village boys who come to us don't. They aren't patriotic and they don't love their individual villages in the way that their parents love them. They are detached – and yet they are still stuck hard in the local soil. They have quite a problem. I am convinced that primary education in the rural areas is to blame for much of this. Country children develop early and yet hardly anything is done at the primary-school stage to cope with this. The state is pouring money into further education, but there is so little for us to build on. By far the greater proportion of boys who come to the Centre are without any development in the personal use of their faculties. We can't do much about it because, at eighteen or roundabouts – their peculiar Suffolk personalities have set like concrete! You can scratch away but you can't shape. It's too late for that. You feel a terrible sense of waste.

You will feel that I perhaps despise them but I am of them and I resent what is happening to them. It was different during the Depression; there was more excuse. But there's little excuse now, it is just a matter of feeding the new shoots. They're young; they should be critical, vital, but they're not. You can never get a critical statement about a television programme. It will either be 'all right' or 'good'. It is a passive occupation for them. They talked about *Cathy, Come Home* because of the hot language – not because they were indignant about the housing situation. They are very careful about not sounding original, yet they often come out with things which prove a strong individuality. They make statements – big, flat statements. They never explore ideas. Nobody has taught them how to use words to convey theories, so now that all the old village story-telling has died out their talk is very poor dull stuff. Although sometimes you'll get a flood of the old richness when somebody has to relate a bit of gossip. There is terrific animation. Eyes light up. The man isn't really gossiping in the trivial sense of the word, he is story-telling. Some of the gossip stories are told many times over and people will begin to laugh at the first sentence although they know the whole tale backwards. The East Anglians are serious people who laugh a lot. You'd hardly call them colourful yet they certainly aren't grey. They have this kind of iron composure. It is this that you are seeing when you look at them – not them themselves. Something occasionally shifts it – one of these funny stories, perhaps – and then you see an entirely new, unsuspected person. Talk about sunshine after rain!

We call them all 'Mr' at the Centre – even if they're no more than sixteen. They like coming here and regard it as a bit of a club. The social function of the place alone is worth half the cost of it. It grades the boys up to the level of friends who are going to Ipswich Civic College and the actual psychological effect is enormous. And it should help to bring the farm-worker's son up closer to the farmer's son – but it doesn't. The farmer's son is of a different mould altogether. He thinks as a manager. He'll talk about buying tractors and the choice of fertilizers. The farm-worker's son doesn't discuss the buying and administrative side of the farm. There is a distinct cleavage between the boys. They don't really mix. The farmers' sons stick together. They have mostly been to Woodbridge or Framlingham schools. Both sides feel strong class differences and the farmers' sons don't really like farm-workers – I don't know whether you realize this. You will find very few farm-workers in the Young Farmers' Clubs. The clubs go with a sort of status and, being full of such brash types, are hellishly snobbish. The boys have sports cars and Simpson tweeds, and they like to take their girls out to dinner at the beamy old hotels. But most of them have strong or easily traceable local accents and a person of genuine culture wouldn't find all that much difference between them and the ordinary village boys. I don't like it. It should all be disappearing but the fact is it is stronger than ever!

Both groups are conservative to an amazing degree – I mean, considering how young they are. I asked my class the other day, 'What about hanging?' There were thirty boys in the class, all aged between seventeen and nineteen, and every one of them was in favour of hanging. It shook me. You find some funny things out. They all have a streak of cruelty. They kill animals in a way which would disturb the ordinary town boy – very few town boys have ever killed anything. But by the time he is twenty a countryman will have killed a considerable number of animals. It doesn't mean anything to them. It doesn't mean much to me. I'm a countryman and I was brought up in an atmosphere of natural killing. On a stock farm you see the animals going away to slaughter. You see cows which you've milked for years and which you have named, and with whom you might have built up quite a little relationship, going off to the butcher and you don't feel a thing. It is logical. The countryman has no reverence for life. Things are born, things die. All the time. Death is as familiar as birth. To take a murderer's life is just sensible to them. What is the good of 'leaving him in his misery' and eating his head off, as it were? Might as well kill him. Killing isn't a dreadful act to the village people. The idea that one mustn't take life doesn't make sense to them. I argued against them in our hanging debate but I could go outside this minute and kill a rabbit with my bare hands or shoot a bullock without the least bother. We also discussed corporal punishment and the class was all for bringing back the birch. It was, 'Give him a good thrashing and he won't do it again'. There wasn't the vaguest sexual interest in these vengeances. This comes later, I suppose. Shooting, of course, is their big thing. It is *the* recreation. The farmers' sons shoot in organized parties and the farm-workers' sons shoot in solitude. Boys who shoot are often good naturalists but you'd have a hard job getting them to invest in a pair of binoculars instead of a gun.

We discussed the colour problem – we have these topical debates, you see – and the class said, 'Get all the coloured people out of England; they don't belong here'. Later on I found out that not one of them had ever even spoken to a coloured person – except maybe to an Ipswich Corporation bus conductor! It isn't simply education which will change things. Think of the Tories in Suffolk – they've had 'education'. Don't talk to me about Tory Suffolk! It is, well, *illiterate*. My mother is one of them, so is my brother – ordinary farming folk, you would say, nice, kind – but how they hate, *hate* all liberalization! It upsets them. They used to say that the farmers round here would vote for a baboon if it had a blue arse and this is as true today as ever it was. This is where the real rural primitivism exists. Not in the cottages. But who really knows about the cottages? They are still mysterious. Much of the life in them is still concealed. Something happened to the East Anglian people during the great Depression. They lost their staunchness and independence. They were made to fear. They won't talk freely.

There is still far greater control in the village than in the town – control of parents over their children, employers over their men, church and chapel controls, etc. The older men pick on the boys and are always looking for faults. The young are watched and criticized, although you would hardly find a better behaved and amiable lad than the average village boy. They rebel sometimes, like the occasion when scores of them from miles around put on their leather jackets and zoomed down to Felixstowe on their bikes. Well, you know what Felixstowe is – a sort of decaying ground for retired people – and when they got these massed motor-bikes surging along the front, there was panic! The boys chose Felixstowe because it was refined. They wanted to make a noise in it and assert their virility. Then the police arrived – then the television cameras! Plenty of pushing around and some resistance. The local papers had a field day. But what happened really – just a lark, an hour of glory. Suppose the bikes and jackets had been horses and riding habits – all these young countrymen sitting up straight and dashing along – the old men might have shivered a bit but I'm sure they would have said something like, 'How splendid!' The truth of the matter is that many of the older country folk are eaten up with jealousy of the young. Fathers see sons of seventeen doing things that they would never have been allowed to do, and are envious. They see things such as the way the boys behave in the local pub. Before this generation a countryman went into his pub to have a damn good session – it was their pleasure, wasn't it? But the young men hardly drink at all. And before transport the pub men stayed loyal to one pub for maybe the whole of their lives. Each man's little ways were known – just as they were in the midst of their families. If you wanted to keep any private life at all it was necessary to watch your step when you'd had a few. But the boys will drive down to Southend or Clacton and let off steam in pubs where nobody knows them. They'll pick up girls and make love to them, and nobody in the village will be any the wiser. They are living in a bigger scene.

The boys at the Centre will discuss sex quite easily. Most of them have had quite a lot of experience and their attitudes are fairly uninhibited. They live in dread of getting 'caught' – of having to marry because their girl is pregnant. Farmers' sons are reckoned good matches and a particularly attractive eligible male from a good farm will be noted down for miles around. A surprising number of men stay bachelors but nobody finds this very extraordinary.

All these discussions we have are extras. They shouldn't be. Every course at Ipswich Civic College has a liberal studies element attached to it, and so should ours. At the moment we allow a certain amount of discussion in order to help the farm-workers with their problems and not with any intention of broadening their lives. Yet we should be broadening their lives, I feel. We don't employ a naturalist, for example. But we should. Somebody should be saying to these boys, 'Let us go and *look*'. I want the whole approach changed. I would have been the first to call this 'broadening' idea airy-fairy nonsense when the Centre first opened but I'm changing. One of the extraordinary things about this latest generation of villagers is that it is too comfortable! They need provocation, stress. They are sturdy young well-fed animals being trained as farm-machine operators who don't feel strongly about anything. They are content for the world to stay as it is, poverty, pain and everything, as long as they are comfortable.

11 · Officers and Gentlemen

What have I done for you,
England, my England?
What is there I would not do,
England, my own?
With your glorious eyes austere,
As the Lord were walking near,
Whispering terrible things and dear . . .
                        W. E. Henley

Colonel Trevor West ·
aged forty-eight · retired army officer
and highly successful pig-farmer

Colonel West is an heroic, complex man who doesn't fit into the conventional mould of the typical retired army officer. Tall, eloquent and with noticeably fine manners, he is like a figure from another age. Ten or so years ago he bought the local 'Muck Hall' – the farm with the jinx, with the legend of ruin and defeat, and has, almost single-handed, turned it into a rich and thriving property. He has the English mixture of extreme practicality and dream. His ignoring of the local jeremiahs and his indifference to the clan activities of the various social groups in the neighbourhood, plus a certain old-fashioned 'distinction' in his personality, sets him rather apart. He is married and has three sons. He is a lonely man, although it isn't Suffolk which has made him so; his is the nature which is alone in any country.

*

I returned from the Middle East in 1956 but long before becoming a soldier I meant to farm. I was taken with it. I was a little bit afraid of what I saw in London – oversensitive, perhaps. Anyway, it wasn't for me. Farming was something I came to. As soon as my sister married a farmer, which was my first real introduction to agriculture, I was taken with it. It was in harmony with what I was – with what I am. But then it was an idyll. I had no notion of the £ s. d. side of it. I just knew that I needed to be involved with livestock, life production, creating an existence in which you yourself was answerable to yourself, and to no one else.

Well, then the war came. I was eighteen. Just before joining up and going abroad I met Elizabeth – the daughter of a farmer. I met her on the farm itself, which was just below where I was stationed. We were friends for just a fortnight and then I went to fight the war. I was away five years and we were married within seven days of my getting home. By this time I was an Arabist and soon, being back in Jordan with the Arab Legion, I was lost to the Western world and utterly absorbed in and devoted to what I was doing. I felt I was part and parcel of an effort. I didn't try to assimilate Jordan or anything like that but my spirit was with this country and I felt that I was living to a purpose and creating something. And then, gradually, everything changed. I stuck it out until the situation became ugly, which I always knew at heart would happen. I – all of us out there – was being estranged from a natural position and being forced into an unnatural position. It is all difficult to explain. The country drew me. I wanted to be there indefinitely. I never thought of my own personal future but of myself as part of a great idea. The money – a pension – was absolutely negligible and not tied in any way to Britain, so that when at last I was forced to resign I came away with little or no money with which to start another life. My wife had little, I had little. Towards the end of the life in Jordan – the last three years – when the stresses were such that you had to act against your will, I made a personal act of conscience. I told myself, I disagree with what I am doing but it is an instruction, so I will carry it out. At home we both said, 'Oh, to get away from here! All this – it is horrific! It is terrible. We are becoming part and parcel of the destruction of the thing which we have spent our lives creating. We are being employed to tear down what we have built up. It was good. Now *we* are part of the bad. We must go!'

We both still longed for the English countryside. For my wife – a farmer's daughter – it was natural, and I wanted no part of the townee life. We wanted to regain something which would allow us to be in complete control again. In my imagination I felt that agriculture was the only life where one could be master of all one did. If you made a mistake you were answerable only to yourself. I also thought that if I obtained this independence it would help me to forget the Jordan horror. And so we came home. At first, farming seemed out of the question – we just hadn't got the money for it. It just wasn't on. As my cousin farmed in quite a big way in Dorset – about 2,000 acres – I thought of asking him for a job. I also thought of other jobs, such as photography. I have always been interested in this and it would have meant that I could work on my own. I had once been a press officer so I thought I could do free-lance news pictures. But I knew all this was a very tricky business and that I hadn't the right to expose my family to such a gamble. But whatever I did, I knew that I must do it quickly, otherwise my little nest-egg would erode. So one day I saw my cousin and said, 'Bill, I have this money, do you think I could begin to farm?' I remember this moment exactly. My cousin was in his car and I had stopped him as he was leaving the drive; the engine was running. He thought for about a minute, staring across a field, then he said, 'I think you could make it. I've got to go now. Excuse me.' And that was all he said. He was a hard kind of man – stodgy, if you like. A good farmer but not what I would call an imaginative one. Every step he took was stolid and careful and he only adopted a new process after a neighbour had given it a good try-out. He wasn't the kind of man I admired but I could believe in him. So I went home and said, 'Elizabeth, let's try and get ourselves a farm. Let's do it!'

I went out and bought a couple of farming papers and then I wrote off to various land agents – and was immediately inundated with 'splendid properties'. I got a map and ringed all the likely ones. Fortunately for us it was 1956, when the first fall in land prices occurred – the first time since the war when people felt that there wasn't a fortune to be made in agriculture. Up to this time, rationing and everything else had created a very false impression of security but now the war-time boost was over – so was the post-war feather-bedding. A farmer who lost money during those years was a man who would lose money anywhere. It took an abject fool not to make a good living then. It was different now. We drove around in my big sports car which, except for my cameras, was my only real possession, and eventually we came to Suffolk. The farms here were extraordinary, mysterious, very individualistic. One, I remember, had sixteen ponds round the farm-house! Anyway, we ended here. I discovered this farm of sixty-five acres which had been bought for £10,000 just ten years earlier, when the prices were up, since when it had been worked – not too seriously! – by a young man who had lost about £1,000 a year on it. I didn't worry about this. I knew that my attitude and the young man's attitude towards the place were poles apart. Elizabeth and I walked round it. It had a 'lifting' feeling for us. We had my cousin with us to explain a few things but we didn't know what we were walking into. The farm was a mudpie – not an inch of concrete. Nothing. But there were nice Victorian red-brick buildings and barns which looked like barns, and not tumble-down shacks. It was one of the Duke's farms and had been built with bricks from his own kilns. There were three cottages and the old homestead – a Tudor house in a terrible state. My cousin stumped around in the mud and said, 'This is all right. It will give you as good a chance as any. Take it.' I got it for £5,000, lock, stock and barrel – a sixty-five-acre Suffolk farm with a house and three cottages.

Three days later we began trying to tidy it up. There were bedsteads in the garden, rats in the house and muck everywhere. It was June but you still couldn't walk anywhere without getting slush over the top of your boots. But we weren't defeated. We were on a hill and on our own. We could breathe again. We went around clearing rubbish from the fields into an old truck. We did nothing else for a whole month. Two village men came and helped us each evening, after they had finished work. The barns were crammed with great worthless machines and junk – it took us two entire days just to strip the masses of old binder-string hanging from their nails. It had been looped and pulled, looped and pulled for generations. When the farm was clean, I fixed a perimeter fence round it – this was obligatory in those days. I now had an empty farm, £1,000-worth of cameras, a hard-topped, long-wheel-based Land Rover – and our TT licence. It was time to begin.

I heard that there was a genuine sale of dairy stock at Bishop's Stortford, the reason for the chap's selling of his herd being that his land was being taken by Harlow New Town. It was a dispersal sale – just what we were looking for. So we drove off to it and I bought six cows – not heifers – so that we should have some milk to sell. Soon after this we bought more stock from an old Scottish farmer. This kind man remembered his own struggles when he first came to Suffolk and often came over to give us good advice. I told the men who came and helped me in the evenings, 'If we get eight out of ten heifers during the calving, I'll buy you a barrel of beer!' And we got eight out of ten! This was the beginning of our herd. I had to install milking equipment, of course. Now this is a dreadfully expensive thing to do but I discovered an al-most new set of Simplex equipment in a country market and got it, pump, motor – the lot – for £60. All we had to do after this was to put the piping in. I was milking. I had tried my hand at it years ago, when I was about eighteen and before I joined the army, and here I was, with the scrub-brush inside the pails again and feeling as though all those years in Arabia had never been.

We then sold the cars and the cameras, and so we cut ourselves off. We didn't employ anybody. We couldn't leave the farm. We had the telephone and we shopped on that. We were isolated. For six months we never went beyond our gates. We continued to sell everything and anything we could do without in order to buy cows. We kept on breeding and buying. We started all this in August 1956 and by Christmas we had ten cows and within a matter of four years we had thirty. We bought in one or two Jerseys to maintain the colour and quality of the milk. Our first sale – of five gallons a day! – went to the Stowmarket Creamery. I was embarrassed to see their great lorry calling for such a small quantity and at first tried to get rid of it by making cream cheese. The whole place was festooned with sheets and bowls, and we couldn't move for cheese so there was nothing for it but get the milk taken some other way. Eventually, we were selling 100 gallons a day.

My wife and I did everything. We had no help. We worked seven days a week and 365 days a year. We haven't had a holiday as such in twelve years. During all this time we have only been away from the farm for three nights. The local people became intrigued by us. 'Who's bought Sinai?' they asked. – 'Oh, a Colonel Somebody ...' '*He* won't last long!'

I pressed on, I mortgaged, I did all the usual things to raise money. I used the bank – I worried the guts out of it. I went on and on. Kept on laying concrete, embellishing, struggling, arranging. My books weren't exciting. The profits didn't show up because I was constantly expanding. 'That Colonel,' the locals said, 'what do he think he's doing?' But I would not work in improper conditions: I meant to have a model farm. It was going to be poised in such a way that it could undertake something of considerable import. It is hard to explain except by saying that I seemed to be fussing with the frame of a picture which had yet to be painted.

There was no water, so we had to bore. No electricity. My wife and I had to start three different engines before we could milk each morning. If only one of the three failed we were foxed. Then I managed to get a great second-hand diesel – and 240w. Each battle had to be fought inch by inch. All the things taken for granted by everybody else were battles for us. The main electricity didn't come for five years and wouldn't have come then if I hadn't raised the roof with the local M.P. I fought all the time. Nobody wanted to do anything when I mentioned Sinai. That is its name – Sinai Farm. It seemed a cursed place. We took every scheme that was available. If there was a loan to be had from the Ministry for draining land, we took it. We drained and drained. It was ironical that with all these neglected wet fields we had to pay such a fortune to get water.

We had to get the water on a three-year plan. It was an expensive game. First we had to get a temporary five-year licence to bore, then we had to put the motor in – this cost £1,000 – and then, in the third year, it cost us £1,200 for the actual irrigation part of the scheme. But it was a great success. We hit the water 100 per cent and have a far better yield than any farm round here for miles.

Our sixty-five acres were originally a poor little arable set-up but we turned them all into pasture. We were one of the first people in Suffolk to go in for zero-grazing – that is, you don't allow the animals to go out and graze, but graze the crop yourself with a flail and bring it to them. This method has many beneficial side-kicks. We tried everything that was new, no matter how odd it seemed. If we sensed some kind of intelligence behind it, we tried it. We got help from the Agricultural Mortgage Corporation. And at the end of all this – our 'first phase' – we had fair meadows, twenty Jerseys each with an average of 1,000 gallons of milk a year and twenty-five Friesians, each with an average of 1,200 gallons at four per cent butter fat a year. In the end we sold the Jerseys because of the premium on the bull-calves. This was the only thing which swung us to the Friesians. We were the first farmers round here to use pea-hulm for silage. The district grew peas on a large scale and by purchasing the hulm we saved our acreage – we didn't have to find winter-feed from the same land.

Well now, here comes the really mad part. Joining our farm was the real Muck Hall of the parish. I mean Sinai had some kind of mysterious reputation for destroying men's hopes but Maris Farm – this adjoining place – was honest enough not to offer any hope at all. Absolute Muck Hall, that was Maris. The laughing stock of the neighbourhood. There it stood, derelict amongst all the local wealth, and no one would touch it. A few acres of its land had once gone with our farm, which is why I began to think about Maris. I thought it would be nice to have them back. Then I began to think, 'I would like Maris very, very much ...' It challenged me. It drew me so much that I had to force myself not to go near it or walk it. I dreamed about Maris, what I would do with it, how I would bring it into Sinai. I spoke about it to my neighbours, who said, 'For God's sake, now you are going mad!' They said it had broken many men and that it would break me, and that it was all right as long as you didn't go stirring its mud up – it would leave you alone if you were content to rot away on it – but try to put it in order and it would turn on you and kill you. That is what they said. Well, with the help of the A.M.C. we bought Maris and I remember walking to it on a September morning and thinking, 'Where shall I begin?' To add to the dreadfulness the last owners had tried to burn the hedges. They had raked the straw up from the fields on to the hedges and put a match to it. It was just a mess. When I measured the hedge stumps I found that these and the roots spread thirty-five feet across and that they would have to be bulldozed out before anything could be done at all. You couldn't get a plough near them. What top was left, and there was plenty of it, was sixteen feet high. The bulldozers arrived and the mud turned into quagmire. I knew that we must get the hedges out before winter and the corn sown. I knew that unless I could crop this Muck Hall I couldn't keep it. I wouldn't be able to find my payments for it. The work went slowly – two bulldozers now. The neighbours drove by; they couldn't bear to look. It rained – how it rained! The farm turned into slurry. I couldn't see the end of it. But a year passed and we cropped Maris, and we got a third again as had ever been grown on it before. The happiness of it – I can't describe it. It made us quiet, thoughtful.

It was this relief which made me realize that my dream of achieving something truly unusual in farming still hadn't come to anything. I had done wonders but it was conventional wonders. So I began to think of new methods. I discussed everything with Elizabeth and we came to the enormous decision to replace the dairy herd with pigs. We sat down and worked and worked at it. Sheep and pigs and corn ...? Just corn and pigs ...? Sheep? Calf-rearing? This was about 1962–3. I rang up a perfect stranger, one of the biggest farmers in Suffolk, and said, 'I want to produce weaner-pigs. Will you buy them? Are you interested?' 'Very,' he said – that was all. So we had a sale of our cows and the village thought we had gone crazy. 'Changing in mid-stream,' they said, 'dear-o-dear!' One of the reasons for their amazement was because they could see me making a concrete road to join my 'Muck Halls' to-gether. 'Two dung-hills tied to each other,' they said. We laughed but it was really very frightening to listen to. Country people aren't all that kind; they like to see a bit of a crash. I suppose it breaks the monotony. But once I could get from one to the other of my farms, I knew I would have a viable 170 acres. Because of its deadly reputation we bought Maris for £100 an acre – a tremendous bargain.

Well, pigs it was. I converted an old dairy to what I believed a rearing house should be. I'd first had a look around and seen other people's rearing houses and had been appalled by them. I knew that I had to *see* my pigs and be able to reach out and touch them. And I looked forward to their arrival; they would be less dictatorial than cows. Four months later the big farmer whom I had telephoned came over to see our first weaners – and we were away! I started off by just buying Large Whites but changed to Saddlebacks on this rich farmer's advice. The Large

Whites converted slowly – so many pounds of food to make so many pounds of flesh over a given period, this is what conversion means. He helped me get a Walls boar. This firm take boars from various breeds, test them at a progress station and then tell one, 'This boar can convert at X'. It will eat, shall we say, 2½ pounds of food and put on a pound of flesh. It will arrive at the Heavy Hog weight of 260 pounds in 170 days. The boar soon improved our stock for, like a bull, a good boar is fifty per cent of your herd. Eventually he is mated to every one of your animals. This farmer came to the quarterly boar sale with me and helped me choose. It was evident that we both had considerable sympathy for one another. I liked his outlook. I liked his appreciation of what I was trying to do. I admired someone who had just got a contract to produce 14,000 Heavy Hogs taking such time and trouble to help me find a mate for my thirty sows. Eventually, he got me a fine Walls Gilt. And soon I became a 'multiplier', breeding foundation stock to produce sows for the rich farmer, who needed a sow herd of seventy-five 'to put him on the ground'. We – Elizabeth and I – had eighteen animals only – sows which we had to breed from their own kind before we could 'cross off'. We had to multiply the original eighteen to seventy-five before we could 'cross'. It was a long haul! Two years of no return, with money just going out all the time. And, of course, more accommodation, more farrowing quarters – and no financial help whatever at this stage.

The bank made a fuss but I said, 'Look. I've lived as a pauper for six years and I've stuck to my guns about embellishing my farm. If my profits don't amount to very much it is because my place has never carried a job which is worthy of all the groundwork which has been put into it. Now there is a worthy project and it should be, "All systems go!"' But it was the A.M.C. who really helped me. I had the kindest, most fantastic response from these people. They went to the very edge to help me.

This business today, well we have literally built it up out of the unwanted mud. It belongs solely to us and we are still independent. The sow herd now numbers 200 and I'm keeping it at that. It means about 2½ thousand weaners a year. Our food bills run at the rate of £25,000 a year but they will eventually rise to between £30–40,000. We run the double farm with four people and have a bit of time and cash left over to spend on the old Tudor homestead, which we are restoring with our own hands.

Round here, there is no doubt about it, they wait for the big trip. They would like to see me stumble. I am positive about this. They say that no man has pigs for two years without a major breakdown – and I have had them for four years. I am resented because I'm absolutely independent of them all. The whole area is a matter of indifference to me. I could do what I have to do in Scotland – or China. The National Farmers' Union means nothing to me. If the local farmers want to sell me straw, they can do so, or they can forget it. If I owe them anything and they send their account, I pay it by return post. It is the way I behaved in Arabia.

We had students to begin with and I would have liked to have gone on with this method. But we find that the material is getting poorer and poorer. It is the idiot who seeks agriculture and, even when he has a degree, he's incapable of implementing what he has learned. It is pathetic. Quite terrible. Labour on all the farms round here is considered untouchable. You should be able to say to a man earning £800 a year, 'I'll give you £1,000 a year if you'll come as my manager', but if you did you'd never live it down. If you offer a local man a better job than he has on another farm in the area it is considered a kind of seduction. I am chided because they say I don't know how to pick good men but I am forbidden by the local customs from approaching the men I see doing good work because they 'belong' to this farm or that. The men should move about freely, getting the best wages they can.

I find the East Anglians cold and hidden. I have never experienced such coldness before. They can be barbarous and there is an innate cruelty in them. You find it all over the village. The strange thing was that, to begin with, I had the feeling that Suffolk had been seriously maligned because when we first came here people came forward to help us. They helped us get the harvest in and I was touched. There was this apparent communal spirit. It was like North America. But now I realize that this 'help' was nothing more than prying. What was I? Was I steel or was I soft metal? Was I going to give? Soon, they withdrew. They will help you in distress but they don't really like to see you not in distress and doing fine. They don't come and say, 'Good show! It's a pleasure to see what you have done!' They never say this. The average Suffolk farmer is one of the hardest kind of men I have ever met. You find the exceptions, of course. I'm afraid the neighbours and myself are a bit 'lost'.

I don't feel entirely settled here. This is our year of truth, the year when the real profits should start. I feel restive. If it all 'happens', as they say, I shall begin to feel that I have done what I set out to do and might want to move on. My mind has to create things and, when they are completed, go on to another venture. But some ventures refuse to be over. I never sleep one night without dreaming of Arabia.

Major John Paul · aged fifty-one · ex-colonial officer, now senior Civil and Home Defence Organizer in East Anglia

The Major has lived in the village for six years. He is a small, dark, authoritative-looking man who expresses himself with quiet lucidity. He is the unexpected rebel, for although his family, house, political and church-going patterns appear orthodox on the surface, there are oblique currents underneath which are tugging him away from mainstream conclusions. He is conservative but anti-traditional. The traditionalists, perhaps from their arrogantly self-assured bastions, may have given him a few knocks, one thinks. Unlike so many ex-officers who have travelled the world, Major Paul is travel-educated. His job is to establish a nucleus of civil defence in every village, as well as to co-ordinate the defence of Suffolk as a whole. The volunteers, between one and four in each village, wear navy-blue uniforms and are required to give fifty hours a year to their training. They have exams and are fully qualified at the end of four years. The work has parallels with that of the W.V.S., the Red Cross and the St John Ambulance Brigade and attracts the same type of workers. When the Major took over, the units were full of people re-living the halcyon experiences of the Home Guard and air-raid wardens of the Second World War; now it attracts young people, many of whom gain such side-advantages as trips to Denmark, Germany and France. These young people have driven out many of the 1939–45 veterans, who were fighting their old battles all over again.

What is the object of the defence? The Major is diffident – 'Relief work, emergency, floods, that kind of thing'. But it is really to do with the Bomb, isn't it? The Major agrees, not so much reluctantly as having to admit a regrettable truth. One senses that he would prefer to put out forest fires or maybe direct famine relief. He has to organize: this is what he really is, an organizer. What do his volunteers think about the Bomb? In what way are they different from the rest of us who see it as a kind of the end of the world against which all precautions are futile? The Major thinks. 'They take a positive attitude to something horrifying ...' he says at last. We return from this brink to such reasonable subjects as the effect of 'abroad' on the villagers, many of whom have never left Suffolk before. 'They were amazed how hard men worked in Holland and Germany. They watched astonished.' Were they impressed? 'No, they thought it was foolish. "Life wasn't meant to be lived like that." ' The young men were quite changed after a week on the

Continent: it was as if they had stepped out from behind their Suffolk masks.

Major and Mrs Paul live in a beamy, chintzy ex-farmhouse, but with a difference. There is no attempt to re-create the country idyll. The garden is in such a state that it approaches a kind of coat-trailing. The lawns flop hairily into the rosebeds and rampageous plants mock the refinements – sun-dial, crazy paving, wrought iron – of a previous owner. Inside, *passe-partout*ed photographs of mess groups from Aden, Kenya and other places are hitched to the beams. Mrs Paul was a nurse in Nigeria – 'They were beautiful, lovely people and marvellous where they had been left alone, but as soon as they got to learn about a few things they got a bit Bolshy, you know.' There are four pretty children, all under eleven. Did they get on well with the village children? – 'It was hard going at first.' How about herself? – 'It has taken a long time to make friends.'

Major Paul, talking with the quiet patience, 'My job is to produce an organization of 600–1,000 people to deal with any sort of emergency. It is done on the parish basis. There has to be someone, or preferably a group, in each village who can deal with any kind of emergency, local or ... national. Farm labourers, factory workers from Ipswich, farmers and their wives, retired service and colonial officers, those are the people who help. I have to weld them into some kind of county organization. People have said that the volunteer spirit has been killed by the Welfare State but this is not so, and this volunteering is the strength, not only of East Anglia but of Great Britain. There is still this tremendous urge, this great centre of the people who want to serve others. My work is basically to train people to help other people within the village unit – but there is a lot more in it than this, of course. Six years ago our average age was fifty-seven, now it is forty-five. Young people from eighteen to thirty make up a third of the Civil Defence force. They are not paid but they get their expenses, petrol allowance – that sort of thing.

'I came here mostly because of my job, of course, but also because of the sailing. It takes a long time to be accepted, especially if you're not prepared to go into a group and re-live your memories. Retired officers like myself – I know any amount of them – they get together, with their wives, a little clique or whatever it is, and they relive memories. I like meeting people I served with but I wouldn't do this as a social habit. I would avoid this sort of thing. After all, it's the past. It has no bearing on what is happening today and it won't matter tomorrow....

'The people who do this are a class on their own; it is their deliberate choice. I think that they gather in groups like this almost as a form of protection. They are rigid in outlook and they keep to their own customs. Their outlook is pre-war and the social changes are so great that to keep this outlook they are forced to live entirely artificial lives. All they do is discuss the past and my view, as somebody from outside and who has come from a different life, is that they are parasitic. They don't make their own groups because they can't get in with the "county" – it's simply a deliberate choosing. It's an inward-looking nostalgia. They are living a life that's gone. Why do they do it? Fear. They know they are regarded as strangers in the village and they cannot bear it. So they look around Suffolk for people like themselves and ignore everybody else.'

All the time they worked abroad, they had a dream of England? They hankered after a microcosmic scene of non-change and certainty. And when they got their retirement and their Suffolk house, they found things were not so, and they cannot bear it. So they bury themselves into their gardens, which are the village where they are concerned.

'I find the average village person, well, not very quick, shall we say. His intelligence doesn't compare with that of the average Londoner. His knowledge of world affairs or even of U.K. affairs is not very high. He's not really interested. But he's kind – they are all very kind people. I am always astonished by their kindness. Their roots are deep in the past, they haven't been what I would call "de-tribalized" and they still look towards their parish councils, which I wouldn't say were very effective. The village is changing but it is still very undisturbed. The people who belong have lived here for ever. They're contented – no, complacent. They all think they live in a very fine place and they're really not bothered by people who say, "We've got something which you haven't got". They like things as they are, whether it's work, religion – anything. They're not keen on the arts.

'Without being derogatory to them – I am very fond of them – I think they look solid, and I'm referring to both sexes now. Their faces, though, they are Celtic. They have eyes which, while seeing obvious things, are also at the same time seeing things in a world of their own. Sailors' eyes are like this. The Suffolk people remind me very much of Cornwall. They have the same intensity. They are very intense people. They are loyal, but more loyal to an idea than to a person. The young are not very articulate, unless they are a long way from the village, abroad, perhaps, as I have seen them.

'There are two bad things about Suffolk villages. They contain groups of retired officers and colonialists who cling together and ignore life as it really is, and the ordinary country people are incurious – and proud of it. And, of course, there is the feudalism, particularly between the Blythe and Ipswich, where there is a tremendously strong 'inward-looking outlook' and everybody from the County Council to the lords are fighting to keep village life intact, and where people go to great lengths to preserve rural life, buildings, customs – anything. The great social changes of the last twenty years have made little progress around Akenfield. It is quite different in North Suffolk. I am new. I travel. I see all the Suffolk villages – so I know.'

12 · The Orchard Men

Adam lay I-bowndyn, bowndyn in a bond,
Fowre thowsand wynter thowt he not too long;
And al was for an appil, an appil that he tok
As clerkis fyndin wretyn in here book.

Anon, *Bless the Time the Appil was Taken,*
fifteenth century.

DIARY OF THE AKENFIELD FRUIT HARVEST

16–20 June	Gooseberries picked. The main varieties grown in the village are *Careless, Leveller* and *Golden Drop*, although the latter are only seen in cottage gardens.
21 July	Laxton plums.
1–7 August	Main plums picked. The varieties are *Earl Rivers* (considered the tastiest), the *Yellow* and *Purple Pershores, Czars* (chief canning plum), *Warwickshires* and *Droopers* (best jam plum).
1–21 August	Blackcurrants picked. The varieties are *Boscrop, Wellington, Mendip Cross* and *Baldwin*.
15 August	Apples picked. *George Cave* and *Scarlet Pimpernel* (these have taken over from *Beauty of Bath*, which used to be the first eating apple of the season).
1 September	Apples picked. *Worcester Pearmain, Grenadier* (first of the cooking apples) and *Lord Lambton*.
20 September	Apples picked. *Egremont Russet, Laxton's Superb, Cox's Orange Pippin* (thought to be the finest English apple. Raised by a brewer named Mr Cox at Slough in 1830. 'Pippin' because they are propagated from pips – the royal fruiterer brought pippins to Henry VIII.)

1 October	*Bramleys* (best English cooker, heavy cropper and easiest apple to sell), *Newton Wonder* (cooks until Christmas, eats after) and *Blenheim Orange* (pips first taken from a garden in Woodstock. Produced fruit 1818. Nobody knows where the original tree came from.)
Mid-September	Plums. *Victorias* (bought by Heinz for baby food), *Burbank,* the 'giant prune' plum, and *President.*
September–October	Pears picked. *Conference, Comice, Orange Pear* (cookers).
25 October	Apples picked. *William Crump, Discovery* (four acres just planted – no fruit yet).

East Anglian apples, some of which can be found in the old gardens in the village but which aren't grown commercially.

Lady Henniker (raised at Thornham Hall, Eye, 1840–50)
Norfolk Beauty (1902)
Norfolk Royal (a very old variety)
Green Roland
Histon Favourite (Cambridgeshire)
St Edmund's Russet (raised at Bury St Edmunds, 1870)
Doctor Harvey (the great winter apple from Norfolk)
Sandringham (raised 1884)
Sturmer Pippin (raised 1880)
Lord Stradbroke (raised 1933, a big angular apple)
D'Arcy Spice (the most valued apple in the Eastern Counties. It was discovered growing in the gardens of Tolleshunt D'Arcy Hall in 1880.)
Costard (not an East Anglian apple but familiar throughout Britain. There are records to show that it was being sold at Oxford in 1296. The original costermonger was a seller of Costard apples.)

Alan Mitton · aged thirty-eight · orchard foreman

His name appears regularly in the church records way back to the late seventeenth century and on a great crop of Victorian tombstones. He is tall, Viking-looking, the biggest man in Akenfield, a natural leader and king-pin of the apple-workers. Courteous, self-assured, he has the 'gentle giant's' good nature. He has never been away from the village since he was born – in the same house in which he now lives with his wife and family – and although Akenfield is his world, it is a broad rich world. He has never felt the need to explore another. He is deacon at the Strict Baptist Chapel and at the Anglican–Non-conformist get-togethers he prays in lucid, mannered eighteenth-century English. If somebody says, 'We will read from First King's Seventeen', or 'Ezekiel One-Six', he opens his Bible in a single movement at the place. He plays football every Saturday, his limbs in their modest knee-warmers contrasting with the crutch-length shorts of the rest of the team.

'Ask Alan to do something, and he will do it,' they say in the village. 'Ask him how to do something and he will tell you.'

*

I am an orchard man. The orchards I was born into, as you might say, are the biggest in the village. There are nearly 140 acres of them and they lie on the slopes to the south of the houses. More people are employed here than anywhere else in the village. I actually started work on this farm three years before I left school, mostly during the summer holidays. And then, when I left school, the farmer said, 'You used to enjoy being on the fruit cart, maybe you would like stay on it regular?' I said, 'I would rather', and that is how I came to be in the fruit all the while.

When they first planted the orchards, before the First War, they began with just a little patch containing two or three trees of each kind of fruit and then they began to lay out the Bramley orchards – probably about five acres apiece. And gradually the orchards spread their way up the hill – because of frost reasons, I suppose. We've got about nine acres of old-established Bramleys left from those days. Some are over fifty years old and if the pruning is done correctly there is no reason why these trees shouldn't go on for always. Right at the bottom of this old orchard there is a row of the original trees planted in the 1890s – just five trees planted at twelve yards square, which is double the space usually given to a Bramley. One of these five trees, which is nearly eighty years old, never produces less than twenty bushels of apples. And the funny thing is that the apples are all big. No one really knows why this tree is so marvellous, why every year without fail, as you might say, it gives eighteen out of its twenty bushels which are first-class apples. In 1965, which was a good apple year, we picked 124 bushels of fruit off this one row of old trees. The next row, where the trees have only half the space, gave 120 bushels.

In the days when I began, out of the twenty men on the fruit farm, only four were allowed to prune. This was because of the old-fashioned idea that when you were cutting a piece of wood you were taking so many apples off the tree. So the trees went up and up, and bushed out and became enormous. They got so thick that it was difficult to spray them and so tall it was hard to gather. And they didn't get enough air. But about fifteen years ago we tried a new drastic cutting method. We said, 'Right! We'll have this bit out and this bit out!' The old men came and looked and said, 'You aren't pruning, you're pollarding!' They were very shocked. 'Poor trees, poor trees ...' they said. All the middles were ripped out; the trees looked like umbrellas. In fact, it looked really shameful. It was always the old boys' pride to keep the shape of a tree, so they were shocked. It was their main art, to keep the tree-shape. Well, nothing was said. The sawing went on. The middles were taken right out and the lower boughs removed so that the tractors and sprayers could drive through the orchard. These trees looked terrible and the next year they grew so much spur-wood where the boughs had been that we wondered if we had done right. Then, the *next* year, the fruit started to come. It was exciting. The apples got better and better. It was amazing; you had to see it to believe it.

So much changed after this. Once, you had to wait five years between planting a tree and picking its fruit, now it is only three. These young trees are no more than three feet high and with a stick no rounder than your thumb. They have had their tops cut off at knee level and have burst out into four or five branches which, a year or so later, have been cut halfway back again – tipping, we call it – and then the third year we have the apples. You can pick as many as twenty pounds of apples from a fourth-year tree. It is all so quick.

We buy our trees from a nursery in Sussex. They come as maidens, which is a first-year tree which has been grafted and budded. We plant them at the end of the year and then, just before the sap rises, we snip the top out. Should any flowering buds appear the first year, we rub them off. We never let apples come the first year. These trees are low and small, so that we can pick the fruit easily. All the big trees are gradually disappearing.

We are expanding the Coxes. Twenty years ago there wasn't a Cox tree on the farm at all. We were told that the soil in the village was wrong for Coxes and that they wouldn't grow. The only field which might grow them, they said, was down by the river. They said they might grow there. But then, they said, the frost will lie in the river belt, so better not plant there. Well, we planted them on the slope with a pollinater and they have borne extremely heavy. Coxes are expensive apples but very popular; there is always a sale for them. You can eat them all the way through from early October to February and they will always be good, whereas an apple like a Worcester can only be eaten in September for the full flavour. It soon goes clung, as we say. We pollinate the Coxes with James Grieves – one James Grieve to about every fifteen Coxes. If it looks like an apple-glut year and we think that the Grieves aren't going to sell very well, we pick the biggest of them in early September and sell them as cookers. The apples which are left on the James Grieve trees won't be picked at all. They will just drop onto the ground. Last year they were all picked and sold because the spring frosts caused an apple shortage.

We're growing Matsus, which is a new kind of apple from Japan which has been crossed with a Golden Delicious. There are more Golden Delicious apples grown in the world than any other variety. We find that the Matsu will hang on the tree longer than any other apple. With Coxes, you've got to rush and pick before the mid-October winds take them off but there is no hurry with a Matsu. It will hang firm until you have finished picking all your main eaters and cookers. Last year, this one particular Matsu which we grew on trial had eleven apples on it. They were great things. We cut one up into pieces for the women to try and they said it was juicy and nice and fine-flavoured. This year, this same tree bore 511 pounds of fruit! The weight of it carried the boughs to the grass, so that it was like an open parasol. Every apple went over the two-inch mark, which is the grade an apple has to be for market. So we are pleased with the Matsus.

Like everything else in the village, the fruit trees are being made to fit into less and less space. We have four acres of apples which Mike Poole and myself trim on the 'pillar' system, pruning away so that a maiden is left with the main stem going up to about ten feet eventually. It is a bit complicated to learn. It means that instead of getting 132–6 trees on an acre of land, you can get over 300. It also means that all the apples are low enough to be picked from a short pair of steps. But we have come up against a snag. With so much pruning you get a lot of little spurs and a density of leaves, so the apples don't ripen all that well.

All the apples go into the gas-store near Beccles when they have been gathered. They are picked straight into bulk bins and are graded when they reach the store. The store has about fifty departments, each one of which holds 200 tons of apples. It operates as a syndicate run by thirty fruit farmers. The apples can stay in the gas-store for as long as they like but once a store has been opened, the fruit has to be got out onto the market within a week. Most of it goes to Newcastle and Glasgow, and some of it may go abroad. We also send our pears to the cold store. These are Conference pears, or what we call 'banana' pears, which are picked round about 16th September, which is really three weeks too early. But the store is being prepared then for all the farmers in the neighbourhood, so there is nothing for it. The farmers say, 'This week it must be Conference pears; it is the only time we can manage them!' So Conference pears it is. They are often still growing and if you had to keep them in the ordinary way they would go clung. Liverish. But they'll come out of the cold store perfectly ripe. A good Conference pear must make $1\frac{7}{8}$-inch grade and we don't pick them if they are smaller than this. We round-up those which haven't made the cold-store grade about 20th October and sell them to the merchants of Saxmundham. They are sweet little things by then. We grow seven acres of pears altogether. Plums are not stored. They are sent straight up to Covent Garden and the London barrow markets.

The year begins after the picking. We start pruning. We look at the trees and say, 'This is the fruit bud, this the leaf bud', and we wonder at the prospect of good blossom. Except with pears, for you can never tell with pears. A heavy blossom show never means a heavy crop. It seems to me that the pears thin themselves out. You'll get a pear orchard covered in bloom and worth anybody's time to walk down, the trees will all 'set' and then, just when you expect them to bulb-up, half of the fruit buds will drop off. It is the tree sorting itself out. Unlike the Bramleys – they won't drop off and during a great blossom year like that of 1965, we had to go round with ladders and thin them by hand. It was a terrible job. You'd find a cluster of blossoms with seven or eight apples in a heap and you have to take three or four out and throw them to the ground in mid-June. Because, always in June you get what we call the 'June drop', when plum-sized apples will drop to the grass automatically. But now we have a spray which does the thinning-out. The Coxes were sprayed by an aeroplane this year. It was done three or four days before they were picked to prevent store-rot.

During the picking season, you'll get twenty to twenty-five young people coming to the orchards for a job. Most of them stop about a couple of days – they don't like ladder work! They come with visions of a lovely holiday, sunbathing, transistors, larking about and a pound or two right easy at the end of each day. But they can't use the ladders. They will lay it flat, like a thatcher on a stack, and break the tree with their weight. The straighter a ladder is put up, the better. I put the ladder up for them and show them how to pick. Just turn the apple up, put it gently into the pail and when the pail is full empty it softly into the box below by letting the apples fall across your arm. They'll do this for about half an hour, then they'll think that they're not getting along nearly fast enough, and you'll hear the apples rattling down in the orchard! They'll be throwing them in the pail. The picking of the tree-fruit is really controlled by nine special women – our regulars, we call them. These nine will pick eighty acres of fruit, earning between £10–12 a week. They come to the orchards at various times after they have managed to get their housework done, mostly between 8.30 and 4.30 and they only stop for a flask of tea. In the old days, when people were hard up, the orchards were crowded with women at picking time. Nowadays, the women work in twos and threes, one picking from the ground, one collecting the middle apples and one picking from the top of the ladder. Each orchard is planted in six or eight rows and the women strip it row by row. It doesn't matter how tall a tree is, there is never a single apple left on it. Although they pick fast, their hands are so gentle that you never find a bruised apple. It is a miracle.

The children come for work as soon as they have broken up for their summer holiday at the end of July. Those who are in their last year at school are often hoping for a regular job. The boys and girls are good on the gooseberries and currants. Top pickers on gooseberries can earn as much as £5 a day. The currant fields are being extended all the time and we now have thirty-six acres of them altogether. About half of these currants are being picked in a new drastic fashion, with the entire bush being cut off close to the ground and fed into a picker made out of a converted hop machine. It is an experiment which, I think, came from Kent. The bushes can be grown very close together and you can get twice as many on the same acreage. The only snag which we have come up against is that the bushes don't grow enough the second year to warrant their being cropped down again. It is a strange sort of picking. There is this great field covered with thick bushes one day, and as bare as a bit of ploughing the next.

This is a good village. It has its faults, but it is a good village. It is in the old Liberal Eye area. The election before last happened to come in the middle of the fruit-picking and the women came down from their ladders and said, 'We're going down to vote in our picking clothes!' So off we went, me driving the tractor and them all in the truck behind 'rough and ready', as they said. When we got to the school, there were the Tory ladies sitting outside with their markers. The fruit-pickers shouted, 'You don't want to worry your heads over us – we're all

Liberal!' Ninety per cent of the old village folk are staunch Liberal but the young men only talk politics round about election time. They always find fault with whoever is in power because they think they are paying too much tax out of their wages. For most people, politics is something to do with your wages. The young people go with the tide – the young tide. They feel safe then. They are very careful, watching the money. We find it with the football club. They'll pay their dues but if we say, 'Can you manage a bit more?' they at once say, 'We can't afford it'. But everybody spends without thinking on a Saturday night. All the rest of the week, you think about what you spend, but never on a Saturday night. Groups of boys will get into a car and spend pounds between six and twelve on a Saturday evening. They don't spend much on clothes. They reckon these are just a necessity, not an extravagance. They won't buy fancy for the fashion. The young men will work all the hours God ever made to get an extra bob or two but if you ask them what they are going to do with the money, they don't know. Some of the boys save and save. They love money.

The village keeps the same pattern. You get more or less the same groups of people keeping the same ideas. They don't mean to get out of their ruts. But it is still very lively here and outsiders don't realize just how much goes on. There is the tennis club, the youth club, the darts club – a club for everybody. I belong to the football club. It was started in the bad times before the last war when the boys couldn't even afford goal-posts and had to use sticks pulled out of the hedge. Then somebody lent them a field. Then they got a committee. Then the war came and everything had to be stored in a barn, then we had to begin all over again. I was fifteen then and I have played ever since. I feel old amongst all these lads, but there, they'll be old too one day. We have two teams and no age limit. Each member pays 10s. a year and we belong to the Third Division of the Ipswich and District League. You have to start at the bottom, you see. We play on a field near the river which has a natural rise and which is under the shelter of a hill. It has been a meadow for years and years and the grass is smooth as well as tough – real meadow grass which the cattle have put into good heart. Our first field was dreadfully muddy. We mole-drained it, we raised the turf with forks, we sprinkled the pitch with sawdust, but we always came off it drenched. This meadow is beautiful. We have thirty players, twenty-two for the first and second teams and a few reserves. We are insured and if any player gets hurt he gets £3 a week. We had a boy who broke his leg and who was off work for seven weeks, so the football money came in handy. The club provides the balls and shirts, but each boy buys his own boots, socks and shorts. We think we did very well last season. We bought a new dressing-room for £60 and still had £70 in hand! But there are always other things. A new set of shirts costs £12, nets £16, a ball £5, a marker £15 and our annual insurance premium £30, so you see why we have to get money for our club. We wouldn't be able to manage without the women. They are mainly the players' wives and girlfriends. They have been brought up with the notion that men have to play football. They make tea at half-time; they wash the shirts and shorts. You are expected to be dazzling clean when you begin a match. We have now got into the Second Division and with good luck we should soon be in the First. The talk is football, football, and only the summer can stop the talk.

Three women sit in a little hut at every match. They have a teapot, twenty-five beakers and a primus stove. 'Who won?' they say.

Michael Poole · aged thirty-seven · orchard worker

Michael is one of Akenfield's some twenty or so bachelors, a good half of which share his age group. They are simply waiting for a time which suits them to marry but he waits in vain for any opportunity which will take him from his parents' hearth. There are scarcely any words left to describe him; the world has become a much kinder place where his sort is concerned. 'He is *simple* ...' people will say, putting a wealth of meaning into the description to make sure that it implies something quite unalarming. Simple is exactly what he is not. He is illiterate and it is this which cuts him off. He cannot read or write a single letter. 'He couldn't learn,' it is explained. While the others thundered their way through the multiplication tables, collects, Alfred Noyes's *Highwayman* and history dates, Michael made rag rugs. He worked with incredible speed and ingenuity, translating bundles of old coats, skirts and frocks into cosy oblongs to lay along the side of beds, warm shaggy islands in the icy lino seas. The women brought the rags and the school provided the time. Nobody seemed to realize that a child who could work so hard and who could make such good designs might have been able to learn if learning had been a less rigid thing.

He is sharp-featured and fair. There is no rest in the 'simple' face, it has the alertness of a forest creature, eyes seizing at every object. Michael must outdo everybody in work, carry heavier loads, bicycle more miles to a casual job, leave everything with a neatness so devastating that it is almost showy. He saves hard and has hundreds of pounds. He actually left the village school with a bank account of £8 – his rug earnings. He drinks a lot of beer and will 'talk with anyone who'll talk to me'. On Sunday nights he sits right at the back of the church, his yellow hair thick as one of his own rugs, his nervous face ablaze. After church the congregation queues up to persuade him to cut hedges, scythe orchards, empty cess-pits, saw wood, cart manure, dig. He takes every job on. He never refuses. It could be the pressure of so much work which makes him do it with a kind of franticness too fast, too earnestly. Unlike most countrymen, it is not pleasant to watch him work, he is all too obviously compensating. He is a discreet gossip and the big news from the village is handed on in one or two pithy phrases with a look which says, 'Make what you can of that'.

*

I used to get up of a morning. I used to take two pails. I used to climb Scarlett Hill to the pump. I used to carry the water home. I used to find the house all dark, all sleeping. I used to clank the pails and shout, 'Come you together now! Let's be having you!' and my dad would jump out of bed *bang!* I used to walk back to Scarlett Hill, to old Mackay's house. I used to hang around his door and then go in and watch him cut fat bacon and slip it in the pan. Then eggs. I used to say, 'Is that your breakfast then, Mr Mackay?' and he'd say, 'That is'. He'd slip a bit more into the pan – 'For the dog,' he'd say. 'What dog, Mr Mackay?' – 'That damn young puppy,' he'd say. I used to take a chair. After breakfast I used to say, 'It's nice for you to have a mite of company like, Mr Mackay'. And he'd say, 'Oh?' I used to be ten then.

I went to work on the fruit when I was fourteen. I never minded it. I got my money and that was the main thing. I grew, my money grew. It was nice to have it.

Summer was best. You'd get the women come and give you a look. You'd torment them and they'd torment you. There used to be a regular procession of old girls who'd bike up from Framlingham for the picking. When I was sixteen, one of these old girls came up to me in the orchard and said, 'Let me see your watch'.

I didn't answer.

'Aren't you going to let me see your watch then?'

I said nothing. Anyway, she could see my watch; it was lying on my waistcoat under the apple tree.

'I shall take it ...' she says.

'Take it then.'

'I reckon you want me to take it?'

'I can see you're bent on it,' I said, 'so you may as well.'

So she took it, for devilry. It was on a chain and she hung it round her fat neck the whole live-long afternoon. I wouldn't let her see it worried me. She'd walk by and shout, 'Come and get it!'

I said nothing. She brought it to me about five, before she set off home. She put it over my head like a necklace and said, 'There you are, you young bugger'.

I wouldn't speak to her.

The next morning, along she comes, straight to where I'm about to start. Her arms were stuck out full length and she was all smiles. She got her mouth on my face and, my God, she must have thought it was her breakfast, or something.

I pushed at her. I said, 'Don't! Look out, he's coming!' – He was, too. Old Fletcher the foreman. She broke away but back she arrived later when I was lying on the scythings, eating my bait. It was long grass all around.

'Don't fret,' says she.

I said nothing.

'The coast is clear,' she says, and comes down on me like a ton of bricks. I couldn't see nothing but grass. There was such a rocking. I couldn't tell whether I was babe or man.

At tea-time the women went rushing home with their aprons full of apples – shrieking, you can be sure. They shruck a bit more when they saw me and a couple of them rang their bike bells. My old woman shouted, 'Don't torment him! He's like his old watch – not so bad when he's wound up!' Laugh! You should have heard them!

It was my first time.

Christ, that was a summer and no mistake.

13 · Four Ladies

Go and ask Robin to bring the girls over
To Sweetwater, said my Aunt; and that was why
It was like a dream of ladies sweeping by
The willows, clouds, deep meadowgrass, and the river.

  John Crowe Ransom, *Vision by Sweetwater*

Marjorie Jope · aged seventy-nine · retired district nurse

Nurse Jope is mother-confessor to the village, a person of absolute trust and fidelity. There is no conscious sense of vocation about her and the idea of doing good is quite obviously unknown to her. She is unsentimental yet at the same time un-matter of fact: one instinctively realizes that a great part of her genius or triumphant personality – call it what one will – lies in her simple belief that each individual is different and that so much difference as a community of 300 souls is likely to display in a working life of forty years, such as she has experienced, must dispel most of the convenient conclusions. For all this time she has seen Akenfield naked in birth, naked in death and, most privately and multitudinously between-whiles, bare and vulnerable in its human despair. The amazing thing is that for all these years it was not only Akenfield which rested in her care, but eight other villages also. She was paid at the beginning a basic salary of £2 a week and, although this sum was haphazardly supplemented by gifts from better-off people, most of the cash she had left over from household and professional expenses went on the purchasing of extra medical supplies. She neither condemns nor feels any nostalgia for Akenfield between the wars. As for the wistful paternalism revealed in programmes like *Doctor Finlay's Casebook* and talk of old-style village self-help and charity, mention of such things causes her to smile and shake her head the merest fraction. 'Certainly people were more neighbourly then. They went in and out of each other's houses to help with what was needed, and thought themselves well-paid with a cup of tea, yet [a small smile at the paradox] it wasn't better than now. It was worse, much, much worse.'

She is a neat, brown-skinned woman with fine eyes. She lives in one of the old farmsteads now called cottages and possesses a cheerful new car which she uses to transport 'anyone who has to go anywhere'. Children picnic in her orchard. They obey her with a special gravity – 'Yes, Nurse: no, Nurse ...'

*

I started in 1925 with Akenfield and three other villages and then, in two-three months, some more villages came under my care until I had nine altogether. I was a novelty, I can tell you. None of these places had had a nurse before; the births and deaths were attended by secretive old women, just as in the olden days. I was appointed by the local nursing association which was affiliated to the East Suffolk Nursing Association. I had a little car. There were no cars then, so you can imagine how important I looked! My salary was £2 a week and at first my father had to help me pay my lodgings. I had to pay all my own expenses but soon the villages had to raise my salary. This was done by individual people paying the Nursing Association 4s. a year. Well-off people paid more. My first lodgings were with an old lady who disapproved if I went out earlier than nine in the morning or got back later than four in the afternoon. I changed lodgings a few times because nobody understood that I had to be free to go out and come in at all hours. The vicar had to be severe with them. His name was Mr Paternoster and the verger's name was Creed. It sounds funny but it was a fact. Anyway, the vicar said, 'We've got a nurse now and we're not going to let her go', and then he searched around and eventually found me a kind of hut. I soon made it into a house and then I was independent. The relief! I paid rent for it and I was always on duty in it, although officially I had Thursday afternoons off. I had the telephone and that was a novelty too. Most ordinary people didn't use the phone: they walked or biked miles and miles with news of accidents, maternity cases, troubles of all sorts. What with the phone and people calling at all hours, it was non-stop. I often wonder how I did it. But I was young and the young find all things possible.

There was a great difference inside the cottages in those days. One had to explain every single thing. The most simple instructions had to be said twice over. Living conditions were very, very poor. Akenfield was an agricultural labourers' village. The only 'people' here were the Cretinghams. They were the only 'people', you understand. So everything fell on me. I was school nurse, too, and once or twice a year, when the school doctor came round, I had to assist him examine the children. I knew them all so well they could have been my own children. I knew their homes and in most cases I had delivered them. There were so many dirty children in those days, dirty hair, dirty feet, impetigo. It was thought a disgrace to have a dirty head, but lots did. There's nothing like that now. Children have never been as beautiful as they are now. There were quite a lot of 'home' children in the village in those days – more than twenty, perhaps. They came from Dr Barnardo's and from the Church of England Children's Home. They were all boys – nobody wanted girls. They came sometimes when they were only a few weeks' old but they were rarely adopted in the full legal sense, perhaps because the foster-parents would lose the home-allowance if they were. Two of these boys became a schoolmaster and a Battle of Britain pilot and both tried to find out who they really were, but they never did. A lot of the Barnardo boys were sent to Australia when they were fourteen and new ones came in their place. Their foster-parents didn't seem to turn a hair when the replacement happened; it always amazed me.

The old people were not taken care of. This is another thing which people like to think now, that grandfathers and grandmothers had an honoured place in the cottage. In fact, when they got old they were just neglected, pushed away into corners. I even found them in cupboards! Even in fairly clean and respectable houses you often found an old man or woman shoved out of sight in a dark niche. People were most suspicious at first when I called. There was no such thing as a welcome, you had to make your own way. They didn't want anybody outside to know their business. I had to ask questions, especially about TB. They hated that. I had to collect long lists of facts about them and they were so unwilling that it often took me days. I had to feel my way, exchanging trust for trust. They had their secrets, like all families, but I had to know some of them! There were families in Akenfield who never told anyone anything. It was – their entire life, you know – all bolted up behind the back door. Not many people were taken away to the infirmaries. They were born at home and they died at home. I now know so much about them all – things nobody else could ever know. In time I heard everything. They told me things they could not tell each other. I knew them body and mind. None of them, neither the best nor the worst, were so very different to each other, if they did but know it. They liked to imagine they were, of course. I suppose we all do. Five years after I arrived in Akenfield it got so that I could walk in nearly every house. Sometimes they all looked so strong and well that I wondered why I had been sent for, then the worry would come spilling out. It was usually about the relations. Practically every family was related. It is the same with myself, except I don't know my own cousins. So many village marriages used to be cousin marriages. It is different now because the young men drive about all over the place and find girls. Nobody moved a yard in the old days.

People died from much the same things as they do now, except there was more cancer then, unless they whip the cancer patients off to Ipswich and one doesn't hear of it. If they thought they had cancer in the old days they would keep quiet about it. They put up with it in secret for as long as they could. Things were more or less hidden – all life was hidden – and then, of course, it was difficult to move the doctors. They didn't bother too much. Time after time I would try and get a doctor to a bad case in the village but most times he never came. He would come when he thought he would. Sick people were on parish relief but the doctors ran their own medical clubs. If people didn't pay into the club, then they didn't get a doctor. A doctor could not be reported for not coming, although I did report a doctor once. It was for refusing to believe that a woman had TB and telling her to get up. She got up and she collapsed. But then there was Dr Denny who would come out any time of the day or night. He was most unusual. There were quite a few country doctors in the neighbourhood but none of them did this. They were important folk then and the villagers were a bit nervous of them. But Dr Denny was different. Even if it was some-body else's case, he'd come. As for the old family doctor – he was for the old families, if you know what I mean.

People think of me as the person who is present at the beginning of their lives but in most cases I have been present at the end of them too. I used to stay up one night or several nights when they were passing. Some talked of God, but very, very few. Even the people who had been brought up in chapel or church rarely talked of God as they died. It is a fact. What can you make of it? I was with them as they passed. Not much talk of God at the last.

Quite a lot of old people spent their last weeks alone. Their absence of family was only noticed at this time. I remember a clean, respectable old man who lived in a hut on the Framlingham Road. His name was Dixon and the name of his hut was 'Travel On'. He had not worked in Akenfield but had arrived there, presumably after he had retired. Some people said he had been a sailor. He certainly looked clean like a sailor. Then people began to say, where was he? Where had he got to? So the vicar went to 'Travel On' and, oh dear! What a sight. Apparently Mr Dixon had been terribly ill and had just laid in his hut. Worse, he had tried to light his oil-stove to keep warm and had knocked it over and burnt himself. The vicar had walked up after midday Communion on Sunday, just to say hello, as he thought. Instead of which he spent all the afternoon cleaning Mr Dixon and scrubbing 'Travel On' out. He was so convinced that it was a case of village neglect that he prayed about it during the evening service, but we later discovered that Mr Dixon had been attended by his own doctor, who, seeing he couldn't last much longer, had simply shut the door on him. There were plenty of things like that. I often found awful, dreadful things. The village wasn't shocked. They expected people 'to go a bit behind at the end'.

I'm making it sound miserable, aren't I? It wasn't really. It is just that Akenfield is still very close to the old conditions. People weren't worried about these conditions because they were the only ones they knew. They were natural but bad. There was no main water. We all drank from the ponds or the pump or from some wells. It was nothing for me to nurse where the boiled water was bright green! As for my equipment, well I will tell you. I had a saucepan for boiling up my instruments, a spirit stove and several enamel bowls. I carried all this stuff about from house to house in a huge American cloth bag which I made myself. I used to have to strain all the village water through muslin before I dared use it. As well as these things, I carried plenty of odd pieces of mackintosh and a big bundle of clean rags – torn sheets from the better-off houses mostly. We never had nearly enough dressings. As for drugs, well there was aspirin and little else. People in great pain might be given occasional morphia by the doctor. Nothing much. On the whole, people took pain and illness for granted; they weren't very frightened. They didn't worry very much. They supposed they would get better. Nor did they seem fearful of death. They had all worked so hard and so long, I suppose there was a kind of comfort in it.

Mothers worried most. Families were so big that there was nothing restful in lying upstairs with a house full of children. Some families, well you knew that they did not have enough to eat, but they wouldn't tell you. Nor could you find out. Not the real facts. I had a case on the Myddleton Road – a young mother – I knew perfectly well what the trouble was. She was hungry. So I saw the vicar and he got some of the church charity money, which was lying in the bank from one year to the next, and we bought her some ordinary good food. That was all the medicine she needed. We always tried to get the mothers to come to the village school when the county council doctor examined the children, but when he asked them what they gave these thin boys to eat the answer was always, 'porridge, eggs, meat, cake...'. You should have heard! All the mothers thought it right to lie. They thought it shameful not to be able to feed their children, not to be able to manage. Yet I knew of quite a few children who came to school without any breakfast and who walked home to dinner after dinner of just potatoes. That was what they ate, potatoes, and for tea, bread and jam. They had meat on Sunday. And suet puddings and jam. It was easier for the children when they were babies for then they came under what we called 'infant life protection visits' and a very good committee which saw that they had food and clothes. There was little or no cruelty where children were concerned. The stick was used but it was thought quite normal and nobody took much notice of such punishments, although there was talk about a man in the next village who used to whip his daughters. They were getting big girls and they would walk freely along the roads.

Did you know about our gipsies? They came every November to winter down by the Drift on the lower road. They used to camp there in what I called igloos – half hooped tents. The village didn't like them a bit, but in those days they didn't like anyone except themselves. They were always hostile, always suspicious. It is so different now. Looking back, I see this hostility as the worst thing. The least question and they froze. Eventually I found out that I had to get my answers without asking questions. The gipsies were so used to cold faces that they took them for granted. They had lots of babies but in all my nursing years I was only asked to visit them once, and then it was a false alarm. The young father had heated up the water on a tripod and the mother was lying in a glittering, spotless caravan. What a difference to the cottages! An old gipsy, Mr Martin, died in his caravan and it was burnt on the day of his funeral. This was in 1936. He had several children including a girl named Ocean who was a famous Suffolk pedlar – cottons, buttons, things like that. All Ocean's children are married and live in houses now. There are eighteen people in Akenfield who are descended from the Drift gipsies. They are the good-looking ones – you can't miss them.

The village people tend not to look old when they are no longer very young. It is hard to tell their age above fifty. They are strong, quiet people. They endure. Some cannot, of course. There was this middle-aged farmer at Plomesgate, well to see him you wouldn't think he had a care in the world above a bit of a bad leg – nothing to worry about really. Then came this message to say, 'come quick'. It's his leg, I thought. When I arrived, there was his wife and all the neighbours huddled like hens in the parlour. A woman said, 'He's through there, nurse'. So I went into a shed, with her following, but when I started to pick up a sack she cried, 'Oh, don't do that while I'm here. Don't!

Don't!' The farmer had slashed his throat in the shed. That morning he had got up and made the tea as usual. Then he took some up to his wife and drank some himself, then he strolled up to the shed with his razor.... He had almost cut his head off. 'Bind that up, nurse,' said the doctor when he arrived. That nearly finished me for laying-out. I had to put it in my report, you see, and except for mothers and children it was against the rules to lay-out bodies. All the same, I did it and I went on doing it after I retired. When people want help they must have it. What matters more than this? I wash and straighten them for the grave. It is such a small thing and somebody must do it for me. It is such a small thing but people cannot bring themselves to do it. They find it hard to think away from themselves. It is sometimes why they are as they are. They are learning all the time.

Mrs Tom Cooper · aged forty-one · farmer's wife and President of the Women's Institute

One of the rules of the W.I. is that we must be non-political and non-sectarian, so we don't discuss what you might call the moral questions of the day, which is a good thing. It still leaves us plenty to talk about. Immediately I mention the W.I. the farmers think, 'Tweed suits ... home-made jam ... a lot of gossipy old women'. Full stop. They don't really understand what it means to us. We – all the women in the village – feel frightfully bound-in at times. When I am without the car – and some of the women don't have a car ever – I feel extraordinarily helpless and locked away. I feel stranded. I feel as if I could scream. Yet some women never leave the village at all. They buy at the village shop. They go simply nowhere. Buying things at the village shop is expensive but they put up with it. They have no choice and have to put up with whatever the shop-keeper decides they should have. You get to know his stock backwards. There is never anything different – horrible sliced bread in cellophane, bacon with the rind cut off and wrapped in plastic, processed cheese, frozen stuff and terrible vegetables. It is like it or lump it. They will put up with this sort of thing and yet demand very elaborate cookery demonstrations at the W.I. – continental food, glorious bread and cakes. They like to make things. They say, 'I've got something to take home to show my husband!' or, 'My John will never believe it!'

When we had a Questions Programme, seventy-five per cent of the questions were about the characters in telly adverts and the women knew all the answers. They knew the names of all the people in the Oxo and dog-food and detergent ads. I only switch over to I.T.A. about once a week so I didn't know what they were talking about. I thought there was something wrong with me. They all came alive during this competition, rushing to shout out things like, 'Leslie Fairy Snow!' and 'Heinz meanz beanz!'

The women get tired of villagey things. They love travel talks with slides showing Russia and Yugoslavia. They are among their most favourite things. They yearn to go to these places. They don't want to go to some big Suffolk garden which is open to the public or to Lowestoft, they like going a long way, Coventry or London. They like eating in restaurants whenever they have an outing. This is very important. Hardly any of them are interested in natural history but they adore arranging flowers and they are very competitive about it. Flower-arranging has become a great craze in Suffolk and more and more churches have to hold flower festivals. There is terrific one-upmanship. The women also like to go to the theatre at Ipswich – and have a meal out, of course.

We have quite a bit of difficulty in getting members – television again. Also, we meet after tea and a lot of the husbands won't stay with the children in the evening. The men like to feel free. They will stay sometimes, of course, but they say, 'Don't count on it'.

I came into the W.I. movement after I had heard how much the women enjoyed hearing about the old country crafts – they are very keen on the Museum of Rural Life at Stowmarket and nearly everybody treasures some ancient family thing. One of these treasures was a corn-dolly about eighty years old. It was a long plaited tube ending in a bunch of ears and with a handle to hang it up by. An old lady then produced her heirloom corn-dolly which was in the form of Mother Earth and dressed in a long cotton frock and bonnet. It was about two feet high and a hundred years old. It had been passed down in the family and she was going to pass it to her daughter, she said. She said she couldn't give it away because it would be unlucky. About this time I also met a farmer from Framlingham who had to take over a corn-dolly which hung in the kitchen of the farm he had just bought, otherwise his farming would be ruined.

The dolly was made each harvest, kept until the spring and then 're-leased' into the newly-sown seed. A woman of about sixty told me that she could remember her grandfather making them. She could recall him plaiting as he ate his bait at harvest-time. She brought one of his dollies along; it was a kind of goddess and she had wrapped it in a plastic bag.

The origins of the dollies are very vague and go right back to the ancient Egyptians and Greeks. They were made because people were scared of extinction. They could have been a gift of appeasement to the gods or a way of preserving the spirit of the corn. They were made in the shape of Ceres or a horn of plenty, or just a corn cage to keep the fertility symbol in until the next sowing. But eventually people made them into the shapes of things belonging to a certain part of the country. In Essex the dolly is made like a terret which can be worn on a horse collar and the Suffolk emblem is a horseshoe because of the Suffolk Punch and because this was the land of the great horsemen. The Cambridgeshire bell-dolly came from the practice of ringing bells when the last load of corn was brought in off the fields. They have a lantern in Norfolk which they think orginated from Rumania. The Roman legions who were stationed in Norfolk came from Rumania and it is believed that they brought their harvest-dolly with them.

Hardly anybody could remember them before I talked about them. Now they are very keen to learn how to make them. Although, when I told the W.I. that they could be turned into attractive decorations for harvest festival an old lady jumped up and cried, 'How dare you think of putting a pagan idol in our church!'

You need ripe corn with a hollow stem. You cut it from the field at ground level. When you have brought it home, you cut the ears off at just above the first node and at an angle. Then you strip the flag off. It takes ages and you must use good-grade straw. You then sort the straw into different thicknesses – I use a knitting needle to measure these and to test that each stalk is hollow. You then temper the straw by soaking it for more than an hour in cold water and you keep it moist by wrapping it in a towel. You only have to do this tempering if you cut the corn and keep it. The men – it was always the men who made the dollies – were able to cut corn and make their dollies at once. It is best to use a basic five-straw plait for the Suffolk dolly. You tie the corn at the thin end where you have cut off the ears – and then you start. It is dreadfully difficult to describe and almost impossible to do unless you watch somebody else. Instructions don't help. All I can say is that you have two straws at two o'clock, one straw at nine o'clock, one at six o'clock and one at four o'clock. You fold the one at three o'clock down to six o'clock, up to midnight and then turn it, so that you've always got two at three o'clock. You must treat the straw with respect and hold it at the point of the work, the left hand underneath, the right hand above, otherwise it will bend in the wrong place. It is very easy to do but very hard to describe.

The women are amazed at the shapes which 'come out of that old bit of straw' and they say, 'But you never made those beautiful things out of *straw?*' The W.I.s began bringing back the corn-dolly art soon after the last war – it was almost forgotten. I have been demonstrating it for two years but so far I haven't met anybody who is really interested. I mean not tremendously so. The women say they haven't got the time to do it and that is that. They say, 'We've got all this knitting...'. They are always knitting. They watch television and they knit, knit, knit.

Mrs Ferrier · Chairman of the Women's Institute

You get some W.I.s where everything gets planned beforehand by a small group who use the rest of the members as a tame audience, but not us. We are democratic. Everybody is expected to offer suggestions for getting out a programme. We're not a bit strict – very informal. We are doing unusually well at the moment – in fact it's absolutely unbelievable! Young unmarried girls going onto the Committee! You'd never have got them to do such a thing once upon a time. They're frightfully keen. We do outlandish things. Somebody suggested we all spent the evening in the pub – and we did it. We filled the pub right up. We had toasts – everything. It was very jolly. The men didn't know where to look.

We've got fifty-six members in our branch, so it is a very big Institute, and we are part of a group made up of eleven branches. We meet once a month and we have a big group meeting in Ipswich once a year.

We are bothered about expenses because everything is going up. We have members who can't afford to go on outings. People are getting poor again. The next two years are going to be a difficult time for our branch. The hire of the hall and the electricity have gone up and we can't afford the best speakers. So many people will offer to address a W.I. although they have nothing to say – or can't say it if they have. We've just had a policewoman to talk to us. She was very modern. She shocked the two policemen's widows who live in the village. She said that policewomen had to get hardened. They had to ask these wretched girls who get what they call 'molested' exactly what happened. I must say, I'd never be able to answer questions like that! 'Did he put his hand down your blouse or up your knickers?' they ask, it seems. The policeman's widow who was sitting next to me said, 'My late husband would never have mentioned such a thing!' All the village women said that the last thing they would want to be was a policewoman. I think they are right. Being a policewoman is a peculiar thing to want to be – even allowing for the uniform. But they're good with children – less frightening than policemen, I suppose. I'm dead against uniforms. They attract funny people. I don't even wear my W.I. badge. I feel like cattle when I'm wearing a badge. I'm the only person on the platform who hasn't got one.

We have a nice lot of power. If we think that something has got to be done, the village has to listen to us. We talk about most things but the Bomb doesn't come into our conversations, although some of the women believe that the bad weather is caused by Russian and American rockets going to the moon and Venus. They got very worried about that hospital affair which let the cat out of the bag about a yellow label meaning 'Don't bother to resuscitate; patient too old'. It was terrible what damage this did. It was diabolical – the talk of the place. The village was beginning to trust the hospital but now it is all uncertain again. What *did* happen when one went there? They were extremely shocked. But mostly they go on about the young people they read of in their newspapers. Wild boys. They forget that when I was young I knew of ploughboys who would steal into a house at night where they hadn't received largess and plough up the lawn. Not to mention the Saturday-night fights behind the pub. Mrs Enders, who ran the pub then, said to me, 'The good old days are gone, my dear. On a Saturday night nobody came out of my front door except on all fours!'

You hear a lot of strange things said about those times, about private service, for example. But people *loved* being servants. There was so much fun in the servants' hall. Such laughter. If you got into a bad place it was usually your own fault. You had probably lost your character, or perhaps your mother had. If people found themselves in bad service you can be sure there was a reason for it. The ladies maids had a lovely time and they could watch how things were done and become educated. It was lovely. But the young women in the village say they wouldn't have any of it! They say it was slavery. They don't understand. They simply can't imagine the pride which Suffolk village girls used to have. Pride, they say, what is that?

Marian Carter-Edwardes ·
aged fifty · Samaritan

Classic English lady, kind, energetic, Vice-Chairman of the Women's

Institute, Rural District Councillor. Opens her garden to the public in July. Arranges flowers in the church – and would scrub the whole place out if she found it necessary. Strict Conservative. Three sons, all grown-up. Surrounded by large dogs and good furniture. Nothing too much trouble. Racy, nothing could surprise her. Good-looking and moves with a girlish, tennis-court freedom. Drives a fast car with dogs looking out of the windows. 100 per cent maternalism for anyone who cares to apply. Total lack of self-consciousness. Influential. J.P. Disarming.

*

When you begin to take on a few village affairs, all the rest come rushing at you. It is, 'She'll do it'. Or you'll even get a letter to say that somebody is delighted to inform you that last night you were elected vice-president of some society you've never even heard of. It's a fight to keep a bit of time for yourself. To read the papers you would think all this kind of thing was dead by now but in fact it is worse than it ever was. Not worse, I don't mean that, do I? *More* than ever it was. (Bessy is coming on heat, that's why she's behaving like that.) But if you live in the country, you have to do these things. Who will if you don't? For instance, they are going to bring Meals-on-Wheels to the village this spring and I'm the only person who really knows who should have them. So now I'm Meals-on-Wheels as well as everything else. 'She'll do it!' Of course, those that need them won't always have them. I can think of one person who wouldn't *think* of accepting them. I can do nothing with her where this kind of thing is concerned. I must put up with it. I couldn't get round her – nobody could. She doesn't accept charity, thank you very much, and that is that. Then there is another cottage where the wife will have the wheel-meal but the husband will not. He doesn't take anything from anybody. 'But, Mr Drift ...' I'll say – you can hear me, can't you! – and, 'Let's hear no more of it!' he'll say. Polite, of course.

I'm fond of the old widowed men who sit quietly in their houses. Most of them aren't so much waiting for food, or whatever, as for a talk. I feel so guilty. I chat my way through a quick cup of tea and they've got a look on their dear old faces like Bessie here, just longing for you to go on and on. I skip the groaners. It really does take it out of you to be groaned and moaned at. I like the ones who say, 'Well, that's life!'

Well, now, Samaritans. We find that we don't reach the village people as easily as we reach the Ipswich folk because it costs so much to advertise and we can't afford it, so that they just don't know. Then there is the other problem. Your village person would as soon undress outside his own front door as divulge his innermost feelings. You see, your real countryman or woman is unpersuadable. Unless he wants to tell you about himself you will never be able to even guess at what is worrying him. And there's another thing, if a country person is absolutely driven to seek help because worry has got the better of them, they'll also take it for granted that somebody like myself will wave their fairy wand and simply 'do something'. Otherwise they wouldn't come. They've never believed in confession being good for the soul. I make tea, offer a cigarette and gossip. It is a kind of priming. Once they start talking I shut up. I never criticize – no Samaritan ever criticizes – and I never offer an opinion if I can help it. And I *never* moralize. I just listen. And I am often listening to something which has never been told to another soul in all the world. Everything is confidential. You never tell anybody anything of what you have heard. And usually, to be quite honest, it isn't worth telling! The things which can worry people to the point when they seriously consider killing themselves often turn out to be small – trifling. You think, *is that all?* But the worry has assumed enormous proportions to the sufferer and you, the outsider, aren't there to belittle it but to break it down. Samaritans don't even try to re-organize a person or start putting his life together. They just listen until they hear the trouble and then they might channel it in the direction where they think it might get the best kind of help. It could be the doctor or the Marriage Guidance Bureau but the truth is that a good fifty-five per cent of the people who come to us are just plumb lonely. Their lives have gone up the spout, and there isn't a single soul they can talk to. So they sit and think and everything gets magnified and soon they are demented.

I try to get people to join the W.I. There is this idea that it is all cakes and home-made jam but we work hard for charity in Akenfield. We help the organization to run a farm in West Africa and we send money to the Cheshire Homes. What the members like most of all are outings, trips to the theatre, mystery tours, things like that. There are crowds of young women. They meet at the apple-picking and say to any newcomer, 'You must join the W.I.' The only women who don't belong are what I call the non-joiners. You'd hardly credit it but there are certain people who won't join anything. We have the meetings in the evening so that the husbands can look after the children. The women don't like their children to come to the parties and things. Even if it's the pantomime, they say, no children! They want to escape them now and then. All the members write on a piece of paper what kind of speakers they want to listen to the following year and then the committee has to try and get them. They like travellers best – foreign places. You don't know the village women until you have seen them in action at the W.I. They would certainly surprise their husbands! I watched them when we're singing *Jerusalem*. I watch Mrs Ferrier.

> *Bring me my bow of burning gold!*
> *Bring me my arrows of desire!…*

What ever can she be thinking about, I wonder.

The biggest age-group is the twenty-fives to forties. You hear, for instance, of the reverse side of the pregnant unmarried girl problem, of the boy who wants to marry her but whose Mum won't let him. The boy is eighteen, maybe, and according to his Mum, he is a 'nice boy' – meaning that the girl has tricked him. But you discover that the boy and girl have been lovers for over a year – something like that. One is constantly seeing the other side of a lot of familiar coins in this job. People with worries are the easiest to deal with. It is some deep psychiatric problem which a person has somehow managed to conceal from the village but which has become unendurable which is the big difficulty. I'm no psychiatrist and wouldn't dream of meddling in this deep water. With the client's permission, I put him in touch with the professionals.

People are amazed when they learn of the amount of suicide there is. Very often, when I am addressing a meeting, I will say, 'Since you have had your tea and have come here to the village hall to listen to me, somebody has killed herself' – and it shakes them. Fourteen village men and six village women committed suicide in East Suffolk this last year [1966] – as against the nine men and five women who took their own lives in Ipswich during the same period. So villages aren't always the cosy, friendly places they are supposed to be, are they? People can be as lonely there as anywhere else.

There are Samaritans like me all over Suffolk. It works like this. A troubled person will pluck up courage to go to the Ipswich office and give his address as Akenfield. So the main office will ring me up and say, 'Well, now, Mrs C-E, you live near, you go and befriend'. Befriending is our word for making contact. So I go and see the woman. I don't find the beginning very difficult; the very fact that they have asked for help gets you quite a long way along the road. I never attempt to explain the Samaritans to them. I say, 'You're worried. Tell me what you are worried about.' And then I sit back. It's surprising. I might be there for three hours and never say another word.

A lot of people just get abandoned by their children. They leave home and simply don't come back any more. There are a few letters, then nothing. There is this frightful law which says that children aren't responsible for their parents. It makes it easy for those who want to shed responsibilities. But, on the other hand, you sometimes find a strong family situation, but where the family contains the last folk who can help. Family emotion gets in the way, family embarrassment. Samaritans mustn't get emotional. You've got to forget yourself and not be conceited. You're there to be kind and sensible. You never act on outside information or gossip. It wouldn't be any good your ringing me up and saying, 'I've just seen Mrs Thingummy and she looks as though she's about to do herself in, so please go and see her'. Samaritans mustn't be people who like giving orders. The last thing you must say is must. If you can get it across that the troubled person needn't be alone any more, then they'll begin to not want to die.

You can't always help. Sometimes you are let into a kind of wilderness and you plod on and on, losing your way and wondering what it is all about. But you mustn't pry. You just wait and hope that soon you'll come up against something which makes sense. And sometimes, having met you several times and told you all their miseries, a person will kind of fall for you – and then what do you do? It's all a problem. You've befriended them and now they're befriending you! It can be a bit awkward – the real challenge, I suppose. However, one must soldier on....

14 · The Young Men

The moon-mist is over the village, out the mist
  speaks the bell,
And all the little roofs of the village bow low,
  pitiful, beseeching, resigned.
– Speak, you my home! What is it I don't do well?

  D.H. Lawrence, *End of Another Home Holiday*

Terry Lloyd · aged twenty-one · pig-farmer

In spite of the sweet reasonableness or dire warnings offered by the
advocates of bigger units, Britain remains remarkably full of farmers
going it alone, or who would go it alone given half a chance. The young
men aren't showing lack of greed but realism when they say 'ten acres
will do'. Whether it is some far cry back to the old pre-Enclosure days
or the same uncooperating spirit which confronts the French agricultural economists with the blunt fact of *two million* or so small farms,
the truth is that the almost sensuous contentment of doing what you
like on your own bit of land persists as strongly now as ever it did. The
Akenfield small-holders will tell you that they have to work all the hours
that God ever made, that they never have a holiday and that they have
to watch every penny. Yet even William, the young shepherd, with his
new estate house, bigger than most wages, responsible work and
generally superior prospects, dreams of 'getting out and having a little
place of our own. My wife wouldn't mind; she'd do anything to help
me. It is all she wants too.'

Terry Lloyd achieved this enviable state the week he left school at
fifteen, when his father gave him four acres and an old barn. At twenty-
one he shows some of the conventional signs of the free-lance, a
precariousness accepted as an ordinary condition of being alive, enough
fear not to do anything silly and quite a bit of unegotistical self-
assurance. He is a small, quiet, thoughtful young man, mature in his
outlook but without that essential limitation or simplicity which makes
things comfortable. He is a thinker. His mind is restless in the way that
the Suffolk rivers are restless. The water hardly seems to move at all,
yet it reaches the sea. He is a natural maverick, a masterless one. There

is a searching quality in his manner, as though he is looking for some-body who will instruct him in the basic grammar of an as yet faintly grasped language, some key which will lead to 'all the rest'. Books? The question brings the inevitable embarrassment. The village people of all ages seem frightened at the mere mention of books. Why isn't this book-fear dispersed at an early time? Why should it exist at all? A seventeen-year-old wrought-iron worker from the village, a good crafts-man and an apparently lively youngster, said, 'Yes, I have read books. I read Enid Blyton when I was at school.' The normality of reading scarcely exists. To nearly every person interviewed, it was a strange thing to have read a book. The book is a kind of frontier across which few seem to have the nerve to pass, even when, as in Terry's case, it is the only way out.

The county day-release agriculture centres are producing interesting side-effects. In the purely social sense, they have contributed more to the destruction of the derelict vision of the farm-worker as a kind of sub-standard human being than any previous plan to improve his status. But something else is also taking place. The mere process of class attendance and an intelligent interest in his affairs by equal-seeming adults has set the learning process in motion for the first time for many youngsters who left school at fifteen. This is what has happened to Terry, now in his last year at the Centre. One master in particular has helped him, and others like him. What has emerged from this still fairly new – about ten years old – governmental further education programme is that one part of a student's intelligence cannot be trained to the degree necessary for him to learn the new sophisticated farming methods without his whole intellectual nature being awakened. Terry is grateful for the extraordinary amount of tangential information Mr Austin has been able to throw off upon such subjects as natural history, politics, current affairs – even art. To an outsider, many of the students appear famished, starving for something more than the curriculum provides, and there seems to be a unique opportunity to accomplish on the young adult scale something comparable to what Sybil Marshall achieved in her condemned Cambridgeshire play-ground and described in *An Experiment in Education*.

The truth is that there is a void where the old village culture existed. Ideas, beliefs and civilizing factors belonging to their grandfathers are not just being abandoned by the young countrymen, they are scarcely known. A motor-bike or universal pop might appear to be a reasonable exchange – but not after you have begun to think.

*

I went to day-release about five years ago. It starts off pretty basically – machinery, crop husbandry, stock husbandry – and then, in the second year, it goes on to the farm institute level. I am taking the management course at the moment. It is made up of two parts, records and accounts and general management. I feel myself that the day-release scheme really offers more than the full institute course. It has certainly made all the difference in the world to my life. There are five masters at the Centre. I get on very well with Mr Austin – we all do. He'll discuss anything with us – insurance, history, morals, religion, sex – anything. It is tremendous. Something completely different. Other industries have had their training schemes for years and, as usual, the poor old farm-worker gets his last! Anyway, we've got it now. It isn't philanthropy. There was suddenly a need to train the village boys to use machinery and understand the new scientific methods. There is such a massive amount of machinery used in farming now. The men are going down, down, down on the farms and the machines up, up. What men are left have got to be real good – different to what they used to be.

I always wanted to work on a farm – but I was born in Leeds! I can't remember Leeds because I was so little when we left, nor can I ever imagine myself as being there. Me in Leeds – impossible! But I was. Then we went to Scotland, where I went to school in a little town in the mountains. Everything was beautiful there. But if you want to know how I came to Suffolk, you will have to hear about my grandfather Merriam Lloyd, who farmed the Dove. And if you haven't heard of him, then you're a newcomer yourself. He wasn't really a farmer, in fact he was a bicycle-shop owner by trade. He came to Suffolk in 1910 and bought the Dove for about £500. He was a bachelor who walked about with a gun – you know the sort. He was very independent and nobody could tell him anything. He knew it all. His farm wasn't much when he bought it, by all accounts, but it was a sight worse when the Second World War broke out. He hadn't done a thing except walk round it. Of course the War Ag. told him to plough up his meadows – told him! Of course, he wasn't having that. He took no notice. So they pushed him out. Some men came and literally pushed him out of his own front door. Then they brought some bits of furniture out and stood it round him on the lawn. They wanted the house, you see, for administration. Well, he went to live in a shepherd's hut in the orchard, where he stayed all through the war and doing absolutely nothing, of course, and the Dove was given to Jolly Beeston to farm. Jolly was nothing then but he's very, very big now. The war made him. He paid a florin a year on each acre for the Dove, just to make it legal. He ploughed it all up, ploughed all his own margins and wastes up, got subsidies – he was quids in. He was made. He's never looked back. The war put him on his feet and, do you know, although he didn't do one single stroke of work, it made my grandfather quite well off too. He was so lazy that he didn't fill-in his compensation claim forms until after 1951 – and he was still living in the shepherd's hut – but eventually they sent him £350 damages for putting Nissen huts in the Dove garden. So he had a good war. I don't blame the farmers for the war fortunes; I'm glad it happened. But, all the same, when I see their big cars and little swimming pools, and think how, before 1939, some of them were riding around on bikes and having to sell a calf on Tuesday to pay the men on Friday, well it is amazing. Some of them really suffered. They won't, they *can't* talk about the old days. Not because they are ashamed of them but because they were so badly hurt. Some of them can't rid themselves of little economical habits which can't possibly matter any more. Like Mr Clary, who must be worth a couple of hundred thousand, but who still sweeps the last drop of barley from the barn floor himself.

The war and the price of the land going up has made them all. And good; the land shouldn't rot. But it has also made it quite impossible for someone like myself to go into arable farming. The net profit on an acre of barley is about £10 and wheat about £17. Put this against land worth £300 an acre with ingoing valuation – it's about three per cent! Well you can't do it. Everybody is trying to manage bigger acres with bigger machines and less labour. Put it like this, to manage 200 acres you need two tractors, but with two tractors you could also manage 250–80 acres. You see, you have to try and spread the machine cost over as many acres as you can.

Then you have another problem – labour. Although labour is being cut and fewer and fewer men are needed to work the farms, it is still hard to find them. They are all going away from the land. An intelligent young married chap simply can't afford to be a farm-worker. Those who stay, the bright ones, I mean, stay because they really love the land. A young man like this can be found working all hours of the sun. This love-the-work business is all very well but sooner or later these clever, hard-working countrymen will have to be seen as experts, and paid accordingly. Otherwise they will simply have to drift off into the service industries like the Milk Marketing Board and the seed and fertilizer merchants.

I am lucky, I work for myself. When I left school at fifteen, my father let me have four acres of his ground rent free. So I got a job on a farm at £4 7s. a week. I gave mother £2 for my keep, put £2 in the bank and spent the seven bob. I never spent notes, only silver. I saved for about six months and then I had enough to buy three little pigs. I fattened them, sold them, and bought five. One of these was a gilt. £45 it cost me. I've still got this same gilt today. She's had ten litters and I'm very fond of her. I kept on selling off the litters because this makes a quick turnover. You buy a gilt in pig and take the pigs off her when they are eight weeks old and sell them as stores, and the money turns over nice and quick. You've got to pay for the gilt's keep from the minute you've bought her. You must turn her out on the meadow, put her in pig, care for her. Anyway, eventually I've built up until I now have thirty sows, which are as many as I can manage. I daren't do any more to it, not yet, anyway.

I've got a boar. I haven't been too choosey about him because I'm not fattening. A good boar is very expensive – about £90. Mine was cheap – he cost me £37. He's a pretty good boy.

I like the work so much. I have to do it all. So I wouldn't step the sows up any more. I feel that the more you get the less well you can do the work. So many people say, 'Ah, we've done very well, we've made so many pounds profit, so look what would happen if we got 100 pigs! We would be home and dry.' But it doesn't work out like this, because you either have to pay wages or not be able to give so many pigs the same attention which you can give a few.

I breed Essex pigs, which are very good mothers. They produce a blue pig which sells pretty well and is very hardy. I do all the buying and selling myself, and have this sense of freedom. It is wonderful. Freedom, if you would like to know about it, is getting up at 6.30 every morning, having a wash and breakfast and being outside by seven to start feeding. I feed all the pregnant sows on the meadow by throwing sow-cake down on the grass. I'm very lucky, I've got this little stream running through my land, so I water from it. After feeding and watering, I start cleaning out. I do it twice a day. The old traditional method was to clean out once a week but it is much simpler to do a bit each day and work right through. Then I water everybody and go home to eat a proper breakfast. After breakfast, I might go to market at Campsey Ash with the pigs which are fit to sell. I like to watch them being sold. If they don't make the right price, back they come! I used to have a man cart for me but now I take them in a little pick-up which I managed to buy. I'm not very fond of people who live by carting animals around, they tend to knock them about and pigs especially look very bad when they are bruised.

The market is full of dealers forming a ring. They're whispering at the tops of their voices, as you might say. It's 'bid for this' and 'don't bid for them'. But if there happens to be a scarcity they will bid for anything. They go mad for pigs. I like to introduce a smart pig right off the teat at eight weeks. You can actually take a pig off at three weeks, but I'm not very fond of this practice. You get five litters in two years with three-week weanings – two and a half litters against two of the eight-week method. But it is a very expensive system because you have to buy a special milk substitute feed for them which works out at £70 a ton. The best way I know is the outdoor weaning system, with your pigs out on grass in little bale shelters. You build up disease if you keep pigs in the same building year in, year out.

I have dinner at twelve, do all kinds of jobs until half-past four, then it's feeding again. I have tea at six and at eleven, just before I tuck in myself, I have a walk round to see if everybody is cosy. Pigs are funny animals and like a sense of being cared for.

It's a long day but I don't mind. I've never had a holiday since I left school. I have been out of the county now and then but I always get back the same day in time to feed. I honestly don't mind. I think that once you've started this animal business, you've started a way of life within yourself. I couldn't live without a pig, which might seem a funny statement to you. I work every Sunday. It seems worse when you're talking about it than when you're doing it. East Anglia is now *the* pig area and the chief thing about myself is that I tend not to join in the huge Suffolk pig world. I may see it all differently later on. Maybe.

It is a very precarious business. Pigs are a difficult stock to control. They don't stay steady, they waver from surplus to shortage. What happens is that, in February, the Government assesses what the nation's pig requirements will be for the next year and guarantee what they call the 'middle band'. The middle band consists of between six and eight million pigs. It has a guaranteed price. This year it was 45s. 5d. a score. If production falls under this band, the Government steps up the guarantee to encourage production; anything over, and the price just drops off. This is how it is supposed to work, but it doesn't unfortunately. There will be pig surpluses at the end of 1968 – even if foot-and-mouth really hits us. At the moment about one pig in 200 is being slaughtered. It is nothing! One gilt will produce twenty pigs a year. You could, if you wished to, keep the ten or so gilts out of this twenty and breed them – and so on. I don't belong to any of the groups like Porcofram. I work alone and sell on the open market. I have to do this, it is the way I am. I am all right now but when the surplus time comes I shall get hit. The price on the open market will sink; I will know all too well that it would have paid me to be in the group.

Walls have really spoilt the pig market round here. When they first introduced their pig scheme they said, 'Right! produce a pig for us as fat as it is long!' They weren't interested in grading. They wanted a big pig of between 250–300 pounds – a heavy hog, a cutting pig. The legs of this pig went into hams, the rest into sausages and pies, and the fat into ice-cream. Well, eventually they got so much of this pig fat stored away into the hangers and Nissen huts of an aerodrome that they said, 'Right! We've got enough.' And so they packed their big pig scheme up – and a lot of pig-farmers came unstuck.

I am a member of the Young Farmers' Club. It is not a thriving club. A lot of these Y.F.C.s lack something, I don't know what exactly. They're made up of sixty per cent farmers' sons, thirty per cent young men from the service industries and a sprinkling of farm-workers' children. The service industry people are reps or officials. The reps join because it's the policy of the feeding stuffs and fertilizer firms to establish friendships between their young representatives and the boys who are soon going to own or manage farms. I joined to get to know people. No, this isn't exactly true; I joined to get an education. That was the real reason. We go on farm walks and that sort of thing. But the fact is that these clubs offer the working man's son very little. They cater for boys with £1,000 a year and a sports car. The clubs are rather snobbish and even if you don't care about snobbery you can't help seeing it. It is the bugbear of the clubs, spoiling everything. To tell you the truth, I feel completely out of it. Some of the members simply don't want to associate with you. You are not in their class, they think. They have been to Framlingham or Woodbridge School. Or even to Felstead. They either won't or can't conceal that they are 'different'. I tolerate all this simply because of the educational side of it but I have learnt that if you don't have certain kinds of clothes, a car like theirs and spare money, then you don't just belong – even if you're a member! All the clubs have this atmosphere. I keep away from the strictly social activities and only attend the walks and talks. Very few girls come to the clubs – at this particular branch, anyway. I often wish that I had joined the Ipswich branch. The atmosphere could be better there. It is so hard to get accepted. I never understood anything about this until I joined the club. I don't want to 'get in', as they say; I just want to go and be ordinary. I am the only member of this club who isn't a farmer's son – my father is a farm-worker – or a rep. The gentlemen-farmers' sons are quite different. For instance, they arrive in sloppy jumpers and jeans

when everybody else wears Simpson's hacking jackets. These boys
haven't a clue what it is all about and obviously can't tell me from the
rest. But Suffolk isn't really a snobbish place. I wouldn't like you to
think that.

The Agricultural Training Centre is a far better meeting place than
any Y.F.C. I belong to the Stockman's Club there – what a difference
in the atmosphere! It is a wonderful club, really useful. It costs 5s. a
year to join – and 25s. a year to belong to the Y.F.C.

Working on my own tends to cut me off from people. I am involved
in the little circle around me but, so far, I have never managed to make
a successful move out of this circle. Even with a car.

I do quite a bit of reading. I have read a novel sometimes but most of
my reading is connected with pigs. It would do me good to broaden my
outlook, I suppose. The trouble with my life is that, except for Mr
Austin, nobody has ever talked to me about anything except farming.
I watch television but if you look back on television – it is the saddest
thing. I like the News. And documentary programmes, like that old film
about the Russian Revolution.

We often have discussions at the Y.F.C. but the members, although
they are not much more than boys, have already learned to shut their
eyes to what is going on in the world. They have firm opinions about
everything. They can't debate, they make statements such as 'The
Americans are doing a good job in Vietnam, stopping Communism'.
Full stop. What is the point of arguing? they seem to say. When I told
my father he said, 'Funf has spoken' – it is an old wartime joke. I told
the Y.F.C. that the Vietnamese were really just farmers in revolution,
but nobody spoke – except to say that the Americans are doing a good
job, etc. I am astonished that they are able to hold such strong, solid
opinions about things which they can't possibly know a thing about. A
lot of them are the sons and grandsons of self-made men who worked
very hard until the war made them rich.

I am a member of N.U.A.W. I think it is a very bad thing when
young men don't join the Agricultural Union. Everybody connected
with modern farming should be united in this way. The pity is that the
young men are affected by the 'beaten' men. But the beaten men are
all so old now – over fifty, so why worry what they say? You take
George Annerley, he has the fear on him still. Farmer-fear – it went all
through Suffolk. George thinks that he is betraying his farmer if he
joins the Union, and I know plenty like him, men who would sooner
admit to anything than that they were socialists. Catch them putting an
election poster in their cottage window! The young men are absolutely

different. They speak their minds. The boys who go to the Training Centre aren't fools; they know that they are able to do specialist work on the farms and that a good worker isn't going to be sacked because of his politics. A good worker can get a farming job in a day. A lot of us think outside all the newspaper talk and believe in the Labour Party – not just the Prime Minister, but in the socialist movement. But I haven't very strong political feelings myself and I am not an outright socialist. I just want to go forward and to stop this everlasting looking back.

I am recruiting for the Union. I got six members in one week! All from one farm, and not one of them had thought about joining before. One of the older chaps said that he couldn't see what good the Union did because it wasn't getting us the money up. But how I look at it is this, unless there is a complete and intelligent new support for the Union, how can you expect it to work? Too many of the members do nothing but look back into the past. The past is finished. Over. Whatever happens, it will never be like that again. These old farm men make you feel so damned miserable. Be what you are, say what you have to say. Stop staring over your shoulder. Laugh at old Sammy Eden. Do you know what happened on his farm during the election before last? All his men stuck red rosettes on the tractors and things and drove around all day before he spotted them. That night he sacked the whole bunch – and then three days later he had to re-employ them all again because he knew he'd got the best men in the whole neighbourhood.

I don't feel all that personally attached to Suffolk. I often fancy Scotland. I dream of Scotland. I think it would suit me. It was the Scottish farmers who came down here before the war and worked harder than the Suffolk men, and began to put new life into the place. A lot of these men farmed on the rock. Think of farming on the rock and then drawing a plough through this rich earth! How surprised they must have been. But I don't think a lot about the future. I find life quite enjoyable. What I would like would be to farm like the Barber brothers. There are four of them and they've got about sixty acres each. They aren't mechanized but they are wonderful farmers. They follow the Norfolk four-course plan of wheat, barley, beans and roots. Mind you, they live virtually hand-to-mouth, as you might say, yet comfortable. Their fields are beautifully clean. Everything is traditional, but without the struggle and misery. I would love a little traditional farm, plenty of muck, plenty of grass. I would go right in and say, 'For the first two or three years I shall rob this land and get a return'. When I talk of 'robbing', I mean that where there's plenty of grass and muck there will also be plenty of phosphate and potash in the soil. My fertilizers would be cut right down. I could rob and get away with a good start, and probably take off three crops of wheat before I had to start spending real money.

East Anglian country people work very hard. The young men will do anything to make a start. The working-class village boy gets on because he won't mind what he does or how long he does it to get a start. A lot of boys start with a partnership. When he has proved that he can make a bit of money, another young man will go in with him and the pair of them won't marry or spend a penny for several years. They live very carefully. They will sell beansticks to the gardens on the Ipswich estates. They don't have such a strong sense of missing things as the town boys have. Not many country boys round here have record-players, so pop music doesn't 'take' in the same way as it does in London. The boys will listen to the music on the radio but they won't buy records. And most of them won't buy the fashions because one of the things about a village is that you never give anyone anything to talk about if you can help it. That is why I admire Hughie. Do you know Hughie? Hair like a girl and trousers so tight you wonder he can breathe. What a nerve he's got! The old women clack about him and the men whistle. But he takes no notice at all. But why shouldn't he do as he likes?

I haven't got a girl-friend. Plenty of time. And I'm not promiscuous either – what a word! Sometimes I go to the dances in Ipswich but it is very, very hard to get a partner. The girls come with their boy-friends and won't dance with anybody else. The boys are mostly mods. Not many boys from the village go to these dances. I have also been to the Saturday-night dances at Framlingham but it seems virtually impossible to meet a girl in this way. The village girls like to get married very young but the boys don't. Many of the boys don't want to marry until they are about thirty, although plenty of them have to long before then. I have a friend whose girl made all the running before they were wed, now he has to beg for it. I sometimes get lonely for girls.

I have been to London three times but have always returned the same day. I have never slept there. It means getting up very early in the morning, getting all the work done in advance, having a bath, getting there – real drudgery! But it is only once a year. I go to the Smithfield Show. But I think I will try and take a proper holiday this year. You might say that I have had an awful warning! It was like this. A chap I know down the lane, a very hard-working chap who started up like me, only twenty or more years ago, has just had to sell half his farm. It seems that he was so busy working, saving, making sacrifices, that he forgot how to bargain. So here he was, buying his clothes from the second-hand shop in Ipswich, getting streaky bacon ends from Sainsbury's at twopence a pound, never having a day off and working like a black. This was how he got on when he started but now that he's getting old – forty-five or more – he has become lackadaisical in the strangest way. You would think that he was working for somebody else instead of himself. You could say, 'This hay is £20 a ton' – and although it might be the biggest rubbish, he'd buy it! Everybody was having him on. Things began to fall down on his 120-acre farm. Then there was a creditors' meeting. It was a wonderful thing for him. He saw the light. He said to me after last harvest, 'Fenner the contractor tried to charge me 7*d*. a bale for this baling hay. A bit dear, ain't it? I said. I cut him down and got it for 5*d*.' Now the deed of agreement has been drawn up, this small farmer has become a saved man. He's paying cash for everything. He's a saved man. Redeemed by the auditors! So perhaps I shall get to Scotland for a week this summer – let my brother look after the pigs. I mustn't get like old Charlie. I am getting on. I shall be twenty-two on Valentine's Day.

But I am forgetting, I do quite a lot of things. I shoot. Commotion – and not just for the birds. I've got these four acres and if I see a pheasant on them, I might shoot him. But no sooner than the gun is heard there is somebody rushing round, wanting to know this, wanting to know that. It is nothing to do with them. They are my fields, it is my gun. I have a licence for it. The pheasant is the god, you see. People like me aren't supposed to pot at the god. But I do – I have just done so. With any luck I am just picking him up when this face appears over the hedge. 'I thought I heard a shot,' says this man. He looks as if he could burst or faint or something. He wants to shout, 'Sacrilege! sacrilege!'

There is something else I do – silversmithing. I learnt it at evening classes. I have made a beer-mug and a chalice.

Bruce Buckley · aged seventeen · forge apprentice: Thomas Dix · aged seventeen · farm-worker

Bruce and Thomas (Tompo) are the classic mates of the 'Til-death-do-us-part' kind and are at present at the zenith of the bosom-pal stage. Time, with its steadying proprieties, is the only thing which will prevent them colliding joyously like a couple of ponies whenever they meet.

Mrs Sullivan pushed them into the same double desk on their first day at school when they were five and told them to look after each other. An arranged mateship which works has followed. At eleven, they were both pulled out of a hole in the ice, drowned to all accounts. At thirteen they ran away to hitch-hike. Where? That was the problem. So after two days of it they walked home. These two events seem to have made them staid, cautious and quite gratuitously contented.

Bruce is thin and fair. His long, pale neck grows out of his leather jacket like an iris stylosa stem out of glossy damp, dark mould. He is watchful, sharp. He thinks quite a bit of himself but his friend manages to rub the edge off the worst of Bruce's conceit without his realizing it. Tompo, in fact, makes Bruce more likeable than he would be if left on his own.

Tompo himself is square and dark, with a ready-to-smile furry, red-brown face and an expansive, roly-poly body. A plain, good-natured Morland character. Both boys giggle a lot and exude a challenging kind of mindless delight. They have an occasional way of tumbling over each other like cubs which seems to irritate older people, who frown. Both have established reputations for accomplishing prodigious amounts of work. They chat cheerfully across each other in an amiably disconnected sort of way. Their world is small and they are determined to keep it so.

TOMPO: What do we do? We read books....

BRUCE: I don't have much time so I read small books....

TOMPO: We've been to Woodbridge this afternoon, just to walk round, and that. We're going to the pictures in Ipswich tonight. We're going to see a film called *Casino Royale*. We only go to the pictures in the winter; in the summer we like to get our motor-bikes out and zoom around. We go into all the other villages and drink Coke and shandy in their pubs. We don't look at things much. I like to see the birds but I can't say that I'm very interested in them. Let them fly about, I say. Suffolk is a great place for birds. Everybody knows this.

BRUCE: Last night I went brushing for Colonel Eldon. They got 210 pheasants. I'm not a good shot myself, I tend to miss everything. The Colonel rears about 600 birds and holds four shoots a year. Yesterday, there were eight guns and fifteen brushers. I like to meet the guns and brush for them because they pay me pretty well. I get 36s., a bottle of beer and a packet of cigs. I like birds too.

TOMPO: We've been friends for years and years and years.

BRUCE: I earn £6 flat. This is what I take. Motor mechanic boys would be lucky to get £3 4s.

TOMPO: Sometimes, when my mates have been with me chopping out sugar-beet, I've made as much as £15 clear. This is on piece-work, mind you. But my usual wage without deductions is £5 14s. 6d. I stick it into my wallet, you know. When I was young I put it in the bank. Now I keep it in my wallet in case I need to spend it. It is nice to have money. I bought this motor-bike six months ago.

BRUCE: Girls take your money – Tompo's had nine girls.

TOMPO: Well, not *had* them....

BRUCE: You *had* one of them –

TOMPO: He gets a bonus on top of his wages – £4 5s. a month. It's a share-out of the profits which the forge makes every month. They must be doing pretty well if they can afford to give that much back.

BRUCE: There's a girl in Saxmundham who would be easy for Tompo but he won't look at her.

TOMPO: Who's talking about girls?

BRUCE: It's all right for you. (Pause) I didn't have to apply for the job at the forge, you know – *they* asked *me*. I'm glad that they did.

TOMPO: I started going to the Agricultural Training Centre last September. The term starts in September and ends in March, so that we have six months off during the busy time on the farm. I am doing a three-year course because I am an apprentice but some farm boys only go for two years. I work for the farmer who hires land from my father, so I am really working my father's farm for another man. I am particularly interested in farm machinery. We have 600 acres and two tractors, and we mostly grow spring barley. Then it will be winter wheat. We have forty acres of sugar-beet and 100 acres of peas for Birdseye.

BRUCE: I once found an old, old book dated 1874. It was full of recipes to cure horses and oxen. It had a cure for foot-and-mouth disease. The master read it and said, 'Rubbish'. My father, who was a horse-man, read it and said nothing.

TOMPO: When I was a little boy I used to come outside and watch the horses on the farm. There were six, then there were five, then there were none. I didn't care. I'd sooner have a tractor any day. This is just my opinion, you understand. They just stick you on a tractor now and say, 'plough the field up'. Easy! You stick your old wheel down and – plough! Who worries if it isn't straight?

BRUCE: Arnie.

TOMPO: Oh, Arnie! Bugger Arnie. (Mimicking) 'When I was your age, I didn't get five or six quid a week, I got five or six bob!' Arnie's old. He's fifty-four.

BRUCE: We shall be fifty-four one day – *in the same month.*

TOMPO: Well, let's hope we both live to see it. We're learning Old Time Dancing at the youth club; that should come in handy. It is a very big club and people come to it from miles around on their bikes. They are nearly all village boys.

BRUCE: And girls.

TOMPO: And girls. Saturday night is the village night out. In the summer we all zoom off to Felixstowe on our bikes. We don't swim there. We swim in the river at Melton. Did you know that there are a tidy few swimming pools in the gardens round here? The farmers built them – I don't know why because they can't swim. We go to Wimbledon to watch the stock-car racing. I used to be mechanic to a stock-car driver. We also go to the wrestling at Felixstowe. It looks pretty terrible but it isn't really. It is all put on. Anyway, the men don't wrestle well if they're not being televised, and you can't blame them. What do we like doing best of all? – motor-bike scrambling. This is the most favourite thing in the whole village. We all belong to a motor-bike club – there are more than fifty of us – and we all go off to the scrambles at Blaxhall and Wakes Colne. The club costs us 10s. a year and we meet every Tuesday night. Our leather clothes are expensive but they keep us warm. We have ordinary haircuts, as you can see. Maybe mine is fairly long. It is just to keep my head warm. When it begins to blow in the wind, then I begin to think about the barber. There's some very fancy dressing now, isn't there? People who want to do it should do it. Why not?

BRUCE: Have you seen Hughie?

TOMPO: Hughie's O.K.

BRUCE: I didn't say he wasn't, did I?

TOMPO: You're a nut.

BRUCE: (Amazed) *I* am?

TOMPO: (of Bruce) What would you do with him? – you tell me. Uproar. Tina, a sheepdog, joins in. Bruce's mother rushes in. 'Clear out you together now! Whenever are you going to grow up? Grow up, do!'

Anthony Summer ·
aged twenty-three · shepherd

A tall, fair, easy-going young man. Married at nineteen, he has two sons and an air of calm authority. He is the kind of person who is put in charge of things and who gets left with decisions. He works on the biggest progressive farm in the neighbourhood and seems either to have turned his back successfully on all which remains of the malaise and emotions of the old scene or is genuinely unaware of them. Probably the latter. He is an elegant dresser, with thick stylishly cut hair and an air of meticulousness which doesn't desert him even when he is 'giving a hand with the beet'. He runs a Ford Anglia, nursing it through the lanes with one casual arm flung across the wheel, and lives in a new estate cottage which is surrounded by about an acre of well-kept garden. The Summer family, seen together, generate the glowing ideal of a family in a breakfast cereal advertisement, plus the added wonder of being actual. Everything they possess, everything they are is fresh, new. It seems just that Tony should be something as Arcadian as a shepherd, even allowing for the intensification of the pastoral scene. The village says, 'That young Tony, he could get a job anywhere'.

*

I was born in Akenfield. All my family is here, my mother, my uncles, my aunties and my granny. But not my father – he was a sailor and was drowned when I was a baby. The ship he was on was torpedoed during the last war as it was sailing through the Dodecanese Islands and he has no grave. When the Greeks put up a memorial to all the British men who were killed helping them, the Legion paid my mother's and my fares to see the unveiling. I was sixteen. The princesses of Greece shook my hand and I walked through Athens. Greece is a very nice place. I think about it. You get such contrasts there. I would like to go back to it. There are no middle people, as in Suffolk, only rich and poor. We drank goat's milk there – just as we have always done at home. I was pleased to see the Greeks drinking goat's milk because it is free from bruc and very good for asthma. I also drank ouzo and ate honey, and sometimes I thought how strange it was that I was walking about in Athens because my father was in the Greek sea.

This was the year I went to Chadacre Agricultural College, which is one of the oldest of the agricultural training places. I had done a year on a farm before going there. It was just a job at first and then I began to like it. My mother said, 'If you're going farm-working, you're going to do it properly. You are going to be a trained man – so no arguing.' So I applied and was accepted. There were about fifty students there and they mostly came from Suffolk, Norfolk and Essex. Nobody specialized in anything: we each took the general course of management, sheep, cows and machinery. The College has changed a lot since it was founded and most of the boys who go there are much better educated than they were before the war. They are nearly all farmers' sons or village boys like myself – hardly anybody from a town.

There were only a few sheep on the farm when I started here at fifteen, then, when I got back from being trained at the college, the farmer took on some more and we had about 250 all told. We did so well out of these that we lost our heads and went straight up to 1,000! Then the profit margin dropped and we soon cut back to 500. This was a good number; it meant that I could look after all of them myself – plus William. William is my dog. He was bought by the farm but he thinks he is my dog, and I think he is too. He does a good half of the work. He can do anything. He can put the whole flock through the footbath without my even being in the field, and he is fond of conversation.

The autumn is the beginning of the shepherd's year, as you might say. The tups go into the ewes about the first week in September. These aren't the proper tups; they just bring the ewes on. We call them teasers. It means that when you put in the proper tups the ewes are good and ready for them, and can be served in one bunch. Let them love together and they'll lamb together, and that will be convenient. A good ram will serve fifty ewes after the teasers have been with them for a month. I work it like this. I put half my proper tups in with the ewes for two days, then take them out and give them a rest while the other half have a go. Each ram has a harness full of crayon strapped round him, so that when he jumps he marks the ewe. I then know how many ewes are coming. I change the crayon – the raddle – every fifteen days. So the first raddle will be blue, then red. In the olden days they painted the jumped ewes with red ochre but now we have this system of telling. If all the ewes are covered the first fifteen days and none of them come back, then I take the tups out. I leave them roughly three periods to come over – about forty-five days all told.

I usually start lambing in mid-February, although one year I started as early as Christmas Day. It was much too soon. The grass wasn't ready so the lambs had to be kept indoors. The food bills were terrific! I don't have to help a great deal with the births, only be there. This is most important. I never leave the flock then, I am there all the time. I only call the vet if there is a big mishap, such as the womb coming out. I take each lamb away from its mother and do all the little odds and ends like. You can't raise every lamb which is born, there must be some loss. I try and arrange things so that each ewe has two lambs. This shouldn't be difficult if each ewe has been well flushed before the tup services her and has had good pasture. You see, before tupping time the ewes are kept on a bare pasture and then, just a week before the rams are put in, I put them on a high plane of nutrition which is supposed to bring down more ovaries. And so two eggs will come down, and I have had three and even four. I had five sets of quads last year but they were poor little runty things.

I castrate the male lambs, the little tups, about an hour after they have been born. They say that what you've never had, you never miss. I wonder. I do it with rubber rings. It used to be done much later. The tails used to be cut off with a hot iron and the balls nicked out with the shepherd's teeth. He ate well that day. But the tups still go behind a bit after they have been castrated. They get thin. It pulls them down. It is a surprising thing to happen to you when you have just come into the world on a spring morning. And, of course, I cut the tails off later on – to prevent fly-strike in the summer-time.

I like to sell the first crop of lambs at about twelve or thirteen weeks old when they weigh about seventy-five pounds. There would be about thirty-five lambs in this crop. Some go to the local market and some to the meat-traders – British Beef. The late lambs are sold about September and a few are carried over the winter and not sold until the following spring. But I haven't got enough grass to keep the store lambs through the winter.

I did my first shearing this summer. I sheared 500 ewes. The wife came out and rolled the wool for me and it took us just under the week – that was everything. We took the ewes out from the lambs about seven in the morning and worked right through until about nine at night. We worked every hour that was possible. I used electric shears and now and then I gave some poor old sheep a nip, but nothing as bad as would have happened had I been using the old-fashioned shears. The year [1967] was better than average for the price of wool.

Nobody tries to keep a really big sheep farm in East Anglia these days. Sheep are fitted in with the crop rotations and are just part of the farm. My sheep are put on to rye grass and they also have hay and pea silage, carrot wastage, etc. The ewes also get two pounds of concentrates each when they lamb in order to prevent pregnancy toxaemia. But they get things wrong with them, bad feet mostly. Foot-rot and flies, these are the bad things with sheep. I put them through a footbath twice a week. There is very little intensive sheep-farming in the villages round here although I hear that somebody is trying it out near Diss. He has his sheep on slats, like calves. Poor sheep! that is what I say. I bring my sheep in during the winter but they're out in the air all the rest of the year.

I sometimes think of shepherding in a big way – all young shepherds do. Here we buy-in old ewes and sell them out for meat. But I quite like the idea of breeding and selling pedigree animals. And I'd like to show. This farm only shows in the lamb carcass competitions which means that you show three sheep, then one is picked out, killed and its carcass is judged. I'd sooner show live. My best friend is a Dorset shepherd and he's got a pedigree flock to show down there. I envy him rather.

I belong to Suffolk but I wouldn't mind moving. I once even thought of going to Australia but then I thought to myself, 'Supposing you get out there and you don't like it – then what will you do?' You need a lot of money to start in Australia. All the same, it is always in the back of my mind to do a bit of farming on my own. I'd like to own something, even if it is only a little small-holding where I can keep pigs. Being on my own is a dream which I want to come true. I don't want to get old and look back and think that I have been looking after somebody else's sheep all my life. But land is dear here – too dear. So I don't know what will happen.

It is easy on the farms against what it used to be. The old men wore their bodies to death but we only wear out a few machines. We all get on very well together on the farm. Ages don't count. There is an old shepherd who still works here part-time and he has helped me a lot. He lends me books and tells me many things. The young men are very fond of him because he is so interesting. It is pleasant here but, all the same, I dream, I make plans. I think you must have some ambition – not just carry on. I mustn't get old and look back at nothing. If you can look back on a farm which you have built up, that is something. If you haven't struggled to do something different – better – by the time you are thirty it is all up with you.

We're all interested in better wages and I think we might have more – I really do. But I have to remember that I've got an up-to-date house for only 6s. a week – it would cost 50s. in Ipswich. The N.U.A.W. isn't all that strong round here – not every farm-worker belongs to it by a long chalk. I don't. I don't believe in it myself. The Union men are always trying to get all the farm men together but they haven't done so yet. It is because farm men are lonely workers and individualistic – not like men in factories. I do my sheep, John does his cows, we're mostly alone and we are happy like this. I don't mean that I don't like other people, only that I am happiest on my own. Of course it makes you think a bit. I think about Vietnam and about Hollywood stars being politicians and the Common Market. I think that nobody is going to benefit from any of these things and that they are bad. I think we need to steer clear of America *and* Europe, only how we are going to manage if we do, stuck out here in the sea, I can't imagine. I have never heard a farmer talk about the Common Market.

I do a good deal more than the shepherding on this farm. I help with the harvest and from May until September I work on the peas, and then I go on the bean machine. Although I am in charge of the flock of Border Leicesters, Suffolks and Kerries – 500 ewes and fifteen rams altogether – I fill-in with other work whenever I can. Peas for a frozen-food firm are the big thing here. Their men go round the county and tell the farmers what to do. It is, 'You'll drill your peas today, Mr T.', and then, three days later, they'll return and say, 'You'll drill another ten acres today' – and so it goes on, so that when it comes to harvesting the whole county isn't ready at once. Each farmer gets a bit of early crop and a bit of late. The peas are cut, laid out in swathes and then loaded on to lorries and rushed to the factory. There are four pea-cutters and four pea-loaders round here; the farmers share in the buying of them. Each pea area combines like this. The areas are given the names of colours. Ours is the Red area and covers about 1,000 acres of frozen food crops. The peas are cut by two gangs working twelve-hour shifts day and night. It all has to be done very quick – vines and peas are rushed to the Lowestoft factory. I drive the lorry then, backwards and forwards to the coast all night and as hard as I can go. When I have tipped the load into the factory, I drive round to the silage shoot and collect the stripped vines and bring them back to the farm. But the beans are stripped in the field. Some farmers drop out of the frozen pea contracts and new ones come in. And we all get a bit fed-up with doing things to the orders of the firm. They might say, 'We can't cut yours until we've done so-and-so's', and by the time they arrive the peas could have gone too far, so they have to be sold for seed. It wouldn't be total loss but it is still loss.

I keep doing most of the time. I might watch telly on a nice wet night but usually I get outside in the garden and keep doing. I mend the house. I go fishing in the river. It is a good pike river. It is a good fish to eat, it tastes like cod. We usually gut it, bung it full of salt and soak it well over night, then we bake it. It is excellent. Perch are also good to eat but roach aren't very sharp. I read about fishing and farming, and I also read the *Farmer's Weekly*. I used to play rugby but I don't now because my wife says that she isn't going to have me keep getting bashed-up just for a game. I got into so many accidents. Now I play table-tennis and bowls. The country is all right if you can get about. You've got to have a car. As long as you've got something to get about in, the country's all right.

I'm never more than 200 yards away from the flock. A shepherd is always close – he always has been, hasn't he?

Roger Adlard · aged thirty-one · factory farmer

My father bought me a farm when I left school because I had decided that it was the only life for me. It was in my blood. I never wanted to do anything else. I come from a family of farmers. Great-grandfather farmed and his fathers before him, for as long as anybody can remember. Some of my family were Suffolk millers and carters, and some ran shops in the village. My grandfather was one of the first people to go to an agricultural training institution – at Chadacre. It was hard for him then and it is hard for me now. We bought this small place to give me a start but things have gone from bad to worse where I am concerned because we have never really had enough land.

You see, some time in 1953, when we bought this farm, the price of land was in the region of £50 an acre, although it could have been as much as £100 an acre; it all depended on the quality. And the agricultural wage in those days was about £6 a week. With land at £50 an acre it was possible – even if you only earned £6 a week – to think of saving up to buy an acre. But now, with wages at £10 a week and land at £300 an acre, there is no hope of extension. It is out of the question and utterly impossible. This is the sort of position which has made the small farm a trap for the young man. The smaller the farm, the greater the price per acre. If you imagine growing corn and realize the little return you are going to get from it, then you can't possibly pay more than £200 an acre. But land value has just gone sky-high. I can never expand. A lot of small men like myself are just packing-up, selling their little farms, getting jobs in Ipswich. You can't blame them. Why work and work, and save and save, and never have the slightest chance of adding to your land?

I do pigs and poultry. It is intensive farming. It is not what I wanted to do. I dreamed of being an arable farmer. This was one of those glorious boyhood dreams of harvest fields, hot sun and of being perched up high on a tractor. I feel that the kind of farming I do now isn't quite 'right'. Certainly it isn't satisfying. I long to do arable; I still dream of it. But where would I get the kind of money for even the smallest possible arable farm? What I have actually got is a farmhouse, its out-buildings and ten acres, all of which have been sold away from one of the big estates.

At first we sold pigs and fattened them. We then found that the old type of farm building wasn't suitable for this so we had to put up a modern factory and do the fattening in this. We think of it as a machine. Everything has to be in a straight line, which was something you never found in the old buildings. They were not only crooked, but too high, too wide, too unaccommodating for the thing we had to do with these animals. After a while, I decided that the thing to do was to produce weaners and sell them to other people for fattening because if you fatten in a small way it is a fiddling business, and, equally, if you are a big arable farmer who happens to keep a few pigs, weaning is a fiddling business. A big arable man doesn't want to have to bother with sows. His arable system will be run with economic one-man efficiency, maybe, and he will want what stock he has to be equally efficient. The idea on these modern farms is that no breeding goes on. It is not a new idea; farming is simply splitting up into specialist groups and getting away from the concept of the old mixed farm. The old mixed farmer had a few hens, a few sows, a few bullocks, a little sugar-beet, a few greens, a little orchard – just about everything. It was all so cosy. What ever you do now you've got to do it big. I mean – twelve sows! We've got sixty and we're still not nearly as large a unit as I would want.

Group-farming has hit this area. The group concept is a useful one. I sell my products through a group called Framlingham Farmers Ltd – through their subsidiary called Porcofram, which is the pig group. I am a weaner-producer of the pig group of Porcofram. This is not riding the tractor in the corn, is it! We're all members of this group, which is a company. We all have shares in it and we accept a certain amount of control in connection with buying and selling. So when I sell my pigs to Farmer A, I sell through the group. I tell them, 'Right, for the next few weeks I will have so many pigs per week and that they will be between forty-five and seventy-five pounds in weight'. These pigs are shipped off to Farmer A and he fattens them. He pays the group, which imposes a levy and which then pays me as the weaner-producer. That is how it is done.

There is a certain amount of control in the type of boar which you must use. The kind of pig which I have is called a hybrid which has Landrace, Wessex and Large White in it. It is a cross-bred pig producing a heavy hog, and these are mostly sold to Walls Bacon Factory, who are the large curers. The heavy hog is not a bacon big, although they make bacon from it; it is a cutter-pig. You can use it for a number of things. It is a dual-purpose pig. There are three different pigs in the butcher's trade. The 'butcher's pig' is a light pork pig going between five and six score dead, the 'bacon pig' goes between seven and eight score dead and the heavy hog goes about ten score dead. But I have a feeling that in time the big bacon-factory men will believe they have a better pig in the heavy hybrid hog than in all these. They will be able to do everything with it. That is the way things are going. It is a fast-growing pig which gets very fat and it can be sent to the bacon factory within 190 days from its birth – about six months old. A pig would normally live about six or seven years, but with our pigs it is a short life – and a happy one, we hope!

Gestation occurs in a gilt at four months old. It runs outside during this period and then it is brought inside to farrow. The young stay on the sow for six weeks and then she goes to the boar again. The running around began on grass but it is now bare earth – mud. There is a move afoot to keep them indoors all the while, and this will come, I have no doubt.

What do I think of the morals of factory farming? It is a question I am very sceptical about. I don't know about the factory-calf men; one hears strange stories about these people. But I keep hens in batteries, which is the same kind of thing and which people say is very cruel, but as I have worked with hens and have a certain knowledge of them, I don't really think it makes any difference to them. Pigs are different. A pig is more of an individual, more human and in many ways a strangely likeable character. Pigs have strong personalities and it is easy to get fond of them. I am always getting fond of pigs and I feel a bit conscious-stricken that one day I must put them inside for their whole lives. Yet, if you start to work out how much a pig walks about and how much time he just spends lying down and sleeping, you wonder if he is going to be worse off if he is confined all the time. Pigs are very clean animals but, like us, they all are different; some will need cleaning out after half a day and some will be neat and tidy after three days. Some pigs are always in a mess and won't care. Pigs are very interesting people and some of them can leave quite a gap when they go off to the bacon factory.

There are an awful lot of petitions going about concerned with cruelty to animals. They are usually got up by people who keep pets confined in flats and I am not sure that such folk are entitled to hold these opinions. They cause a lot of trouble to us. But I suppose that one must be democratic and allow them to have their opinions. I do have moral qualms but I also know that everything has got to go this way. Dreams of the past, like my dreams of cutting the corn in the sun, have got to be abandoned. Farming is not this lackadaisical business of yesterday. Yet I think of my grandfather and his father, and I think that although they had small profits for so much hard work, they had a carefree life.

All our factory animals have first-class veterinary treatment – that is something they didn't have in the past – and their food is far, far superior to what animals once had to eat on a farm. Of course, you've got all the additives to make them get fat quickly. But then we have all kinds of additives in *our* food. Take bread, it isn't natural bread, there are all sorts of things in it. It is bought all cut-up in cellophane and is horrible, but we eat it. We eat it because it is the food of our time.

My factory farm is a farm of our time. We have got 9,000 chickens in cages. Four years ago this would have been a lot but today it borders on the small. The battery-hen men are failing; those who have failed during the last couple of years are those who just kept 1–2,000 birds. If you run a battery-chicken farm entirely on your own you need to have at least 5,000 birds in order to make a living. I can remember the day when we could make £1 per bird profit each year; now you're jolly lucky if you can make 2s. 6d. profit on a bird in a year. 1967 has been a very bad year indeed for the egg-sellers and a lot of people aren't making any money at all. It is high input, high output. The foodstuffs present the most fantastic bill – £12–15,000. Our capital turnover on a nine-acre factory farm is higher than that on a 200-acre arable farm.

When the chickens are sold off they go to a processor who buys them live and who leaves you with a clear house in which to begin again. Most of them go into tinned soups. The old hens are best for soups because if you have a stringy old hen a lump of its flesh will remain in the soup after the rendering process. People who eat tinned soup like to find these lumps because they prove to them that the soup is made from real chicken. The feathers are no use because the chickens are wet-plucked, so there is only a mess. We don't bother with feathers. We buy new chicks from one of the six huge hybrid chick-rearing companies. We take them as day-olds and expect to lose five per cent to 'point of lay' – within the first sixteen weeks, that is. I take in just over 1,000 a month for nine or ten months. The pundits don't advise doing this; I do it because it happens to suit my equipment. I don't want a great 'harvest', as it were. I should have to employ extra temporary labour, usually untrained, so what use is that? By having 1,000 new chicks each month, I have 5,000 in a pipeline of various rearing moves.

I wouldn't dare to say how many hours I work a week. I don't start at the crack of dawn. Usually I don't get outside until 7.30, then I work till six. I work seven days a week but I might take Saturday afternoons off to play cricket. Sometimes I stop and think, 'All this work, this little profit – is it worth it?' Friends in Ipswich leave their work on Friday evening and don't see it again until Monday, but if I take a week-end off I have to get-forward all through the week, which means hard slogging. I have had three ten-day holidays in seven years. But in some ways I don't think I am missing life. I am thirty-one and I don't get as excited about things as I used to. As well as play cricket, I sail on the Deben and in the winter I go to evening classes to learn navigation and welding. I have never found time to read. I am a participant.

I don't have a strong village feeling. There is a little pub and that is where most people go, although I tend to avoid it. The village always wants to know what you are doing and if you don't have too much contact with it in the pub, then they don't learn too much. I just keep them guessing.

The new people want a great community centre. People who have just arrived in a village always want to do something in it or to it. What exactly they are going to have in this centre I don't know. They keep talking about 'amenities'; I suppose they mean a car-park and a big smart room. The young village people don't want this. They don't want to be organized and run. When their work is over they want to go off on their bikes to the bright lights of Ipswich. They don't want two-penny-ha'penny dances with a record-player, they want to see the latest group. The new people have a desire to hold together all the old ways while at the same time making sure that they have all the latest things for themselves. The old village people don't see it like this at all. What they see is a choice between what is old and what is new. So they choose the new. You don't want more old things when you've had old things all your life, do you? The new people are often just kidding themselves that they are real village people. They don't just want to be accepted, they really want to take over the gentry traditions. This is why they have come to live in a village. They want to do things 'for the village' and it is all very exhausting if you happen to be an 'old villager' and you just want to be left alone. The newcomers know all about that magic word 'grant' and know where to get grants for this and that. So you can't get out of doing something because you haven't got the money. It really is exhausting. It's no good saying, 'But we can't afford it', because the new people will say, quick as a flash, 'But there's a grant!' So they've got you. What I can't fathom is why a person who has got the wit to make enough money to come and live comfortably in the country, and have a centrally-heated house and a car, should want to put on entertainments in a hut. These people are just playing at village life – kidding themselves that they are genuine country folk.

They wear us out. When their work is done they want to play in the village and when our work is done we want to play outside it. I suppose that sums it up. Of course, what they really want is the old power but they can't have that because it is dead.

The village men are changing. We are seeing the growth of the specialist man on the farm. The agricultural apprentice scheme is getting the kind of lad who can't get into an agricultural training institute off the ground. The farmer is going to get the qualified man in the future, there is no doubt about that. And one is going to have to pay this man a bigger wage than we pay today. And there are going to be fewer and fewer farm-workers. If you get an intelligent boy going on to a farm today you can be certain that he isn't all that concerned about money; if he were he'd stuff a concrete-mixer for twenty quid a week. The distance a village is from the big town is most important. Where the distance is only two or three miles you won't get youths to work on the farms. The older men are different. They are the genuine people who have started off working to the old patterns. They can do anything. They haven't been divided. But I can remember at least four young men who left school since I left school who went to work as boys on the land. Two of them have stayed but the other two have gone off to operate mechanical diggers on building sites, and get £20 a week at least. Then one has trouble of a different kind with the older men. The average age of the field worker in Akenfield is the top end of fifty, which I think is rather frightening. They are the remnant of the old pre-war fantastically large labour force – that is why there is all this talk about the farms looking so neat and tidy then, you know. Labour was dirt cheap and there wasn't enough for everybody to do, so it was clip this and straighten that, and tar the barn. Now you may be lucky and have one really good man, and then stand the chance of losing him, either to industry in Ipswich or to some farmer who is more progressive than yourself and who has lots more machines. And so it works out that some farmers don't have the funds to keep pace with modern technology and agricultural development, and because they aren't up to date they can't get the good young workers, who go for these things. It is a vicious circle.

And then there is housing. If you have old workers you may be in the position of a farmer near here who is bogged down with two old-age pensioners in his cottages. This farmer is a gentleman, so he isn't likely to sling these old workers out on to their necks. But he is likely to get 5s. a week rent for his farm cottages, which stops modernization. I don't know what will happen to this farm, perhaps it will just sink into the ground. Of course there was another side to it in the old days, for you would often find the farm-workers using their great skills but the farm failing because the farmer himself was inefficient. This was often happening, although nobody likes to be reminded of it now. Having an old worker in your cottage is a nuisance but I suppose one has to think of all the work they did once. Farming was so hopeless round here during the thirties that when one went to buy a farm the agent used to say, 'What do you want it for, hunting, shooting or fishing?' There is still a lot of heathland near the river which the old people can remember as ploughed fields. Newcomers think that it is just 'natural and wild', as they call it, but it is the old rich land gone to waste during the Depression, with great holes and tracks made in it by army manoeuvres during the last war. The village changed then and it changes now, but nobody likes these changes because they go against the grain of what we have a right to expect.

Derek Warren · aged twenty-nine · ploughman

Everybody likes Derek, which could be odd as he is clearly unsociable. He 'likes a drink' but doesn't go to the local, doesn't play football, doesn't attend either chapel or church, or join in any of their multifarious activities, and doesn't have 'much to say' with the other young men. Yet it would be hard to find a more village-locked, village-absorbed person, or someone more readily smiling and easy to get along with. He is not only head ploughman on the biggest estate but *the* ploughman of Akenfield. Fields which once engaged dozens of horse-teams and even quite a number of tractor-drivers nowadays see nobody but him. He ploughs solidly for eight and ten hours a day for two-thirds of the year. When one cannot hear his tractor, the village experiences a similar kind of dragging silence to that caused by a clock stopping in a room. He and his wife live in an estate house becalmed in a great park. They have been married for five years but Sheila still misses the little manufacturing (farm implements) town where she was born, and where they met one Saturday afternoon. Derek's answer to her occasional complaints, although they are happy enough, is a kind of impenetrable sweetness. His smile is not unlike that of certain convinced fundamentalist Christians who 'know' but who aren't prepared to argue. One feels at first that one would like to shake such an assurance – until one discovers that Derek is as innocent of this as of anything else. He is a naturalist – birds, butterflies, moths, rats, bats, mice – and the behaviour of human beings has to be pretty drastic for him to notice it at all. He'll talk about his work obligingly enough but he doesn't even attempt to convey his particular village vision other than mentioning things like the rarity of linnets, the prevalence of rooks – sops, really, to one's interest in an experience which lacks for him a sharing language. He is lightly-built and rather Irish-looking with his open yet defensive laughter. He helps to ring bats on the rubbish dump, where they feed on the swarming insects. 'You must come and see me,' he says. 'I am in my height and glory.'

*

I have been ploughing continuously since last June. All the time. Now it is February and I haven't stopped. I have ploughed every day, Sundays too, for eight months. But it is nearly finished now. There will be a break until after the harvest, then, as soon as a field is cleared, I'll be on it. There are about 400 acres of corn-land and I plough it all. All the fields are different. They have their names and they feel to be different places. It is how it should be. I wouldn't like the village to become a Tannington where the hedges have gone and the ploughman doesn't know where he is. A well-kept hedge is a good sight and tells you where you are. The hedges belong to the village. You get so used to seeing them standing there – they are like buildings and you miss them when they are knocked down. Some hedges are important and when they go you feel as bad as if a wood had been taken away. I think that there are certain hedges which the farmers shouldn't touch without asking the people – although I can't see this happening.

I'm contented here. I haven't got the education for a farm manager's job and I wouldn't like it even if I had. All the same, as things are today you really do want some education whatever you do. But if you haven't got it you must learn contentment. Without education you can pick up plenty of practical experience on the farm, but you'll never grasp the new theory or understand the money. If I had gone to the agricultural college it would all have been different, no doubt. I started off working with the cows when I first left school. I didn't like this. I hoped I was going to be a keeper, you see. Ever since I was a boy I wanted to be a keeper but it never happened. 'You won't like it,' they said. 'It is seven days a week and a young lad likes his week-ends off.' I don't know why they said this. They knew I had no Sundays, so to speak. I was in working clothes and round the woods of a Sunday, just as of an ordinary day, so I might just as well have been paid for it. You see, keeping is *the* job for a man who has an eye to nature. There will be something different to look at every day and you'll have never seen it all. But there is no keeper in the village now. The last keeper had the double job of forester and keeper. He had to plant trees when he wasn't feeding pheasants. Whether you can really do both these jobs together, I don't know. There wouldn't be much time to think if you did. You'd have to be two men, which one man can't be if he's to stay honest. But there you are, that's modern demands for you! All the same, keeping would have suited me wonderfully.

I started ploughing, with a reversible plough, when I was eighteen. Somebody took me up to Scarlett Hill and said, 'This handle turns this over, this does something else – and away you go!' I kept straight as I could but I don't trouble so much these days. I don't know why. Because of the plough I suppose. With the old plough you had to have everything marked out and the furrows had to be kept straight if you wanted to finish up anywhere at all. The old men criticize. 'That wouldn't have done,' they say. 'You'd have had to have made a better job of it than that when I was a boy – God's truth, you would!' But they forget that they had the labour to do these fine things. There is double the arable in the village and few men wanting to stay and work it, so fancy fine ways aren't needed. The old men will tell you what an interest they took in their tasks – you could call this their main argument. They were brought up on quality work. Now it is quantity work – you've got to cover the ground. I can plough up two acres of the clay land in a day, and more on a light field.

I am a man on my own. I am not interfered with much. I am on the plough and that is where I keep. I am alone nearly all my work time but I can't say that I feel lonely. Not ever, not at all. People say, 'There's Derek, by himself up on that great old field, turning round, going back … he's lonely. He must be lonely!' Not at all – and what is 'lonely'? I am watching the whole time, you see. I might have more than a hundred birds in my wake. It is surprisingly interesting. The gulls are with me. But now and then it's nice to see a face and have a chat. Somebody will come past and speak, and that is good. It makes a break. After all, I'm a man and not a bird! But, honestly, if I knew that I was lonely, I'd pack it up tomorrow.

I think my wife feels she misses something by being in a remote village like this. She used to live in Leiston before we were married and she still misses being able to shut the front door and walk along to the shops and such-like. She says that going to the village shop isn't shopping. She didn't know anybody when she came here and she still misses her friends. But she is settling down. We have a car so she isn't stranded. I hope she is happy here. I like my work and I like the open air. I couldn't be put to work inside. Although I knew a man from this village who went to work in an Ipswich factory after being a gardener here until he was forty-five. He settled down easily. He put his mind to it, you see. I couldn't put my mind to it.

There was a junior branch of the Suffolk Naturalists when I was at the school – this is how I began to take an interest in birds. About fifteen boys joined but the club is disbanded now. They learned a few things but probably the only thing they still keep up is a spot of fishing – if you can call that natural history. As for wild birds, they might pick you out a sparrow or a swallow, but other than this they won't know much. I may be wrong. It is difficult for me to explain to you what all these living creatures mean to me. I can't really say that I study them although I write down anything unusual that I happen to see. It is just that I seem to know where they all live and what they do. The pesticides are having a nasty effect. I mean a bird can adapt itself to most things but it can't adapt itself to poison. Dressed corn is poisoned corn. It must kill. The kestrels are getting scarce. There were always several pairs in the air here when I was a boy. You could always look up and see them hovering about on the wind then. Now you'll be lucky if you see as many as three pairs on the entire estate. Linnets, too, used to be a common sight but I don't recall seeing a linnet for many a year. It is a seed-eater, so you can imagine what has happened to it. The wrens got very scarce after the hard winter [1962–3] but they're recovering. And the hard winter took the kingfishers off the pond, where I'd seen them for six years. They had a nest where the old boathouse used to be – where the stream runs away from the pond and down towards the bottom pasture. I saw one flash there last summer while I was fishing pike. There are new birds up on the old aerodrome – waders and red-shanks. They feed in the shallows where they have pulled the concrete runways up. We have had a flock of waxwings on the big cotoneaster up at the Big House, and there are always the martins. Each house seems to have so many people in it and so many martins. You must never bang their mud nests down or make them unwelcome, it is very unlucky. It is thought poor manners to destroy a martin's nest while he is abroad.

A lot of my friends have left the village. Most of the old gang. I am about the only one still here. They've all got jobs away. They got married and their wives took them away. Kelsale, Leiston, Ipswich, they've all gone away.

I don't go to the pub. I haven't been inside the door for six years. It is something you've got to like doing – to go in two or three times a week – I'd have no interest in that. But the young chaps who work with me would sooner go there than anywhere else. I watch television with my wife. I like travellers' tales abroad. The tribes of people faraway.

15 · The Law

Mrs Christian Annersley · aged fifty-five · magistrate and Chairman of the Bench

I think that what I actually enjoy about the Bench is that it is simply endlessly interesting. How people live, how people behave, how they think – and all at this vulnerable, naked moment in their existence. I often ask myself if I have a sense of power at this moment – does it give me this? I think it probably does. I think I am probably better than other people – then I know I'm not! (Laughs) I see how fond I am of people. Good people in a muddle, bad people and just poor low people who never have an earthly. I like my fellow-magistrates very much and we think of ourselves as a nice team who are passionately interested in the same things. We've always been a very soft Bench. In fact, people who have been had up in other areas often ask to come up before our Bench. I suppose we would be called upper class – in fact, we could hardly be called anything else. But apart from this our actual Bench status is certainly not greater than it used to be when I first sat twenty-five years ago. People were more frightened of the magistrates than they are now, when it is realized that the magistrate is a conscientious person and not just a stick-wagger. And there is no doubt that today's magistrate is a far better person than his predecessor. He goes to conferences, he goes to prisons, reads the law and does try to find out. Whereas before it was simply Colonel Bloggs who prided himself on being just an ordinary decent chap, and all that this implies. Rigidity. Ignorance. If I am going to send a country boy to an approved school I want to know what the school is like. I visit prisons and study after-care. So do we all. It is something of a status symbol among modern magistrates to have visited a great many institutions.

Our court covers four market towns and their surrounding areas. There are seven magistrates but we never sit more than five at a time. I have been Chairman for the past three years. We elect our own Chairman every three years, also our Deputy and the Chairman of the Juvenile Bench. Then there is the Licensing Committee; no magistrate who is in the brewery trade can sit on this. As I have said, we have always been upper class, which I think is a bad mistake. We did have a working-class magistrate years ago and he was always right. It was fascinating. We'd have this great strapping fellow come up, a horse-coper or something, and we'd all agree to fine him so much, when our working-class friend would add another £10. Then out would come a huge wadge of notes, fingers would be licked and ten of them would be peeled off. He always understood who could pay, who should be made to pay and how much. In those days we were all people with special sympathies. My aunt, for instance, was always sympathetic with people had up for speeding. She identified with them, you see. We all knew she drove twice as fast herself. Then this working-class magistrate, he always showed a special sympathy towards chapel folk who had got into what they call a muddle. But he was always down like a ton of bricks on a village toughie. Then we had a retired colonel to whom anything sexual was red rag to a bull. He would thrash it out of them, given half a chance!

Things were simple then. It was just after the war and this part of Suffolk was very basic. There was incest and bestiality on the one side, an American soldier getting drunk and driving into a brick wall on the other, and people riding bicycles without lamps in the middle. We get much more variety now. In the village there was always the Bad Family. Every village had one and we knew them all. They came up over and over again, and we watched them going slowly, inevitably downhill. I remember one young man and his predestination as a Bad Family person seemed to shine out of him, so that he simply hadn't a chance. He deteriorated. He deteriorated and we watched. It was terrible really. I have remembered him all this time, one of the small percentage of people who go wrong and who will keep on going wrong whatever you do. It is a dreadful thing to say, but nothing can make any difference for some people. Since then, I have visited schools and borstals, prisons and hospitals, and there they are. One can pick them out. They are cursed in some way. Nobody knows what with really. Even abroad, in Denmark, for instance, where conditions seem so perfect, you get identically similar results and statistics. I don't think that these poor men feel cursed themselves; they just think that although they haven't managed to beat the law this time, they might the next. Hard to help – hard to reach. I think that they feel shame but I'm not really sure. Our village Bad Family – father and three grown-up sons – doesn't feel any shame I am sure. Their lives are a little war, winning and losing, mostly losing. When they lose it is simply, 'That bloody old policeman has got me again!' Our Bad Family isn't bad at all – just stupid. But they'd sooner be called bad than stupid.

I wouldn't say that the sexual *mores* of our district have been changed very much by the freedoms and ideas of the past few years. I think they are very much the same, in fact. People know more about it now, that's all. Anyway, ordinary sex wasn't as restricted as people imagine. You can sum it up by saying that it used to be in the hedgerows and now it is in the back of the car. There was more incest in the past and it was always fathers and daughters, never brothers and sisters. It happened when mother had too many children, or when mother was ill, or when mother was dead. And very often it didn't matter a bit. The daughter usually proved to be very fond of the father and there would be no sign of upset in the family. No, I think it was quite an understood thing that a daughter would take on the father when the mother was ill or dead. It would always happen in a 'basic' family, of course. Then somebody would give them away. Or it would come out when the daughter became pregnant. You would then come up against a strange form of innocence. Not ignorance, innocence. You would hear all about it from the police notebooks, pages and pages and pages, and you'd wonder why the man didn't look like a monster. Then you'd realize that what he'd done and what we were saying he had done seemed to be two quite different things. We had strayed into the dark, into the deep – the hidden ways of the village. They aren't all light now. All explored. But things are less strange and secretive than they were – even as little as twenty years ago. We've had families where we never had a clue about what was going on. You would find sub-normal boys, a crippled girl, and you would beg the parents to let them attend special schools. But they wouldn't. They felt they had to have these children close by them to offer them some kind of extra loving. We had an instance of this only last month – a fourteen-year lad who had been stealing girls' panties off the lines. He was one of a family of eight and needed help. Poor old mother brought the boy to court – father wouldn't appear. Mother had no idea what it was all about and was upset. We deferred the case three times in an effort to get both parents together and obtain their consent to allow the boy to go to this school, where he could have stayed until he was sixteen, been brought forward educationally and helped emotionally, but no. They flatly refused to let him go.

Stealing women's underwear off lines is a fairly recent thing. Perhaps women didn't have dainty underwear years ago or perhaps it is because all the underwear ads are so extremely erotic now. Pantie-stealers and indecent exposure people are the same type of man, lonely, nervous, fantasist. Of course, they are always put on probation. We never treat them unkindly. We send them away for a medical report. It is the report in the local newspaper which ruins them. They are shunned in the village. Young boys caught doing this kind of thing have a bad time after the publicity. It is difficult for them. Nobody ever forgets it.

Then we get worrying sex things like the half-witted man who had been had up for interfering with little boys coming up again on another charge of the same sort. There were six little boys this time, and they all told their tales with giggles or blushes, according to their nature, except for the last boy, who was only seven, and he had simply been struck dumb with shock, I think, at being brought into court. It took us something like two hours to get him to say enough to convict the man, and it had to be done because everything depended on his evidence. I shall never forget it. I was absolutely pouring with sweat by the time it was over. He wouldn't say, he *wouldn't* say. He could not bring himself to say what had happened. I thought it was dreadful to go on. But they insisted on us going on to make him say – the prosecution. This child sat on a chair right up close to us and we asked and he couldn't answer. His eyes and our eyes were stuck together for hours. God knows what harm we did him. I felt myself dying inside with horror and wretchedness. Real corruption it was. That's the kind of thing which makes one ashamed of a legal situation. Finally he said it. He was seduced into saying it. We seduced him.

On the whole, and over the years, there have been few child-sex cases and those I have dealt with have always involved men of low mentality or of 'innocence' – this weird innocence I have already mentioned and which is hardly believable until you have come up against it. There was the thirteen-year-old girl who had become her stepfather's mistress and everybody cried, 'Oh, what will happen to her now, poor child?' This was after the case and when we were trying to decide what to do with her. After talking to her I was absolutely determined that she shouldn't be sent to a girls' approved school where ninety per cent of the inmates were already hardened little tarts, and who were destined to be tarts for the rest of their lives. This child, for all that had happened, simply wasn't a tart. In a sense she simply wasn't touched. There was nothing remotely criminal about her; she was simply an under-privileged little girl and what she wanted to do most was to get on with school and get on with her needlework. So this was one of those times when I kept on deferring the case until we had found exactly the right place for her, which was a rather nice ordinary school run by nuns. I remember how aghast we were at the time of this case but now, looking back, I honestly feel that it left no scar at all on the child. Her sexual experiences fitted into the lowness and crudity of everything else about her, her mother having babies all over the place, the dreadful eating arrangements, the bedrooms like stalls and her stepfather as instinctive, rough and direct as an animal. Really, what had happened to that girl was little worse – in the context of her existence – than having to eat off a dirty plate. One is so anxious when these things come to court that they won't suddenly present something previously simply 'accepted' in the most awful light to the child. 'They are saying that what has been happening to me is vile – absolutely terrible....' But it was plain in this instance that while it was going on it wasn't terrible to the girl at all. It has got to be stopped, of course, but one has to take care that, in the stopping it, the real damage isn't done.

A thing we used to get so often but which we never get now is the Peeping Toms. Scores of Peeping Toms! This was a real old village thing. You never really hear of it now. It was all part of the old frustrated, cooped-up feeling, I suppose. It usually happened when the culprit had had a few drinks on a Saturday. What a fuss there used to be!

Only once in my experience have we dealt with shop-lifting – and that was when two ladies from Ipswich turned up for the church fête and pinched something off a stall! But the subject fascinates me and I have just returned from a week-end conference examining this very thing. Women usually do it, of course. I remember a very well-to-do woman who stole a leg of mutton and a fruit pie. It turned out that she was separated from her husband for some time, that they were going to meet but he didn't arrive – so she stole these strange things. A month or two later she stole something else. Then she had a breakdown. Most shoplifters steal what they don't want. Magistrates like to put it down to the change of life when it concerns respectable middle-aged women and to loneliness when it concerns old men. But it could have something to do with the way the shops thrust their goods at one nowadays.

We have high spirits. A boy dressed up for Saturday night and a few beers inside him shouting, 'Fuck off!', to the local policeman. It honestly does seem to me too unnecessary and boring to bring a case for this kind of thing. Admittedly, the last boy who carried on like this shouted 'Fuck off!' three times. It was all very silly. The trouble is, the village boys do like to congregate in their hundreds at a certain place on Saturday nights so the Bench is bound to support the dignity of the police. This is something altogether new in our quiet little set-up. These are the same naughty young men who 'Commit a Nuisance' – they always look pretty non-plussed when the case comes up, I can tell you! One pound and their name in the local paper. Furious parents. Big blushes. Or it could be some old rustic twelve-pinter who is past caring.

I think that the relationship between the police and the Bench is very good, although they get a bit fed-up with us because we are so lenient. The police are, on the whole, straightforward and trying to do their best. Now and then you get a bad 'un, a type who must go too far. But when you consider how they are provoked, they are marvellous people. I think that the provocation of the police is too cruel for words. And the village policeman has a wretched time really. His loneliness is rarely understood. He is advised not to make too many friends when he arrives in the village and the loneliness of his wife is a very real and sad thing. She mustn't chum-up with people. They are both advised to keep themselves to themselves. People change the conversation when they come into a room. The village policeman is a man in a corner and they have to be pretty strong characters to endure such a life. The gamekeepers used to have to live something like this – as men apart. I really don't know why any young countryman should choose the police force as a profession. It is a tedious, trying, unnaturally isolated job – and poorly paid.

We deal with a good many marriage troubles of one kind or another. All very much the same as those that fill the papers everywhere. A sad normal thing which happens is the financial problem of a youngish husband who leaves his wife to live with another woman and finds that he can't pay for keeping up two establishments. The deserted wife takes him to court because she can't manage on the allocation. We then feel frightfully sorry for the wife, who has usually been left several children, so we increase the allocation. But the man may only be earning £10 a week and he has to keep his second 'wife' and his children by her out of this as well, so one never really knows what to do. In nearly every case the man is with the woman he loves, and the cold facts simply aren't the real facts. Great lists of hire-purchase debts going back years and years emerge – from both sets of families. What has happened is this – a commonplace thing. A young couple have made love and 'got caught', as they say, and are pushed into marriage by their parents. But they don't love each other and nerves get frayed as more babies arrive. Then the husband really does fall in love and he simply runs away from a situation he finds unendurable. It is easy to moralize but what do you do with a farm-worker's wage, two houses and two families?

I think that in a village it still matters absolutely, *appallingly*, if you are 'respectable'. One ghastly day – I shall never forget it – we all sat waiting for a man to appear who had got himself in some kind of fix – nothing remotely criminal – about the stamps and things in his little sub-post office. The police had been to make enquiries and he had been called to come to the court. We waited and waited but he didn't turn up. We asked, 'Had the summons been served?' Yes, it had. He'd mistaken the time, perhaps? Well, we allowed him that. At last we sent a police car to fetch him, and there he was, hanging in the back of the shop. Terrible! We looked at the charge – something to do with these few stamps. Nothing really to worry about. We all knew him; he was a nice little man. We couldn't speak. Very respectable people – *good* people – will often go all to pieces – crash – at the mere hint of an enquiry.

The young people in Akenfield seem hardly to be touched by things like television. Not yet, anyway. Those who appear in court seem little different to the youngster I dealt with twenty years ago. We used to be put out if a young man turned up with long hair but now that it has become universal we never think about it. But we're all still put out when they come in chewing gum or with their hands in their pockets. 'Take that gum out of your mouth,' I'll say, but I'd never make a remark about anybody's clothes or appearance. Most certainly not. On the whole, our Bench is very against making 'little god' speeches. I might say to some young man, 'Now look here, Jones, we've discussed this *extremely carefully* and we all feel *very* worried about what you have done, and we are going to put you on *probation* rather than send you to *prison,* which you must realize *we could do,* and you *must* see that you've got to mend your ways or, *next time,* you *will* be sent to prison. You've got all your life before you. Please, *please* stop doing-whatever-it-is. And pull your socks up *and don't do it again.*' But the truth is, of course, that in more cases than not the guilty person is in such a state of confusion that he simply cannot take in a single word you are saying. So if you must say something to him, you must say it baldly in hard, ordinary sentences. I also use words like 'shut up'. I don't say, 'Bloody well stop it' but I might say, 'Cut it out!' Basic words.

Again, when we are dealing with children – in the back room because they're not allowed to appear in the ordinary court, of course – I talk very very slowly and quietly as I would to any child. Not necessarily severely but clearly. I press everything now and then by a 'Do you understand?' But on the whole we get no response at all and I often wonder if there is any point in it. If tears spring to the eyes I know that I have got through, as it were. I don't want this to happen but in nine cases out of ten it is the only sign that what I am saying is registering. I always make a tremendous point of talking to the parents and there *is* a place for making a speech here. I make them feel that there is plenty of time. Sometimes it is very rewarding.

An average day at our court isn't very spectacular. Four licensing extensions, three motor-car slight accidents with written-in pleas of Guilty – £5 – £10 – £20 – £30 each and licence endorsed. Then, the police having had their radar stationed at various points, you will have about ten cars doing between thirty and forty miles an hour. There is an automatic scale of fines for these offences. Then five bicycles with insufficient brakes or something. Then the young man who got drunk on Saturday and shouted you-know-what, or perhaps he hit somebody with a brick. Then you might have a defended case of dangerous driving, which will take time, or a bit of breaking-and-entering. We never have any of these dear young modern protesters – they don't come our way. We have to pass plans for all the pub alterations. No murders – I have never had a murder case in twenty-five years – and no poachers now. No lead-stealing from the church roof – that was the most popular crime in Suffolk just after the war. But there has been a great increase in stealing valuable things from inside the churches, and the thieves are rarely ever caught.

We also get occasional animal cruelty cases but never cases of child cruelty. The animal cruelty cases are nearly always in connection with dogs which have suffered through the ignorance rather than the viciousness of their owners. I see cruelties which never get anywhere near the courts. Markets – they're nobody's business! I have seen some disgusting cruelty to animals in the markets round here. I remember passing a slaughter-house in Ipswich where some pigs were running in the yard and seeing them being caught by having a hook jabbed into them and being dragged off. This is quite a regular thing. Imagine the uproar if somebody was caught doing this to a dog! Then we have American servicemen who buy Alsatians to guard their wives and families who are living in rented cottages – all so unnecessary in Suffolk, where do they think they are? – and who keep these dogs so tied-up and fierce that at the first opportunity they bite the postman, so it has to be shot.

When we need a new magistrate on our Bench we ask for a specific person by name. A special committee chaired by the Lord Lieutenant considers our choice. This committee is made up of magistrates from all the Benches in the area but the actual membership is kept very secret. It meets twice a year, when various names are brought forward and approved. It is getting more and more political, that is the trouble. In the big cities it is almost entirely political, but in Suffolk it is probably less political than anywhere else. We all feel very strongly about these political considerations and pressures and do our utmost to get a true cross-section of the social element in the local villages. We aren't succeeding but it remains our aim and object. It is still difficult to have a really working-class person because they can't get off work and also because one really does need to be fairly well educated to do the work. Of course, you get a lot of so-called educated middle-class folk who are frightfully stupid, so one can't generalize. One of the best magistrates in Suffolk is a railway porter. He is now on the administrative committee of Blundeston Prison.

It is getting harder and harder to get lay magistrates, especially now that they are wanting younger and younger people. Few young men can afford the time and young women have no one they can leave their children with for two or more whole days a month. And although travelling expenses are allowed, there are still a great number of people who simply couldn't afford to be a J.P. So the trend is towards more stipendiaries. All the same, people still like being magistrates – love it!

All of us worry about sentencing. It is our chief worry. We attend all kinds of courses and conferences to discuss it and how to achieve uniformity or something approaching it. When I first started, the basic rule was to find out a person's means and fine him accordingly. Was he

married? What was his rent? How many children? We even did this
with the bicycle-lamp cases! But now, with affluence, the whole picture
has changed. When you can afford a car you can afford a uniform fine,
this is what it amounts to. But disparity occurs all over Suffolk still, so
justice certainly doesn't appear to have been done. I think that one can
say that the problem is almost entirely confined to motoring offences.
People remain puzzled by the seeming haphazards of sentencing, one
Bench in the west obviously fierce, our Bench notoriously soft.... And
now we've all got to get used to a new thing altogether – the suspended
sentence.

We sit every fortnight but it is soon going to have to be every week.
We used to get everything finished by lunch-time but now it takes all
day, and yet we are a little backwater so far as Benches go. We know
everybody and it can be a bit embarrassing when a personal friend
comes up! Then you can either pretend it's all a great joke or you can
sit back. Any magistrate can push his chair back if he doesn't want to
sit on a case. We're rather a dull Bench really but people come to watch
us and everything we say is lavishly reported in the local press. I must
say that these reports are not very good. In fact, not at all good. They
often get it all wrong and the cases, to my mind, are still too much part
of amusement and entertainment. The Boy-in-the-Suitcase murder has
been front-page news on one of our local papers for the best part of a
year and even *The East Anglian Daily Times,* which is a superior
provincial newspaper, is full of rather trivial court cases. I do wish
they wouldn't do it to such a needless extent. I suppose it is puritan
country and that puritans will want to read where they won't want
to do.

None of us women magistrates wear hats – we're unique, I think! I
won't wear one. I get confused in a hat. My head gets hot and I get
hopeless. The Magistrates Association offers us little words of advice –
Never come into court laughing and smiling between yourselves! Wear
hats and plain dark, sensible clothes! We are very strict among ourselves
about something more important than this – we refuse to be those awful
whispering magistrates who go into a huddle before the defendant and
the court. We *always* retire for our considerations. This means that not
only do you take greater trouble over your decision but that you look as
though you do. This is a very important thing.

After all these years I'm beginning to feel that I shan't be sorry to
give it up, because there are so many things for which there is no answer.
There are so many ways in which you know you're doing the wrong
thing – because there is no right thing to do. You know at heart where

prison is no answer, yet the man will be sent to prison. The prisons – I
visit so many of them – are still way behind everything. And then there
is this conflict of reform versus punishment. And I'm really honestly
and truly, having been liberal and 'psychological' for all my life,
coming to the conclusion that punishment is a good thing. That
punishment really gets it off the chest of a great many people. They
think, 'Well, I've paid!' If people can accept the fact that they have paid
they can either go on being a happy criminal or they can stop being a
criminal. So I don't think that punishment is a bad thing. I used to
think it was, but I don't now. There now, after all my years as a re-
former! It is rather a cleansing thing. Certain people are destroyed –
killed – by the present method. Justice is not done to these people. A
very wrong result comes out. . . .

And then there are the risks you take with human beings. There's a
boy and you think, yes, he's exactly the right sort to send to a detention
centre. Well, he may *not* be. It may do him good, it may leave him quite
untouched, but – and this is more likely – it may do him great harm.
You, sitting there on the country Bench, may in a word send this boy
whom you have never seen before to complete destruction. This is what
weighs on one's mind. I always come home frightfully worried and
wretched if I've sent somebody to prison or to a detention centre. I am
so moved by the plight of many of the people who come up, but I'm
harder than I used to be. The truth of the matter is that most of the
people who come up at a court like ours don't come from 'bad backgrounds'. Most of the boys in borstals are from bad backgrounds –
town and city backgrounds usually. Only two per cent of the borstal
inmates are village boys. This fact tells one something.

Persis Ede · aged forty-eight · odd-job man

Persis has been committed. The whole village is talking about it and, as
usual when he has been in front of the magistrates – 'Morning, m'lady,
Major, Mr Philips . . .' – Persis is out in the bright day of his council-
house garden demonstrating to the world that he has not got a forked
tail or hooves. This time it is serious: he has been sleeping with his
'niece', who is no relation but the daughter of his mate, dirty old
Malyon up at the Tye. The 'niece' is fourteen and the magistrates were
informed that Persis has been 'assaulting' her for just over two years.
For the village it is a case of rapid translation from the inverted commas.
There is one aspect of the affair which is plain enough. It was Mrs

Persis Ede who reported it to the police. 'Linda is a grut grown-up girl now and she'd get into a muddle. It's got to stop.'

Linda Malyon is a stringy, brown-faced, notch-haired girl who looks like a boy. She is the antithesis of country child freshness and she is as un-Juliet-like now as she will be at forty. As a member of 'that lot', as the Malyon family is known, she has inherited in one large generalized lump the shortcomings of two or three generations of her kin. According to the gossips, Mrs Ede is angry with neither Persis nor Linda it seems. She just thinks that it has got to stop and it was entirely with this in mind that she took the bus into Ipswich and made a statement. The Welfare lady called on Linda a few days later, thinking of care-and-protection, and Linda trailed round the cottage, putting the *Mirror* and her brothers' socks under the chair cushions, and the kettle on. The brothers, all small, were heaped up in armfuls like puppies and tossed into the garden. The Welfare lady took the opportunity to mention their ferocious energy as her opening gambit. They could be little buggers at times, Linda agreed. Would her mother ever return, did she think? (Mrs Malyon has 'gone off to London'. Everybody who disappears has gone off to London.) Not if she's got her head screwed on, says Linda – 'though, seriously, it's better if she don't'. The Welfare lady remembers Mrs Malyon and the uproar she created, and mentally agrees. She is pretty well foxed about the current Malyon problem all the same. She expected some boy to arrive, fairly soon, and compound Linda's already miraculously complex existence of schoolgirl – house-keeper and sister – mother, also hardened smoker and paperback addict (Georgette Heyer, James Bond, Barbara Cartland) but the wilfully managed affair with Persis amazes her. She would genuinely like to know why.

'But *why*, Linda?'

Linda tries to find an answer. She thinks of doing the washing before breakfast, getting the two youngest dressed and packed off to Mrs Ede's council house until the two eldest collect them on their way back from the village school, of doing her homework on the bus and doing the shopping in her dinner hour, of coming home and clearing up and listening to her father talk the hind leg off a donkey. Of a great camel's hump of jobs and demands. And then going off to find Persis where he hedged and ditched – so slowly, people said, that bushes grew out of his reach while he was stretching for them – and enjoy his bothered kind of happiness and listen to his awful stories. But there is nothing here which is going to help the Welfare lady, who looks as helpless as Linda has ever seen her.

'I'm not pregnant,' she reminds her.

'But Mr Ede – don't you understand – he'll go to prison.'

'Whose fault is that?'

'Yours – partly.'

'I'm sorry for my part then.'

Linda is sorting the mending. The cottage is acridly sweet, dirty and cosy. Fish fingers wait to be cooked in the pan. The brothers are dribbling what looks like a toy cowboy hat through some stagnant cabbage stumps in a paroxysm of laughter and howls. Quiet! shouts Linda, and they are quiet.

The Welfare lady has written:

The case in which patient is involved is due to come to court on June 30th: the girl he is accused of assaulting is aged 14 years. Patient has known her and her family, who appear to be a rough lot, for about two years. Informant (patient's wife) said that the girl was very well developed and precocious, looking much older than her age. She is said over the past two years to have followed Mr Ede about the place continually and Mrs Ede thought that she was as much to blame as her husband. Mr Ede is said to have intercourse with the girl frequently and over quite a long period, and the girl is said to have been a willing, indeed enthusiastic partner. Mr Ede is also said to have given her and her family money and cigarettes at odd times, and informant thought the girl's father knew about and condoned the association with the patient. Mrs Ede herself finally informed the Police of the affair because (a) she realized that the girl might at any moment become pregnant by her husband and (b) that she resented the time and attention he paid her. She appeared to bear him no real resentment, remarking that her husband was easily led.... Asked if she considered her husband over-sexed or in any way peculiar in this respect, she answered stolidly 'No'. They have intercourse about twice or three times a week and she has never refused him. Patient, when not involved with girls, is said to be a good father and generous with money if he has any. Mrs Ede said that she would never think of leaving him, nor would she ever....

Persis stays out front as much as he can before the sentence (eighteen months), digging the garden, shouting cheerily to passers-by, insisting on his ordinariness. The men pass and say, ''night, Persis', because he can't very well be ignored. He has been county-courted for as long as anyone can remember. Poaching, nicking lead, failing with his hire purchase, fighting, driving uninsured, dozens of little illegalities. Two quiet, artful-looking sons, Tony and Arch, slipped away from home as soon as they could and long before anything could be known about them. Mrs Ede has sent them each a copy of *The East Anglian Daily Times* containing an account of the case but they won't answer. They have never written a line, not even at Christmas. They work in a supermarket in Ilford, but nobody in Akenfield knows this. 'They done well for theirselves,' Mrs Ede tells whoever may be enquiring. She is thin – almost as thin as Linda – and is rarely seen. Her face is heart-shaped and tiny with a big, strong handsome nose. Older people remember her dancing during the war at the American base, hokey-coky-ing night after night in her platform shoes.

Persis' war was even more sensational. While on guard duty in the army he had shot his sergeant for not giving the password. There had been a court martial and Persis had to be acquitted of manslaughter. This business was unknown to the village on account of the wartime morale laws but it is now used by the defence in the Linda case to establish Persis' state of moral irresponsibility. It astounds Akenfield. Persis, they read, is of 'low intelligence' and a kind of murderer. There is no connection here with winking, flannelling, girl-chasing, cheating Persis. Mrs Ede stays inside and paints the entire house from top to bottom, with Radio Caroline turned up so high that she wouldn't hear a knock if it was made with a hammer. Linda brings her two little brothers to be minded while she is at school and Mrs Ede looks at her with a silent 'now look what you've done' but no more than this. Her father says, read, read, read – you must want your bloody head seen to!

16 · Limitations

You will say that I am in the scheme of things,
  A unit in the crumbling earth;
Trees are barren:
  Chance I'm a barren tree.
Link me with circumstance if you must ...

Herbert Read, *The Analysis of Love*

Lana Webb · aged twenty-three

Could Lana be spoken to? Yes, apparently, provided that one did not demand an answer. She belongs to the village and she is emphatically not a recluse. If folk avoid her, that is their look out! She makes it plain that she has not withdrawn from life, complicated though life may be. She is here, smooth and still, washed and tidy, decent enough for anybody who might drop in. Her name is written in as many different places as that of anyone else, the chapel register, the school attendance book, the electoral roll, at the newsagents (*Secrets, Honey, Lucky Star, True Romance* – she is a great reader and is well known for always having her nose stuck in a book) and at the National Assistance Board. Everybody in Akenfield knows Lana and if they don't come to see her, 'Well, that's their loss!' laughs her Gran. The joke is a good one and momentarily engulfs them both. They emerge from it like divers from a pool, shaking their heads and dashing moisture from their eyes with the backs of hands.

'You're lucky that it's only your eyes that are running!' says Lana.

Gran turns away with a '*hoop-hoop*!' Her shoulders shake. 'Now don't start me off again, there's a good girl,' she says.

They both have to raise their voices in order to be heard above the crackling pop coming through the fretwork sunburst of a thirties wireless. The lino is translucent, like sucked toffee, its pattern all licked off by the duster. Shining ornaments, shining blacklead, shining skin on Lana's strong bare legs hanging out of their mini-skirt. Regularly, and much louder than anything else, there is the dungeon-like rattle of a chain being wearily dragged in and out of a barrel. It is Terry, Gran's dog. He is a collie aged thirteen with fat dusty haunches and golden eyes which need wiping. He was fastened to the barrel when he was one and has never been unfastened since. 'Terry!' calls Gran. 'He has what we have – don't you, boy?' 'Good boy!' shouts Lana.

The cottage is partly a soldier's resettlement hut of the First World War and partly a railway carriage, and is quite inordinately pretty. The two units are set in an L and the join is covered with house-leeks and stone-crop, cushions of grass and Paul Scarlet roses. Brass carriage handles glitter behind leaves. Little paths maze around and are edged with beer bottles, their necks driven into the earth. It is a toy house for playing mothers-and-fathers in. Except that the fathers, big, clumsy, nasty things, have long since been ousted from the game. Their speckled photographs glare down from the walls. Both dad and grandad have been dead for years – 'Why, you hardly knew your dad, did you, Larn?' cries Gran with relief. 'Now my husband,' she points to a boy-scout with his hat set on a bamboo table like a meal, 'he lasted for a long time.' Her eyes show patience, resignation, God's will being done.

Lana glances guiltily at the pictures because of Ken. He is in her handbag, along with a facsimiled autographed photo of Ringo Starr, her birth certificate and her horoscope. But somehow there is no need to fret about Ken, who is a kind, stout man of perhaps thirty-eight with his pockets stretched out with bibles, and change for his insurance round. Ken has known Lana since she was twelve. 'And it shows the kind of chap he is that it never made a scrap of difference to his feelings for her,' says Gran.

Lana prinks in the armchair in which she has been sitting all this time and there is the distinct flap and squeak of drenched rubber.

'The doctor himself said that it was nothing to be ashamed of,' declares Gran.

'Of course not!' one agrees in a fiercely 'civilized' voice.

Gran and Lana's eyes meet in wordless discussion. Yes? Yes. Gran goes to a cream-painted door and opens it with a flourish in which candour competes with pride. There is evidently another addition to the toy house which cannot be seen from the road and which makes it an F, not an L. It is a long white room with windows wedged open on either side, and the wind hurtles through it. It is blowing some twenty pairs of knickers. Pink, white, blue, flowered, plain, nylon, cotton, they jig happily above a galvanized zinc bath in which sheets are steeping. Gran closes the door and Lana, her expression faintly amused and challenging now, rises from her chair and goes off somewhere to change. The movement causes an odd Alice-like transformation. Sitting, she is a slumped odalisque. Standing, she is a very big little girl. The door of the second-class compartment clicks behind her.

'You should just see her room,' says Gran. 'Like a little princess's, and she does it all herself. Of course, it hasn't been all honey. It's been a struggle, I can tell you. Only He knows. But neither of us would say thank you to a change now. What with my bit of pension and her bit of National, we're quids in.'

Lana's past is as much an open book as her present. Her father was an American, her mother Gran's daughter. The daughter was known as a 'good girl' and had thus been tricked, bewitched or raped by the American. But it all worked out for the best and from the time Lana went to school until her mother's death from a heart attack when the child was fourteen they were 'all in all to each other'. Lana didn't have children as friends; there was no need. She had Mum, who walked her to and from school until the day she left. She slept with Mum in the second-class compartment and it was in this room, with 'Smoking' frosted on the windows, that Mum cut out and made all Lana's clothes from give-away patterns in the women's magazines. Every Saturday night Ken arrived in his black-japanned Morris and drove them to his Mum's in Ipswich, where they watched television. Gran now went on this outing with Lana, who sat on a pile of *Daily Expresses* which Ken provided. The whole village agreed that Ken had been wonderful.

Lana had wetted the bed as a child, of course, said Gran. But you couldn't call that Incontinence, could you? This had begun six years ago and Lana hadn't been dry since. 'Wet as a ditch, day in, day out.' She got through fifteen pairs of knickers a day, not to mention all her bed-linen. *And* pads *and* rubbers and anything you like to mention. She had had two operations and they had made her worse (Triumph). She don't feel a thing.

Lana returned to her chair at this point. Did she knit, perhaps? Do anything? 'Glory, no!' laughs Gran. Both shook with merriment at the very idea. 'You see,' explained Gran, 'Incontinence is a way of life. Those were the doctor's very words, weren't they, Larn? She can't go to the pictures, not to the chapel, nor nowhere.'

'And Ken?'

'Ken's got his Mum, hasn't he?'

Gran picks up a jug and begins to water her pot-plants. A swing-wing bomber from Bentwaters knifes up the iridescent Akenfield afternoon, its scream momentarily and intolerably trapped in the cottage.

'Blessed Yanks!' says Gran – 'If ever I should swear!'

17 · The Vet

The creatures outside looked from pig to man,
and from man to pig, and from pig to man again;
but already it was impossible to say which was which.

George Orwell, *Animal Farm*

Dr Tim Swift · aged fifty-five · veterinary surgeon

Tall, intelligent, with the red-brown skin and clear eyes of the 'Ipswich'
period Gainsboroughs, Tim Swift has been forced to take more than the
usual complacent or pragmatic look at the new animal farming methods
which have engulfed Akenfield. Since he arrived in the village twenty
years ago he has seen, either a miraculous improvement of livestock in
the area, with subsequent cheap and easily available food for all, or an
unparalleled exploitation by man of the animal kingdom. He is quite
unsentimental, but birds and beasts happen to be his patients, so he has
to recognize their interests. A line has to be drawn between what is
economic or simply convenient, and what is cruel. Where animals are
concerned, cruelty is a bent noun. The number of creatures in Britain
which meet agony and strange deaths via vivisection, sport and factory-farming is incalculable. Special pleading is re-worded every ten
years or so to accommodate the torture and slaughter. Emotion, anger,
pity, retribution are siphoned off into the R.S.P.C.A.'s advertisement in
The Times – 'Dog left seven days without food' – or in such splendidly
dotty animal concern as that which drove two English ladies to succour
the cats of Venice. Rural society created this dichotomy of feeling in the
first place. The countryman knew how far the code allowed him to go
with the various creatures which were his friends, servants, amusement
and food. The code wasn't particularly humane by enlightened standards but, when observed, it stopped men being disgusted by each other.
Bear-baiting, cock-fighting (mains are still held in Cumberland and
Westmorland), otter-hunting, coursing and stag-and fox-hunting chan-
nelled off the more primitive blood-shedding instincts while using, as do
armies, ritual graces for the kill. In a word, people knew where they
were. But now, with a decade's intensive stock-breeding resulting in

huge new animal populations in every village, there is moral confusion.

The vet lives in a large attractive house with tennis courts, an aviary, a double garage and cedars of Lebanon spaced out around it. He is married with two sons and two daughters. The gardens and paddocks are full of convalescents, a donkey, a Betty-cat whose life has to be saved at all cost, a parakeet, a peacock hanging gaudily from the ash tree and moody dogs. The atmosphere is that of a Victorian pet-loving rectory.

*

Only twenty years ago, when I first came to Akenfield, every farmer had so much corn, so much stock. The stock was small and 'knowable', as you might say – twenty cows, each with a name, each milked by hand, more often than not; five or six sows with their litters and their funny old ways. The farmer would milk, feed and then go off to the field until-dinner-time, and then about four he'd milk and feed again. After tea he went to the barn to grind the feed for the next day. His wife kept the chickens and maybe a few turkeys. She'd most likely buy 100 turkey poults and lose about forty of them. This would be acceptable. If she'd still got fifty come Christmas-time, she thought she'd done well. To have reared seventy-five out of 100 was excellent. This was her pin money. She'd pinch food for her fowls from the barn and also give them kitchen scraps. Her other animal was a pet pig.

All around, the country was as it always was – nice old parks, oak trees, rabbits, a few stags to make things look grand, sheep by the lake's edge, cattle up to their udders in the pond. That is how it was when I came here – England as it used to be. But it will never be a Constable again. Most of the farm-workers had a sow in the backyard. Then wages went up and the price of pigs dropped, and the sows disappeared from the cottage gardens. The parents of these farm-workers had lived on bread and fat bacon – the farmer supplied the pig, either very cheaply or for nothing, and it was fed on house scraps and mumble which the children collected along the hedgerows. The cottage people grew their own potatoes – great stretches of them to keep them through the winter – and they got skimmed milk from the farm. The meat they ate had as much as four inches of fat on it. A pig was fattened to forty score – now it is fattened to eighteen score. It was a world of great pigs. The villagers needed all this fat to make their lard, which was often eaten on bread instead of butter. They had to eat all the fat they could to keep them warm. They had such poor clothes and often nothing to change into after having been out in all sorts of weather. Many's the time I've seen them, men dressed in rain-hardened boards and little capes of sacking

hanging down from their heads. The Suffolk women won't buy fat now
– perhaps it reminds them of these shivering men in the lea of the wind,
eating their bait and chopping at pure white hunks of the stuff. The
fattest pig-meat from Suffolk now goes to Yorkshire – the miners still
like it very much.

It was fun being the village vet; the work had just that kind of
fascination which you get with anything to do with medicine. Animals
often lived a long time, particularly horses, of course. I would be treating
a horse with a discharging joint for months – maybe for years. Many of
the horses were lame and had to wear surgical shoes. Nobody would put
a horse down until it was absolutely useless. The sick animals were
often affectionately treated but they suffered a lot. I had almost no drugs,
no antibiotics. The sick horses would be nursed and worked until another
day's work couldn't be got out of them, then they were shot. If you
could keep a horse going, you did. Ethics were different then. My job
was to keep a horse on his feet.

I saw the great Suffolk pastures just before they disappeared. Tremendous, they were. It has all vanished under the plough, except down
by the rivers where the meadows get flooded. All the cows have gone.
There is not a cow in Framlingham parish, there is not a cow in Saxted
parish, there is *one* cow in Bedfield parish, there are no cows in Monk
Soham parish and when you get to Wilby I wouldn't be sure but I
think that the main herd there has just been sold out. But there is still
a cowherd in Akenfield because of the stream and in the river valley at
Debenham there are still a couple of herds – although there used to be
eight. But there are no cows on the high land any more because the
farmers can make more money by ploughing up the old pastures. It is
awful – although one is not supposed to be sentimental about anything
in the countryside these days. It is such a comfort to see the small herd
of Jerseys at Earl Soham. But even where you still get a farmer with
a modern cow set-up, the dairy feeling is all changed. Supposing he is
milking 120 animals, it is most unlikely that he will be employing a
cowman and paying him a wage. He will be far more likely to contract a
man to milk at so much a gallon and who will undertake to feed the
animals at so much food per gallon of milk. The man who takes on the
job will be in complete charge on the understanding that the more milk
he produces, the bigger his wages. Next year the herd may still be on the
farm but the village people will never see it. Cows will no longer graze
under the sky. They will be in herring-boned sheds all their lives. No
mud – and no sun. Most of the beef-fattening animals are already indoors. The time will come when villages like Akenfield will have

thousands of creatures living in them, but they will be, for all that the ordinary person knows, non-existent.

It is because our land is so valuable. Because we can grow such very high quality corn and catch crops. We can no longer afford to let animals roam on fields as valuable as this. They have to be locked up. They will never eat another blade of living grass. It is unprofitable. But they will have a ventilator to every pen and thermostatic heat control, sawdust floors, and automatic feeding and watering. Hotel conditions. The stockmen must change too. There is all the difference in the world between a man who just feeds stuff to pigs for a few weeks and a man who calves a cow, milks it with his hands and walks with it daily to the pasture. There is only one man I know who has managed to carry the personal touch into the animal factory and he is an ex-German prisoner-of-war named Hans Faber. Hans can walk into a shed where there are a thousand pigs and point at one of them and say, 'That is number 734'. And it would be. He is probably the greatest pigman in Suffolk. He is paid £1,500 a year.

This is the biggest pig district in England. Pigs and barley. They go well together. You can pack all your pigs up so that they roughly work out at 1,000 animals an acre – and an acre of buildings is an awful lot of building! – and there you are. All tidy. An average Suffolk farm will have 300 pigs but many of the farmers are going for them in a big way and one farm near here has 2,000 animals. As they are fattened through four times a year, it means that 8,000 pigs spend twelve weeks out of their twenty-two-week lives on this farm per twelve-month. This is real factory-farming. This farmer doesn't breed at all; he buys, fattens, sells. The pig is a wonderful animal for this sort of farming. There is nothing to waste on him. The Chinese even export the bristles. The only part of a pig you can't sell is his squeak.

But there are problems. I don't know what to think. Everything is being so drastically simplified. The pig-farmer will come down to me and say, 'I know what diseases I've got. I just want a few pails of this drug or that and I'll treat them myself.' He does. He injects, and that is that. It costs £1 to have a vet call at the farm and when you are working on today's superfine profit margins you are going to think twice before asking him to. So they rarely ask me to the pig factories – unless they've got an unusual epidemic. It will be the same when all the cattle are locked up.

We've got cannibalism coming up. The imprisoned creatures are eating each other. Everything is being controlled except their natural instincts. These are frustrated, so they have problems. Tail-biting among pigs is becoming a quite incredibly large problem. They just bite each other's tails right off. You go in first thing of a morning and find three pigs running around with a mass of blood on their buttocks. Then you have to sit and watch for hours. At last you see a pig walk up to his neighbour and go *chunk*! and there is the most dreadful scream. Then more screams, for it takes about three good snaps to get the tail off. It is boredom which causes this and they are now considering taking the tails off baby pigs to avoid it. There is a lot of argument about whether a law should be brought in to prevent tails being cut off without an anaesthetic. De-tailing pigs is still in the basket – although in New Zealand they de-tail cows. They do it to stop the cow swishing muck into the milk bucket and to prevent dirt collecting round the cow's bottom. It was the clean-milk production people in New Zealand who started this practice but the whole of the British veterinary profession are dead against it. We say, 'We are not going to turn cattle out on a hot summer's day to get covered with flies and not to be able to flick at its tormented ribs'. The New Zealanders say, 'If the cow wasn't mucky, there wouldn't be any flies'. We don't agree; it is often the sweetness of the udder which draws the flies. Many of the farmers like this de-tailing idea but we are fighting it. We are having to face up to a great ethical question – to what extent can an animal be mutilated in the service of man? Allowing for the fact that one believes that the animal exists for the benefit of man.

There is castration. We've tried to get that more and more humane. We've brought in a law saying that every animal over a certain age must be anaesthetized before it is castrated. But it is economically impossible at present to do this. We haven't got an anaesthetic which works quickly enough. Imagine a big pig factory with hundreds of pigs waiting to be castrated. Each animal would have to be injected twice, put down, given a quarter of an hour and then stood up again. You simply couldn't do it. Think of the vet's fees. The farmer simply wouldn't put up with such a loss. If we had something we could spray, that would be easier. But we haven't. So you have the big question – can you ethically castrate a pig without an anaesthetic? And the answer for most people is yes. Because most people will never separate ethics from profits.

It is accepted that you dock lambs' tails because if you don't all the fat runs into the tail and, also, the whole thing is likely to become a seething mass of maggots in the summer. So the farmer will turn round and say, 'If you dock lambs, why not calves?' He is being reasonable. So you have to answer with a very reasonable point of view. He will remind you that horses had their tails docked because they caught in the reins when one drove, and were dangerous. He might even have cheek enough to remind me that I hunt! I hunt partly because I like it and partly because a hunting vet attracts the horse-work in the district. I have the horse-work for miles around. And all vets love horse-work. I suppose it is because the horse is a noble animal, if I dare say it. He's clean. He's above every other animal. A horse is pleasant to treat. I am making distinctions between animals, you see. It is wrong – unjust – but I am making them. I am caught up in this new confusion. I must get myself right by thinking of the chickens.

They hardly bear thinking about. They are our great cruel compromise. I don't know how many chickens there are in Akenfield but there must be many thousands. People prefer to think of them as little machines which wear out in ten months and are then replaced. They are all deranged. Once you get such a fantastic number of birds together in one big room a kind of mass nervousness sets in. Each bird is surrounded by as many as 9,999 individuals. When you open the door of an enormous broiler house, the inhabitants will end up against the far wall in one vast shrieking pile. Or that is what happened. Now you play them music. You play it loud, so that there isn't that sudden extra sound when a door opens. But the chickens work themselves up 'over' the music, as it were. They are like a lot of women gossiping, gossiping until the uproar forces them to shout. The Bramble Report permits more than one battery hen in a cage, which is interesting – rather strange. Ethics and profits once more, I'm afraid. The battery hens are bewildered by their lives, so there is all this cannibalism again. They eat each other. First they pick a feather and taste blood, and soon some poor hen is disembowelled. This is a very frequent thing. The only answer to this is de-beaking – taking off the top part of the beak. But the Bramble Committee says you mustn't de-beak. To allow more than one hen in a cage and not to allow de-beaking is a good example of their strange compromise between what is economic and what is savage.

We have a new broiler house at the top of the village. There are six sheds which hold 10,000 birds each. You fill the site, fatten out and then empty the whole place, and give it a rest to keep it clean. The farmer used to just empty one shed at a time but he found that this method didn't keep disease under control. The broilers are ready for the fried chicken trade in twelve weeks. They are taken to a processing factory ten miles from Akenfield, hung by the legs to a conveyor belt, made to travel about two feet, stunned by an electrified plate, bled, bathed, dressed and packed into the deep freeze – and all in about ten minutes. Between one and two thousand birds are killed and dressed each day at this factory. And that is poultry-keeping as it is now. I'm not really wanted in this business – not the same bird-doctor me, that is, who attends the parakeet bird farm where every creature is a special living thing. Talking of birds, a ploughman told me that he counted thirteen different kinds of birds following his furrow this week [12 November 1967].

There are lots of dogs in the village. The pet population of England is fantastic. Of course, it is different in the country. All our village animals are economic, with the exception of the dog. The difference between a town veterinary practice and a country one is that in town you are dealings with pets which have become members of human families, lovers, partners – anything you like – so when they are sick you can charge their owners anything you like. They will spend fantastic sums. In the village you only treat an animal up to the economic level. Cats don't rate as high in the country as in the town, although they are intensely useful. You see a farm where the cat population has been wiped out by enteritis and then you'll see something! The rats and mice arriving – in armies! A farm will have as many as a dozen cats queened over by some great 'Betty-cat' who is the mother and great-grandmother of them all. They live pleasant, active, unsentimental lives. They are lucky.

18 · Not by Bread Alone

Speak but one word to me over the corn,
Over the tender, bowed locks of the corn.

William Morris, *Summer Dawn*

There is a Southern saying – fine words
butter no parsnips.

Sir Walter Scott

The Poet

I think that living in the country, for all their sentimental denials, is something which is held in contempt by most people today. They believe that one has opted out of a concern for all kinds of problems. The country is where one doesn't get on. But if I was interested in getting on, as it is called, I wouldn't be a poet. Writing poetry is a way of life. Money is necessary for this way of life, of course, but it has to be earned in some way which doesn't injure the poetry. This is the most important thing. I think a poet should have a job which he likes. He will be a better poet if he isn't nagged by unsuitable work. The work I happened to love is cultivating the land, raising plants, eating my own vegetables and fruit. So much of poetry is oblation and the putting of the seed into the ground is also a religious rite – perhaps the oldest religious rite that there is. Like the rest of the villagers, I grow not only for myself but to give away. This is important. All country gardeners do this.

When I was a boy I lived in a country suburb of London – it was still possible to talk of a suburb being in the country then. After Oxford, I worked in London, where I wrote a poetry of despair. It was a continuous cry for what I had lost, for the hills and fields, and the vixen wood, with the dog-fox barking at night. I imagined myself dying inside and so I came to this village to find my health. My wholeness. That is what I am here. It was not my village but to say that I had returned to it seemed a true way of describing what had happened to me. Suffolk amazed me – the great trees, the towering old buildings soaring out of the corn. The huge clear spaces.

I am now at home here. I know everybody and everybody knows me.

Words have meaning for me here. I am lucky, I came here to get better but I have in fact been re-born. I have escaped into reality. There are no nameless faces; I am identified and I identify. All is seen. Although you may not be capable of loving your neighbour as yourself, you can at least know him nearly as well as you know yourself.

One has to have a leaning towards village life. It is often a life of poverty in contrast with that of the towns. Poverty is sometimes believed to be a great stimulant of art, but I don't believe this. Except I am willing to forego a lot of the things other people now take for granted in order to keep Akenfield, by which I mean the deep country. The power of wonder is here. In spite of machines and sprays, I still find Nature with a capital N in this valley. It is man's rightful place to live in Nature and to be a part of it. He has to recognize the evidence of his relationship to the great natural pattern in such things as flowers, crops, water, stones, wild creatures. Where he destroys such evidence, in the towns, for instance, he gradually destroys a part of himself. This is where poetry comes in; it has to utter the response to the reality of the whole man, and it is only by living *in* Nature that the whole man can develop. City life fragments a man. He is not complete when the reminders of the great natural complex of which he is a part are absent. The business of poetry is to mend the fragmentation which occurs when men forget their place in the natural creation. City poets are in danger of blocking the imaginative river with concrete and hearing so much noise that they miss the voice of the Goddess! Of course much excellent poetry is written in cities, but I sometimes think that it is informed by an improper, a Satanic fury. And with clever words disguising the lack of wonder. This is the dichotomy of city life. The city poet records an alienation which began perhaps with Blake's awesome poem 'The Mental Traveller'. I understand the reason for this way of writing but living here, in touch with the earth and the woods, I can hardly believe it. I don't want to believe in their alienation! For in a sense, in not believing, I myself am alienated from men who do not have and who do not wish to have my experience of the village. I think that it is their tragedy that they don't want such a thing and can even call it escapist and 'uncommitted'. The twentieth century, with its great comforts and its great crimes, has produced immense alienation experiences. People need the seasonal design of country time to remind them of what they are.

Time in the village is quite different from time in the town. You enter time when you enter a town – you rush through it. In a village time enters you, slowly, naturally. I knew so little about time and its importance when I came here. Eventually, its poetic value has been revealed to me.

They say that I have opted out. That is what they say. I am out of all the great events of the day – or so they tell me. The accusers come yearly and usually in the summer, for none of these kind of people have patience with a village in winter, and they point their finger at me for having turned my back on what they call current affairs. They tell me that a poet should not avoid what is going on in the world. A poet should be with the mass of mankind, they say; a poet should carry a banner. I do not march, I do not protest, I have not the people's cause at heart – so I am guilty! I do not argue about the colour question or the religious question. I am a guilty innocent, I suppose. Can one be that?

19 · The Northern Invaders

Where the mowers mow the cleanest,
Where the hay lies thick and greenest,
There to track the homeward bee,
That's the way for Billy and me.

 James Hogg, *A Boy's Song*

Jamie McIver · aged sixty · farmer

The McIvers farm a tenancy of 180 acres east of the river. Forty years of
East Anglian life have made little or no mark on their Scottish positivism
or Scottish sentiment alike. Jamie is a man who doesn't change his views
to suit the times and, now that he is getting older, he clings more than
ever to the clear-cut rules laid down during his boyhood. He is didactic
and authoritative, stating strong opinions in a way which contrasts
dramatically with Suffolk caution. Like most of his countrymen, he has
remained both emigrant and exile. His son Lister, leaving for a Queens-
land farm in the autumn, might achieve a more total break. Jamie is
toying with the idea of joining him. His wife wouldn't mind a change,
and, what does it matter, Suffolk or Australia, if one isn't back home?

*

I came here in 1932. Most of us who came here after the First War came
from Lanarkshire and Stirlingshire. We came because we were land-
starved back home and needed – what did the Germans used to call it?
– *Lebensraum*. We were all young men in our early twenties, strong and
adaptable, and mostly farmers' sons. There was no official scheme. One
came down and then another. The first people to come down were the
Alstons, the Lawsons, the Wilsons and the MacMasters. News about
East Anglia got around fast. It was the land of Goshen compared with
Scotland. A better climate, easier working soil with no damn great lumps
of granite pushing out of it. It was, 'Come on, Wully! Come doon here!'
It was, 'Send home for brother Angus and for sister Mary and her man!'

There were all these fine farms standing idle and no great rush by
anybody to work them. We got our jackets off and got stuck into it. A
neighbour came south first and did so well that his Suffolk landlord

wrote back to the Scotch landlord who had previously employed him, did he know of another Lanark man who would come down and take a farm? That is how I came. We were always tenant farmers. It is our tradition. The Scotch don't try and buy their farms. Scotland is all estates – even in these days of change and economic chaos, there are still great estates. And there are still more tenant farms in Scotland than ever there were in England. Tenantry suits us. I think it was because the agricultural revolution was late in hitting Scotland and when it *did* hit the country, the changes were made fast. We jumped a period. Everybody had learned a lesson quick. We adapt easily, that is the truth of the matter. When there was no room for us on our fathers' rocky little farms in the Lowlands, we came South. It made sense. The circumstances were attractive and the climate, after what we had been used to, was wonderful. We were always exporting our population anyway.

What a scene we found when we arrived! I don't know how to begin to describe it. Dereliction. The fields were wet, the hedges like forests. The East Anglian farmer had lived with his decline so long that he couldn't move, he couldn't think. There he was, bogged down in the best corn area of England with ruin right up to his farmhouse door. The thought of having to restore it seemed impossible, so he didn't think about it. It was a God-sent opportunity for us Scots. Apart from its being heavier land than we had ever seen before, it was the Garden of Eden!

There was something else about the Suffolk farmers we Scots couldn't understand – their snobbery. In Scotland there is no distinction between a farmer's son and a farm-worker's son, for instance, but it was quite another tale in Suffolk. We couldn't understand this. Labourers' sons as well as farmers' sons came down to restore the southern farms, if the southerners did but know it. But I supposed they couldn't tell us apart. The Suffolk farmers' snobbery was quite unjustified – they were just ordinary working farmers who weren't working! That was what was happening. They were all copying the Big House, Colonel This and Sir That. Their wives were sitting in the best room with village girls as maids. A village woman would scrub a farmhouse through for her dinner and her insurance stamp – that is what times were like. But the farmers hadn't twopence to rub together and owed money everywhere. Yet it didn't stop them looking surprised when they saw our women working out on the land. As for the labourers, what a bad deal they had. Some of them didn't get paid for weeks on end. We were more punctilious about this. I'm not boasting, it is a fact. Anybody will tell you that the Scots *paid*. The corn merchants and the blacksmiths came to rely on the payments made by the Scotch during the Depression. Ask any of them and they will tell you. Well, that is how it was. Fancy feudalism in 1929. The ordinary village folk were being pushed about all over the place by the classy farmers. Classy! They thought they were classy – that was about it. I tell you, we had never seen such airs and graces. The cottage man here was also subservient by nature. He'd be touching his forelock whereas a Scot would be saying, 'I'm as good as you, Jock, any bloody day!'

The village men came to work for us and we saw how different they were. They were slow, their horses were slow. A Suffolk man would plough to the end of the field, stop there, then gradually turn his horses round and plough back again. Whereas a Scotch ploughboy would thrust up the field, kick his horses round and be back in no time! A Scotch farmer is used to this quickness, so the first thing we noticed in Suffolk, after the ruination, was the unhurrying pace. The lack of competition between the labourers. It worried us at first but gradually we came to a meeting point where both sides improved. I think that the man–master relationship on a Scots-run Suffolk farm in the thirties was very, very good. Much better than it was between an English farmer and his men.

We found the Suffolk men much more tolerant than ourselves – not nearly so critical of each other. The Scots are hyper-critical of their neighbours and the village people in Akenfield seemed strangely un-malicious. The men lacked aggression. One of the things we noticed most was the childish way the village men boasted about being first. They liked to go to the pub in the evenings and boast that their particular farm was taking thirty sacks an acre off a field, or that they had started their harvest before anybody else in the neighbourhood. They would pick peas as thin as paper just to say that they were first to eat the new crop. Their wives were as bad. They would get up at four in the morning to get a line of washing out before anybody else.

We were, generally speaking, more able, more industrious, more enterprising, less fearful. When a new machine was introduced, it was always a Scot who had brought it in. A Suffolk farmer would wait for ten years to see whether a new method was foolproof – and then he would adopt it.

It was strange when we arrived. I shall never forget it. I was in my twenties and just wed. My farm was falling down, my fields ran with water and my hedges were like jungles. You never saw anything like it. Nothing had been fertilized or cared for for a generation. It was the Garden of Eden gone back. It was the hedges which amazed us most.

Just when we thought we'd seen the tallest one you could get, we'd discover another twice the height! 'Come and see this one, Alasdair!' we'd shout. We'd laugh but we felt like crying. We found weeds which we'd never seen before and clay which sucked your boots off. The Suffolk farmers had what they called their 'best fields' – the ones near the road or which could be seen from the house. But out of sight, at the back, lay the wilderness. We had come to a system that was passing away.

We all started with a small farm – 150 acres at most. Those who went to West Suffolk, Sudbury way, could manage bigger farms because of the light lands there. They went for the 200-acres-plus touch. We each employed about five men, two horsemen, a stockman, a labourer and a boy. There was always a boy. We brought cows from the North and produced a race of cowmen which had never existed in Suffolk before. Before we came, the average Suffolk farm had about five cows but we introduced herds of thirty or more. Then came another problem – there were no creameries to cope with all the milk. So we introduced a milk-collection system which was being used in and around the Clyde Valley, and which was the first system ever to take milk in bulk from the farms to the big cities. We brought very fast Irish horses into Suffolk, fast-stepping jennets which would pull the milk floats from the farms to the railhead. Then it went to London. The supply was far ahead of demand locally. A little place for retaining the milk was built at Wickham Market and all the farmers for miles around rushed their milk to this centre.

This was what Suffolk was like when I, a young man from Lanark owning nothing more than a plough, came here a little more than thirty years ago. Some were better off than me and came with full equipment, stock, furniture and everything packed on a special train, but I came with a plough.

The old threads are still present here. Suffolk's slowness is saving it from destruction by the commuters. But you are getting more and more of the retired type of person moving in. Most of the good ideas for the village come from these people and they do nearly all the voluntary work in the neighbourhood. The ex-colonials circulate in their own tight little circle and they seem to resent the business side – the farming side – of village life. They are all out of place. So they hide in their gardens and feel safe. Gardens are the only energetic hobby they can pursue. They haven't got enough money to keep a horse. There is something else about them, too. They always walk on a tarred road. They never dare to strike across country. You rarely meet them in the fields, even where there's a known footpath. They're scared to leave the tarmac. It is their suburban upbringing. They're living in the country and they know nothing of it. They couldn't tell a red-fellow from a rook. They buy all their garden plants straight from the Woodbridge and Ipswich nurserymen and spend hundreds of pounds on hybrid roses. They can tell you all the names of the roses but they couldn't walk up my lane and pick out the wild flowers and grasses. It is not they – or the Scotch and English farmers – in this village who will provide the continuity.

It is the cottage man who is the continuous factor. There are three main families in this village and they are all working class, and they are the ones whose names cover the churchyard right to way-back. I call myself middle class and I will go from here unremembered. So will all your Major Blanks, your commanders and your colonial Sirs. We'll have left no record. But the village men are the descendants of the old farmers who lived here when this house was built, centuries past. They have come down while others were going up. They are tied in here by history but they don't know it. I know it. I can scrape up scraps of the old pattern everywhere. The villagers don't resent the newcomers, they ignore them.

We Scots stick together here to a certain extent. We keep our distinction wherever we are. We need to talk to each other. If you have English friends you will talk gossip but when Scotch friends get together they will work their way into a philosophical argument. The Scots are more concerned with life than with politics. They have to find a meaning in things. We are still religious, I suppose. We find Christianity in England is a very superficial thing.

The big skies leave the East Anglians empty. The skies are nothing. The horizons are too wide. There is nothing for a man to measure himself by here. In Scotland you have the hills, the mountains. They diminish a man. They make him think. They are there for all time. Every man who has lived in Scotland since the world began has looked at these same mountains. He knows they last and that he doesn't. There is nothing like this in East Anglia. The water moves in Scotland but in Suffolk it stands still – or as good as. Because they are a flat-land creature there is a lack of imagination and excitement in the Suffolk character. You get very few real characters here. You don't meet many men who are outstanding. At home we make a point of being very individual. Every day you will meet men who will not conform. The Suffolk people conform easily, they are natural conservatives.

All England is changing, of course. Too fast. My son is emigrating to Australia and if he makes a go of it, we may follow. These are poor days in Britain. Too much sex. I like reading. My wife goes to the library and grabs three novels for me. I look at them and I say, 'How on earth did the authors get them published?' That Iris Murdoch – she must have some funny friends. Did you see Muggeridge interviewing Lord Reith? What a great man. He made Muggeridge look small, didn't he? Lord Reith is a leader. He is what we want today. We need to be told where we are.

Duncan Campbell · aged sixty-six · sheep-farmer

A lot of us Scots came to Suffolk between the wars. Things have changed mightily since then; they were tough times. My wife and I have been here for forty-two years. Before this I was a sheep-farmer on the borders of Scotland. My father had a lot of sheep in the Border country. The flocks are very big there. They roam at their own sweet will, as they do in Wales. The hills are where the great art of shepherding is practised, where a man has to work subtly to get the best out of his sheep. They have to 'go over the ground', you see. They like to lie on the driest part of the grazing, which is on the mountain top. So the shepherd has to incline them out all the afternoon and evening in such a way that they reach the top at night. Then, at daybreak, they will leave the tops and gradually drift low into the valleys until they reach the stream. And so they go over all the pasture all the time, over all the hill and valley in one day. And that is the art of good shepherding, to work them gently, to let them go nicely out and in daily. The shepherd will go to his flock in the afternoon, moving straight along the valley to set them out. If there are any slow sheep, he will put his dog round them and gradually they will all slowly walk the little paths they have made on the mountain, one after another, grazing higher and higher, until they reach the top – and sleep. It is a lonely life – my word, it is! A shepherd spends nearly all his life quite alone.

Very few Suffolk farmers keep big flocks now. There were many more sheep when I first arrived. There have been great reductions in East Suffolk, the numbers have gone down by many thousands. It isn't because they are unprofitable but maybe because other animals are easier to farm and offer a better return. One of the reasons why I haven't got so many sheep on my farm is that I am growing sprouts, peas, beans and other things for the frozen food factory. It is these new green crops which have made the wonderful change in the farming round this village. Before these came along, I used to go in for ley farming, taking my leys round the farm, ploughing up after they had been grazed by sheep and cattle every three-four years, and then catching the fertility. I can assure you that, compared with these deep-freeze crops, there isn't a finer way of keeping a farm in a high state of fertility than taking the leys round. It seems *right*. You feel that you are doing things the way they should be done and it makes you glad and satisfied. It surprises me that some people who do not get good root crops don't practise ley farming more. I know hundreds of farmers who would benefit from having a couple of hundred breeding ewes on their land. This present continual serial cropping won't, in the long run, prove so beneficial as a flock of sheep going over the ground every little while. The artificial fertilizers can never give what a flock can give.

The farm was in poor condition when we came here. There was a lot of grass on it, so that was a help. But they had made hay off the same bits of pasture so often – continually hay, hay, hay, imagine that! – that at last they couldn't have got more than a ton per acre. Well, that won't pay, you know. I make very little hay and I'll tell you why. Because you can buy nice hay at £8 10s. a ton. Now if the most you can grow is two tons – why waste the time or run the risk of losing it because of bad weather for £17? We only make hay when it has been a growing year. This was a growing year and we cut acres of beautiful hay.

I missed the mountains when I first came to Suffolk – I still do. My wife and I, we missed the hills and the weir-running streams. I shall always remember these four lines:

> *Says old Tom, ' Give me a Border burn*
> *That can't run without a turn,*
> *And with its bonny babbles*
> *Fills the glens among our native hills ...'*

They were written by J. B. Selkirk. They make me homesick. I remember saying them for the first time when I was a young man and standing in a Suffolk field which was being ploughed with horses by an old man wearing a long black coat with tail buttons, a bowler hat and carrying an umbrella! I shall be homesick here, I thought – and I have been. That old ploughman, he was a grand old man. So good.

We have farm students now. Just one at a time, and just for a year's practical work before they go to the agricultural college. We don't mind what trouble we have to go to to teach them farming ways, so long as they make use of all we tell them later on. But some get tired of it and go into something else. It is disappointing when this happens. They are usually boys aged about sixteen. We don't take them into our house; they have to find lodgings in the village. We give them a turn with cows, then tractors, reaping, sugar-beeting, everything as it comes along. The older men sometimes resent the student. If they do it is because he is putting on airs and being too clever. He has forgotten how much the older men know – such wonderful things. Students should watch their step, keep their eyes open and their mouths shut. I give them a reference when their year's 'practical' is up. And they have to make a statement of all that they have done during the year, what the acreage of the farm is and what happens on it, the date when they started the harvest and what machines were used. Many of these young men get depressed because they can never see any way of getting a farm of their own. They are so dear now. But it was hard for us, too. We young men from Scotland had to struggle along carrying an agricultural ruin on our backs. It is a wonder that any of us can stand upright! I tell the students that farming is three-quarters practical and a quarter theory. And that a farmer must be able to do every job himself before he orders another man to do it. I have the sons of quite well-to-do people as students. I tell them, 'Irrespective of your position, you must be taught to work'.

I am really a shepherd. I could work a dog before I left school. My father would let me have the old ones which were finished for the hills and I would teach them and learn from them. Therefore I got into the art of handling dogs when I was a child, and I've never been without them all my life. And my dogs have always been the Border collie sheep dogs. They are with me in Suffolk and I have trained scores for all the East Anglian farmers, but they come from my homeland. The best of them were registered on both sides of the Border in the nineteenth century and eventually the National Sheep Dog Society, with its own studbook, was founded. They are the best sheep dogs in the world. They say that there are sheep dogs in Wales, but I've never seen a Welsh sheep dog.

A really trained-for-trial-work sheep dog costs between £1–£300 – as much as that! But it will be as valuable as a man on the farm, have no doubt about it. They will even collect cattle if you will let them. I have become an authority on these wonderful animals and have judged the English National Trials on two occasions.

My method is this where training is concerned. I select a puppy from intelligent parents – I am not interested in the puppy if his parents aren't good workers. I feed the puppy well and give him cod liver oil once a week. Then comes the hard part. He loves you now and is all over you the minute you show up, kisses and everything. But he has to learn to stay away from you and it is against his whole nature. You start by getting him to stay still at five yards, then you walk a little farther – 'Now, Ben, sit down – *sit!*' You are taking the frolic out of him and putting the confidence in. After much effort on both your parts he begins to become a sensible dog, instead of jumping and running to no purpose. Once you have taught him stillness you're getting somewhere. When you come to work on the sheep and you can stop them (high short whistle) and make them absolutely still from a distance, then you are getting somewhere. You can stop 'em and start 'em. You have made great progress.

I might work on a dog once or twice a day for a month and after this, when we get to the sheep, the principle is to get the dog to go to the *other* side of the flock. And to get there he must go in such a way as not to disturb the sheep. So if the sheep are in the twelve o'clock position, the dog must start getting to the other side of them from the nine o'clock position. Then he must come round in a curve. Now, how are you going to teach it to do all that? Well, my method is to start the dog off with five sheep placed about fifty yards in front of me. I walk half-way to the sheep leaving the dog motionless. I then ask him to come round. Naturally, he comes straight, so I step out towards him as he's rushing past and shout, 'Git out – Git out, Ben!' and before he knows where he is he's running to the side. Then I whistle him to sit down. He should be about ten-twenty yards off at the side of the sheep by now. And then I start to give him his come-on whistle, or I say, 'Come on up, Ben'. But I don't let him do this right away. I stop and start him a number of times. It is a game now and Ben is enjoying it. There is no dog so anxious to work and to please his master as a Border collie. Well now, he's gone round the back of the sheep and bringing them towards you. You mustn't teach him too much at once. He must do nothing more than this for a fortnight – just to run out keeping a nice circle line and bringing a handful of sheep up to you quietly. Then you teach him flanking, running to the right or to the left. If the sheep try to escape to the right you must have a command to make the dog come round and head them off. A short double high whistle means 'come to my right' and one long low whistle means 'come to my left'. You have to give him encouragement and lots of kindness after each command. And all the time he must be quiet and gentle with the sheep – never to worry them, you understand. And there is another important thing. When you have given a command and the dog begins to respond, never add another command until he has completed the first one. And don't repeat the command. So long as he's doing what you have asked, don't say anything. Never shake his confidence in any way.

You need to understand sheep; they are very special animals. Down-bred sheep are very placid and those which come from the hills are timid and wild. Their fright is infectious, it fills the air. It is some old habit which makes them keep together and if there weren't dogs to manage them I don't know what we would all do. I've often said that the British sheep industry would suffer to the extent of a thirty per cent loss if it weren't for the collies. They are the brightest dogs in the world – and all due to the National Sheep Dog Society.

Sheep have to be maintained in a splendid condition, once they begin to go down there is no pulling them up. You have no end of trouble with them if you let them go down. You must understand how to flush them and make them thrive, so that they bring you a good crop of lambs. And how to winter and summer them. And all the time you must do the job as economically as possible, and yet still present them in nice condition at lambing time.

Some East Anglian farmers have no use for sheep at all; others are sheep-minded. They know the value of them on the farm and just wouldn't be without them. Sheep keep a farm in a high state of fertility and also provide a tidy little income. Double purpose creatures, they are.

There is an important sale in Bury St Edmunds during the third week of August and last year I had to come home from holiday in order to get my sheep to it. I had 130 sheep and I took them all. And why? Well, the year before the Queen sent a flock of sheep from Sandringham to this sale – which deals with between 13–14,000 animals altogether – and I saw her get the highest prize. She had sent shearing ewes – ewes which are ready to go to the ram as soon as you get them home and which will lamb in the spring – and they made a lovely pen. Now, I told myself, I would like to beat the Queen. By jove, I looked about and bought a very nice pen of ewe lambs, brought them home, brought them up, took them to the Bury sale the next year and – what do you think? I got the highest price. But only just. I beat Her Majesty by five shillings!

A chap comes up after the sale and says, 'How did you manage it?' Well now, I says quite simply, 'I kept them clear of worms – dosed them in the autumn and again in the spring. I cleared every parasite right out. Then I dosed them for such things as pulpy kidney. I injected them – the scientists have done a tremendous lot for agriculture, make no doubt of it! Things are incredibly better since I started farming years ago – and then I fed these lambs all the winter as economically as I could with sugar-beet pulp, and on the fields before the grass faded and the goodness went out of it. I was never too late or too early with the different cares they needed. I was being a good shepherd. That is how I managed it.'

There is more in the business than making money, you know. I always wanted to be a farmer. I was quite sure. It is a great life. You must praise the land as well as take from it. And order it. There's a field out there – now what have I done to that? I've put humus and nitrogen on it, and now the cows will graze it. I'll fold it twice over and then I'll plough it up, then sow these hand-picked beans. I took over five tons an acre off it this year – two crops in twelve months! The beans go to Birdseye to be frozen. I am growing eight acres of sprouts for Birdseye. Thirty-two boxes of them left the farm yesterday, and thirty-two the day before. I kept a pedigree herd of cows on only forty-two acres of grass. I add fertilizer to the good natural humus in the grass and freshen it all up with irrigation. The rule with land is to give – then you can take.

The days are better now but people refuse to believe it. I felt quite angry at a meeting in Ipswich the other day. A man got up and read a paper called 'The Countryside through the eyes of the Urban Dweller' – and how he criticized us! Taking down hedges! Putting up ugly buildings! It was awful. We just ignored him. But one man did get up and answer him. He said, 'In spite of all you say, we have still got hedges and the land is fertile, and there is no more beautiful sight than fertile land'. The farmers are thought to lack feelings. I have sometimes accidentally put my big foot on a skylark's nest, eggs and all. It is damn awful – it is you know! 'Clumsy fool brute! *Brute!*' I tell myself. But it is done. Robbie Burns once ploughed-in a mountain daisy and wrote:

> *Wee modest crimson-tipped flower*
> *I've met you in an evil hour*
> *For I must crush among the stone*
> *Thy slender stem. To spare thee now*
> *Is past my power – thou bonny gem!*

Have you seen the townspeople in the spring-time, driving out to the lanes and woods, and tearing up the flowers? It is a shocking sight.

20 · In the Hour of Death

There Dewy lay by the gaunt yew tree,
There Reuben and Michael, a pace behind,
And Bowman with his family
  By the wall that the ivies bind.

      Thomas Hardy, *The Dead Quire*

To bring the dead to life
Is no great magic.
Few are wholly dead:
Blow on a dead man's embers
And a live flame will start.

     Robert Graves, *To Bring the Dead to Life*

William Russ · aged sixty-one · gravedigger

'Tender' Russ is a widower and lives by himself in a severe brick cottage called Malyons. The cottage is built endways to the road and into a bank so high that blackberries can hang away from their roots and trail on the slates. The garden is planted but rank. Rows of sprouts have rotted until they have become yellow pustulate sticks; potatoes have reached up as far as they could go and fallen back into faded tangles. Tender sows but apparently doesn't reap. He has retreated to one room in the cottage and closed all the others up. It is a Charles Spenserlahye room, a jackdaw's nest of saved matchsticks, preserved newspapers, clung-to coronation mugs and every kind of clutter. In a corner a bakelite radio gives every news bulletin there ever was. Tender's two budgies, Boy and Girl, drown announcements of famine, war, murder and sport with an incessant chatter. He is short but strongly built. Vivid blue eyes strain and flash to add meaning and explanation to what he feels are inadequate words.

Tender is a monopolist and a pluralist. He amalgamates graveyards and pounces on cemeteries. Although there has been little or no competition for this great accumulation of burial grounds, Tender has a right to feel unique and powerful, privileged and indispensable. He has buried 608 people in thirty different churchyards since 1961 and keeps his own records of 'where they lie and *how* they lie'. And this is only the work of his maturity. Before this mortuary climax there were decades of interrings. Tender has never had a day's holiday, never missed a church service on a Sunday and also never missed an opportunity to carry on his rancorous love-hate debate with his God, the clergy and the quick. The dead are exempt from his fury and he is on their side against the living. He has all their names in an address book contrived out of shelf-paper and a bulldog-clip. The young and the old, the rich and the poor are listed in violent pencil at first, and in biro later.

He works incredibly hard and with great independence, travelling from village to village on a moped to the carrier of which is tied a gleaming spade and fork. He drives well out towards the centre of the road and the Anglo-American traffic has to swerve and swear to avoid him. Quite a lot of people recognize him, however, for he is a famous person, and give him a wide berth. They know they are seeing Time's winged chariot with a two-stroke.

When people need Tender they need him badly, and will make much of him because of this. The need over, they avoid him. Or is it that he avoids them? His eloquence is enormous and violent, and seems to be only indirectly aimed at God and man. He is arguing with the mindless knife-bearing wind which carries the ice of the sea to the vulnerable flesh and fields of the inhabited places. He is a religious man who is listening for God in a hurricane. There used to be certainties but now the parsons say they aren't so certain after all. The Bible itself has whirled past him – a mocking paper-chase of discarded views. Almost every day he hears about the 'resurrection of the body' as he waits tactfully behind a tree, filling-in spade covered with a sack. Most days he is left alone with the new dead. The pity of it all! The muddle of it all! Automatic bird-scarers go off in the pea-fields like minute guns. Something has gone wrong – very wrong.

'Why "Tender"?'

'Oh, that's not *his* name,' said the woman at the pub. 'He inherited it from his father. We call him Tender because of his father, but that's not his name.'

*

I started digging graves when I was twelve years old and before I left school. I began by helping an old man and by the time I was thirteen I could do the job as well as I can now. I dug graves before my voice broke – there now! People would look down into the hole and see a child. The work didn't upset me; I took it in my stride. Right from a little boy – if Mother was alive she'd be able to tell you – I used to bury guinea-pigs, rabbits, all sorts of things. I had about fifty rabbits and when one died I would make a coffin for it, get my choir surplice from the church vestry and read the Burial Service over it. So burying has been in my blood from a child. I never wanted to do anything else; graves are my vocation.

I've been at the church, official-like, since 1918. I was the legal sexton when I was thirteen and I've buried damn-near the whole of the old village, everyone of them. I remember the first grave I dug. It was for a man named Hayman. I've got all my burials down since the day I started, men, women and children.

So far as funerals are concerned, we've gone from one extreme to the other. Bodies used to be kept in the house for twelve days. Everyone kept the body at home for as long as they could then; they didn't care to part with it, you see. Now they can't get it out quick enough. They didn't like hurrying about anything when I was young, particularly about death. They were afraid that the corpse might still be alive – that was the real reason for hanging on to it. People have a post-mortem now and it's all settled in a minute, but there's no doubt that years ago there were a rare lot of folk who got buried alive. When a sick man passed on the doctor was told, but he never came to look at the corpse. He just wrote out the death certificate. People always made a point of leaving an instruction in their wills to have a vein cut. Just to be on the safe side.

There was an old man near Framlingham, old Micah Hibble, he was laid out for dead three times. The last time he was actually in his coffin and waiting for the funeral to begin. When I asked, 'Anymore for a last look before he's screwed down?' there was the usual nuisance pushing his way through the mourners and saying, 'Yes, I do!' Trust somebody to get you fiddling about and making the funeral late. The bell was going, so you know how late it was. Anyway, when this man looked in the coffin he saw that Micah had moved. Well do you know, he re-covered! And what's more, he is supposed to have written a book about what he saw, although I've never set eyes on it. He reckoned he saw Heaven and Hell but he wouldn't say what he saw in Hell; he thought it would be too much for Framlingham. He lived for years after this.

And there was this old lady at Wickham Market and she was in three different coffins. They called her Cheat-the-grave at last. All these things happened because people will insist on checking on death with a mirror, which isn't a mite of good. The only way is to stick a shred of cotton-wool where the lips part and if there's the least little wind of life it will flutter. I can always tell if a person is dead by looking at the eyes. I never make a mistake about dead eyes. I see at once when the seeing has gone.

Village folk have been buried over and over again in the same little bits of churchyard. You have to throw somebody out to get somebody in – three or four sometimes. I always put all the bones back so that they lie tidy-like just under the new person. They're soon all one. The parson said to me, 'How is it that you get so many in one grave?' and I always tell him that I must have disturbed a plague pit. Parsons will believe anything.

The rich people are buried in vaults, you know. I had to open a vault the other day and put a woman in. She joined six or seven others and I had to shove 'em over and say, 'Come you together now, make room for a little 'un!' Vaults are sweet places. Everybody lies in lead first, then wood, so there's no smell. I went into the vault at Stanton when Lord Eastham's wife died. It was full and I had to lay her on the floor because her relations had all the shelves. It was first come, first served. The coffins were all made of panelled oak, great black things as black as a fireplace. Good God, they last for generations!

I've dug for all denominations, from Catholic to Plymouth Brethren. The chapel people are the worst. First of all they're a good three-quarters of an hour in the chapel while the preacher spouts about the dead man and estimates whether he's saved, and then, when they get to the grave, on it goes again. There's no end to it. They forget we all knew the corpse. And then, when they're none too sure about the saving, you should hear them then! There was Jed's funeral – well we don't need any telling about Jed! Well Jed might have been a bad lot but he wasn't a bad sort. You know. I mean he was Jed, wasn't he? Well, this chapel preacher stood there by the hole I had got ready for Jed and was as near as damn-it saying that Jed wasn't saved although he *hoped* he was. So after the funeral I went up to him and said, 'My God, you've had some talk about Jed, haven't you? I know you're here to say a few words – but you've said too much!' I said, 'Do you reckon that *you* are saved?' He said, 'I hope so'. 'Very well then,' I said, 'but do you remember when you get in front of your Maker he won't ask you what Jed has done – he'll ask what you've been up to.' You could see he didn't like it.

The parsons aren't much better. But there, you don't find many *parsons* now. Only men who have done their life's work serving as a colonel or a schoolmaster and then get themselves ordained. I don't really call these people parsons. I don't mince my words with them. When you bury between 180–200 people a year you can afford to be honest.

Dust to dust they say. It makes me laugh. Mud to mud, more like. Half the graves round here are water-logged. Foxton is a terrible wet place; the moment you get the grass off, you're in the water. I float grass on the water so the mourners can't see it but when the coffin is lowered it has to be held under with a pole until you can get a bit of heavy soil on top of it. At Dearburgh the graves fill up to within eight inches of the top. I've drawn as much as fifty pails of water out of a grave at Dearburgh, the last when the funeral was coming up the path. And still the coffin had to be held under three feet of it. It all comes down from the cricket pitch.

The bodies are washed and dressed in shrouds. Except for a parson, and he's buried in his robes. When you bury a parson you always bury him 're incumbent' – the opposite way to everybody else. Everybody lies with their feet to the east so that when they rise they face the Lord. But a parson, you see, you bury him with his feet to the west, so that when he rises he faces his flock. And serve him right, I say. I had a bit of bother about this once.

An old canon had died and was cremated, and the ashes were kept until his wife passed on. I put the jar of ashes on the wife's coffin and lowered the two together. Well, of course, as everybody knows, all that family, particularly the daughters, were over-educated. They were old maids. They weren't cranky because they hadn't had a man but because they'd had too many old books. Their brains were strained. Well, a month after I had buried her mother's corpse and her father's ashes, along comes Miss Bolt to my house to kick up hell. 'You haven't buried Father right,' she says. 'Oh?' I says. 'You knew he should have been buried re incumbent,' she says. 'What *are* you talking about, Miss Bolt?' I say. 'I put your Father's urn on your Mother's coffin, and if you can tell me the difference between the way I put him and the way you want him, I'll dig him up and turn him round.' So then she says that I should have turned her mother the other way round as the reverend was on top of her! I mean if parsons' wives are going to get themselves buried re incumbent, where's it going to stop?

We've got a man in the churchyard named Tyler. He used to be secretary to the golf club. When he died he was buried facing south so that when he rises he can see the links. And it was done! I told the parson, 'If a person of my walk of life expressed a wish like that, you'd say I was qualified for the tall chimney' [St Audrey's Mental Hospital].

I never had any qualms about my work. When I was young I delighted in death. The funerals were big and grand and slow. You learnt a lot about everybody. They crept about in the deepest black – now they come to a funeral in all the colours of the rainbow. And afterwards they don't even walk up to the churchyard to cart the dead flowers away. They have one word for the dead when they have got them into the ground, and that is 'forgotten'. I tell them, too. They're upset, but it's the truth. They'll put a stone up with a 'There you are, we've done all we can for you, now bugger you!' They'll even put crazy paving on top of the grave so they don't have to pay me to clip the grass. And the price of it all! When I started you could get coffin, wreaths and every-thing for £5 – you could actually get a coffin for 30s. Now you wouldn't buy a coffin for a stillborn for under three quid. As for an adult's, it will cost you between £40–50.

And talking of money, I must mention the Table of Fees. Each church has got a Table of Fees which says where the money should go at a funeral. There is the incumbent with his price, there is the clerk with his price and there is the sexton with his price. You would think it was plain enough but I have to read the damn thing aloud to half the parsons or they'd diddle me out of a mint of money. When I do a funeral I'm entitled to 10s. for the service in the church – any church. I don't often get this because the parson takes it. Of course you could argue around this because the Table of Fees says, 'Where no clerk or sexton is employed the incumbent can take the money' – which of course is fair enough up to a point. But believe me when it comes to *little* money matters, parsons are the biggest swindlers on earth. They are. They're that quick on the small change you don't see the passing of it. The burial fees are terrible. It costs a £10 church fee for a parishioner to be buried at Weston – in his own churchyard!

Every parson you come into contact with will have different ways about death. You can't keep 'em in order, you know, these damned parsons! They'll all think different if they can. They'll either cut things out of the Burial Service or stuff things in. It's no use giving the mourners a book so they can follow what is going on. Now old Canon Watson, he'd give you the Service, no more and no less. But the majority of parsons use the 1928 version – which, I agree, is much more cheerful. There's nothing in it like that bit of Job where it talks about the skin worms destroying the body, for instance. Nor that bit about corruption from Corinthians. They say these things are morbid. Well they *are* morbid. It is what people need when they are staring down at the grave-dirt.

It's the same with the Litany. I said to the old Bishop, 'How often could you walk into a church now and hear the Litany read? Or the Athanasian Creed – and that should be said at least three times a year!' 'Ho! ho!' says he, 'it's all out of date.' I said, 'What was good enough for your forefathers should be good enough for you.' 'Ho! ho!' he says.

The clergy don't stick to religion as we knew it. They do things that are forbidden. They are pulling the Bible to pieces. Altering, altering. ... I said to the Bishop, 'What do you think of parsons, my lord?' He said, 'What do you?' I said, 'Well they don't preach hellfire. They used to, why don't they now?' He said, 'What, are you blaming the parsons?' 'Certainly,' I said. 'All these parsons preach is the love of God. But they leave out the wrath. What is the use of love without wrath? Tell me that.' I said, 'You are told what will happen to you if you obey His will, so it is only fair that you should know what will happen to you if you don't.' People aren't frightened any more, that is the trouble. If they had to do my work they would know that life is a frightening business. I had a parson say to me the other day, as I was digging a grave, 'Do you think these people will ever come out there again, Tender?' I said, 'They'll have a damned job after I've finished with them!' He said, seriously, 'Once you're in there, you're finished'. 'Never!' I said. But we don't know, do we? We've just got to leave the body after it has been covered up. The people I've accidentally smashed to pieces in my time, they're going to have a rum time of it.

I'll tell you what I think. In the Burial Service it tells you that when you are dead you go into the earth like a grain but it doesn't say anything about your coming out in the same form as you went in. You might come back as a cat! I love cats. I have a family of ten cats in the churchyard. They used to sleep cold among the tombs but I've made a little hole in the charnel door and now they're very comfortable indeed. They cost me 10s. a week to feed and they don't even belong to me. They don't belong to anybody. They watch the funerals from afar off. It's a healthy life for them. There are worse things than coming back as a cat.

I'm not a Christian. I do a lot of things I shouldn't do, so I can't count myself as one. Life isn't as comfortable as it used to be. Nobody wants to know you. I have been widowed for ten years. I go to church every Sunday but nobody speaks to me unless they want something. Snobbish. They're all snobs now. I'm not blowing my own trumpet, but almost ever since I was born I have been at everybody's beck and call. I have no family, none at all. No one in all the world is my relation. I never did read a lot. I never could give my mind to it. I talk too much, that is my failing. I come into contact with many people at a serious time, so I have picked up serious conversation. What most folk have once or twice in a lifetime, I have every day. I want to be cremated and my ashes thrown in the air. Straight from the flames to the winds, and let that be that.